TROLL

STUDENT
ENCYCLOPEDIA

Library of Congress Cataloging-in-Publication Data

Dempsey, Michael W.
    Student encyclopedia / by Michael Dempsey and Keith Lye.
        p.   cm.
    Summary: An encyclopedia of brief articles on topics ranging from
aardvark and abacus to zodiac and zoology. Includes additional
entries for geographic names.
    ISBN 0-8167-2257-9 (lib. bdg.)   ISBN 0-8167-2258-7 (pbk.)
    1. Children's encyclopedias and dictionaries.   [1. Encyclopedias
and dictionaries.]   I. Lye, Keith.   II. Title.
    AG5.D45   1991
    031-dc20   90-11116

Published in the U.S.A. by Troll Associates, Inc.,
100 Corporate Drive, Mahwah, New Jersey.
Produced for Troll Associates, Inc., by
Joshua Morris Publishing Inc. in association
with Harper Collins.
Copyright © 1991 by Harper Collins.
All rights reserved.
Printed in Belgium.
10 9 8 7 6 5 4 3 2 1

TROLL
STUDENT
ENCYCLOPEDIA

by
Michael Dempsey and Keith Lye

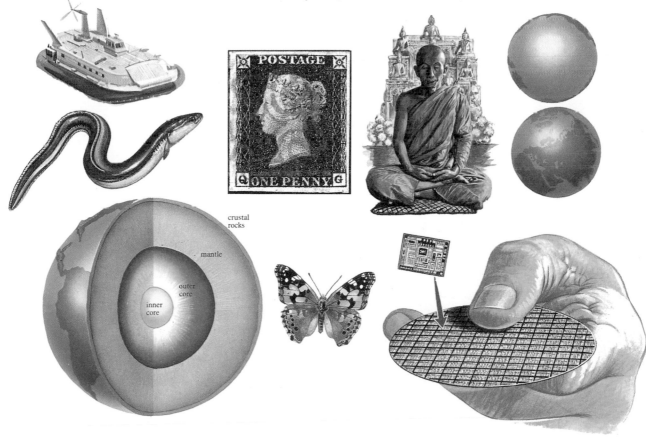

Troll Associates

HOW TO USE THIS BOOK

You can use this book to find out about people, places, events, animals, ideas, and things you might have wondered about. The entries are listed alphabetically, so you can look up a word by turning to the section of words all starting with its first letter. Then look at the other letters in the word in order, to find your entry in the section.

For example, suppose you want to look for information about President Abraham Lincoln. All the people in this book are listed according to the letters in their last names. Turn to the section of words beginning with the letter L. The first entry in this section is Labor Day. Then move to the second letter in Lincoln, i. The first Li word is Liberia. The third letter of Lincoln is n and the fourth is c. So you will find Lincoln on page 62, between Limestone and Lindbergh.

Looking up an entry can sometimes give you clues about other entries in the book that may interest you. In the Lincoln entry, you will find many terms that are explained in other places in the book. Try looking for President; United States; Slavery; Civil War; and Booth, John Wilkes.

Even reading just a few entries each day will help you learn more about the world – for yourself, for your schoolwork, or even for sharing with friends.

A

Aardvark A stocky, burrowing animal of southern Africa. It licks up termites with its long, sticky tongue.

Aardvark

Abacus A simple calculating machine made up of a frame with rows of beads strung on wires. The first row of beads on the right is the ones column, the second is tens, the third is hundreds, and so on. Addition, subtraction, multiplication, and division can be done by moving the beads on the wires.

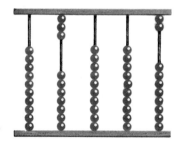

By moving beads up and down on an abacus all arithmetical processes can be carried out.

Abbreviation A shortened form of a word or group of words, such as St. (street), and N.H. (New Hampshire).

Aborigine Term used for the original inhabitants of a country or region. It is used particularly for Australian Aborigines.

Abraham Biblical figure regarded as the father of the Hebrews and the founder of Judaism.

Absolute zero In theory, the lowest possible temperature. It is -459.67 degrees Fahrenheit (-273.15 degrees Celsius).

Acceleration Normally used to mean an increase in speed. To the scientist, it means the rate of change of velocity, which involves changes in direction as well as speed.

Accelerator, particle Machine used to study the structure and behavior of atoms. Tiny atomic particles are accelerated to very high speeds. They then smash into other atoms, and scientists study the results. These machines are also called atom smashers.

Acid A group of chemicals known for their sour taste. Some, like sulfuric acid, can eat away even the strongest metals. Citric acid is harmless and gives citrus fruits, such as oranges, their sharp taste.

Acoustics The study of sound. An acoustics engineer designing a concert hall must control the way sound is bounced off of and absorbed by walls, the ceiling, and even people.

Acupuncture A medical treatment which uses long, thin needles that are put through a person's skin in certain places. Originally from China, it is used to treat illness or relieve pain.

Adams, John (1735-1826) Second president of the United States (1797-1801) and the first vice-president (1789-1796). A leader in the American struggle for independence, he helped write the Declaration of Independence. As president, he kept the United States out of a war with France over American ships. He was the first president to live in the White House.

Adams, John Quincy (1767-1848) Sixth president of the United States. He was the son of John Adams, the second president. In 1814, he helped make the peace with Great Britain that ended the War of 1812. Adams was noted for his anti-slavery views. He was president from 1825 to 1829.

Addition The process of combining two or more things. The mathematical symbol for addition is +.

Adirondacks A scenic mountain range in the northeastern part of New York State. Highest peak: Mt. Marcy, 5,344 feet (1,629 meters).

Adjective A word that describes a noun or pronoun. It can tell how many (seven, some), what color (blue), what kind (small), or which one (that, her). Adjectives may also tell degree (good, better, best).

Adverb A word that describes a verb, an adjective, or another adverb. Adverbs tell how (quickly), when (now), or where (upstairs). Many adverbs end in -ly.

Aerodynamics The study of air moving around solid objects, like the wind flowing around a car or the wings and body of a plane.

Aerosol A gas that has solid or liquid particles in it. It is used to propel paints and other products from cans. Though used less often now, the use of fluorocarbons in aerosols has harmed the atmosphere.

Aesop (6th century BC) Greek slave popularly believed to be the author or collector of many Greek fables, or stories.

Afghanistan Mountainous, landlocked country of southwestern Asia. Area: 251,826 square miles (652,225 square kilometers). Capital: Kabul.

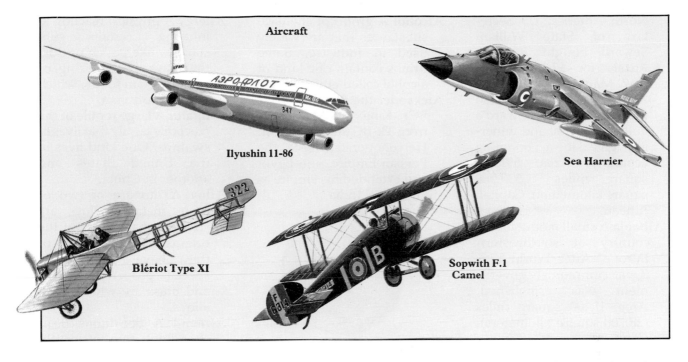

Aircraft

Ilyushin 11-86

Sea Harrier

Blériot Type XI

Sopwith F.1
Camel

Africa The second largest continent. It lies south of Europe and is connected to Asia, the largest continent, at the Sinai Peninsula. Africa was probably the birthplace of humans. Most African countries are poor, but there is great mineral wealth. The people are trying to develop their countries by building factories and improving agriculture. Area: 11,684,000 square miles (30,262,000 square kilometers).

AIDS (Stands for **Acquired Immune Deficiency Syndrome**). A disease caused by a virus. The virus kills white blood cells and destroys the body's immune system. People with AIDS become unable to resist infections. The disease is usually fatal.

Air A mixture of gases surrounding the Earth that is vital to all living things. Air is 78 percent nitrogen and 21 percent oxygen. It also contains tiny amounts of other gases.

Aircraft Machines that fly. The airplane, airship, heli-copter, rocket, glider, and balloon are aircraft.

Air Force, United States The branch of the US military that uses aircraft for defense and warfare.

Airplane A heavier-than-air aircraft. It has one or more wings and is driven by propellers or jet engines. The first successful airplane was flown by the American brothers Orville and Wilbur Wright in 1903.

Airship Also called a dirigible. A lighter-than-air aircraft. It is a cigar-shaped balloon filled with a gas, such as helium, that is lighter than air. It is driven by a propeller. An airship can carry passengers and cargo.

Alabama One of the southern or Confederate States in the Civil War. Alabama had earlier become the 22nd US state. Its economy was once agricultural, but manufacturing now dominates the economy. Area: 51,705 square miles (133,915 square kilometers). Capital: Montgomery.

Alaska The largest state of the United States. It is in the northwestern corner of

Airships were used by Germany to bomb London in World War I, with little success.

North America. US Secretary of State William Seward bought it from Russia for $7,200,000 in 1867. Many people thought Alaska was a wasteland, so they called it Seward's Folly. Today oil and minerals give it a booming economy. Area: 591,004 square miles (1,530,700 square kilometers). Capital: Juneau.

Albania A small mountainous country of southeastern Europe. After World War II, a communist government was established. Area: 11,100 square miles (28,700 square kilometers). Capital: Tirane.

Albany State capital of New York, on the Hudson River.

Albatross Large, black and white seabird of nearly all oceans. Some have a wing span of more than 11 feet (3 meters).

Alberta The westernmost of Canada's three Prairie Provinces. It produces much of Canada's oil and natural gas, plus coal. Beef and wheat are the chief farm products. The largest cities are Calgary and Edmonton. Area: 251,870 square miles (652,330 square kilometers). Capital: Edmonton.

Albino A person born with very pale skin, white hair, and pink eyes, because they have no coloring, or pigment. There are also albino animals and plants.

Alchemy A mixture of science and magic, which was popular from ancient times until after the Middle Ages. Alchemists tried to change ordinary metals into gold. They also tried to invent a substance that would make human beings live forever. Modern chemistry developed from their work.

Alcohol A group of chemical substances that are widely used in industry. Some drinks contain one kind of alcohol called ethanol.

Alexander the Great (356-323 BC) King of Macedonia from 336 BC until his death. He conquered Greece, the Persian Empire, and Egypt and extended his empire as far east as India.

Egyptian coin showing the head of Alexander the Great.

Algae Simple, flowerless plants. Most live in water, others in damp places on land. About 25,000 different kinds are known, including seaweed.

Algebra A branch of mathematics in which letters and symbols are used to represent numbers or quantities.

Algeria Second largest country in Africa. Most Algerians live along the coast of the Mediterranean Sea. The Sahara Desert, to the south, has large deposits of oil and gas. Area: 919,595 square miles (2,381,741 square kilometers). Capital: Algiers.

Allen, Ethan (1738-1789) US Revolutionary soldier. He organized the Green Mountain Boys, soldiers from Vermont. In 1775 he helped seize Fort Ticonderoga in northeastern New York from the British. Later Allen was captured by the British at Montreal and held prisoner. After his release, he fought for statehood for Vermont.

Allergy A physical reaction to inhaling certain substances, like pollen or dust that may cause sneezing, or eating certain foods, which may cause a rash.

Alligator A large reptile of the crocodile family that lives in swamps. One kind lives in the United States and another in China.

Alloy A mixture of two or more metals. Alloys are stronger than either of the original pure metals, or they have some other special property. Bronze and brass are widely used alloys.

Almond A deciduous (leaf-shedding) tree of southwestern Asia that has been grown worldwide for many hundreds of years. Some are grown for their nuts, others for their pink blossoms.

Alphabet A group of letters, or signs, that stand for sounds and are used to write down a language. The English alphabet comes from the ancient Roman alphabet which had every letter but J, U, and W.

Alps Largest mountain range in Europe. It stretches from southern France through Italy, Switzerland, Germany, Austria, Yugoslavia, and Albania.

Aluminum Light, strong metal that resists corrosion. It is used in the construction of automobiles, railway cars, ships, and airplanes. Cooking utensils and soft-drink cans are also made of aluminum.

Amazon Second longest river in the world, after the Nile. It flows from South America's Andes Mountains near the Pacific Ocean through Peru and Brazil to the Atlantic Ocean. It carries more water to the ocean than any other river in the world. Length: 4,000 miles (6,437 kilometers).

Amber Hard substance formed from the resin of pine trees that lived millions of years ago. The finest amber is used for jewelry.

American colonies Also called the Thirteen Colonies. Originally ruled by England, they united to win independence in the American Revolution (1775-1783), becoming the United States of America. They were: Connecticut, Delaware, Georgia, Maryland, Massachusetts, New Hampshire, New Jersey, New York, North Carolina, Pennsylvania, Rhode Island, South Carolina, and Virginia.

American Revolution The war by which the American colonies gained their independence from Great Britain. Fighting began at Lexington and Concord, Massachusetts, in April 1775. On July 4, 1776, the Declaration of Independence was adopted. The British were defeated in 1781 and recognized American independence two years later. George Washington became the first president of the United States in 1789.

Amoeba One of many kinds of microscopic protozoans

Common toad

(single-celled organisms). They move and feed by pushing out false feet called *pseudopodia*.

Amphibian A cold-blooded animal belonging to the vertebrate class called Amphibia. Frogs, toads, salamanders, and newts are amphibians. They live in or by water or return there to breed.

Amsterdam Port and capital city of The Netherlands.

Anatomy Study of the structure of plants and animals.

Andes Mountain system in South America, running along the Pacific coast for the entire length of the continent. It is the world's longest chain of mountains.

Andorra Small European principality located between France and Spain. Area: 183 square miles (430 square kilometers). Capital: Andorra la Vella.

Anemia A shortage of red blood cells and the hemoglobin they carry. Anemia makes a person's skin look pale and causes lack of energy.

Angler fish A saltwater fish with an enormous head and huge jaws. A long, thin cord on the top of its head lures other fishes, which it then eats.

Angola Republic on the coast of western Africa. A civil war began there when it gained independence from Portugal in 1975. Area: 481,351 square miles (1,251,513 square kilometers). Capital: Luanda.

Animal A living being that moves freely and feeds on plants or other animals. Worms, insects, fish, birds, dogs, horses, and human beings are animals.

Annapolis State capital of Maryland, on Chesapeake Bay. It is the site of the

United States Naval Academy.

Ant Social insect related to bees, wasps, and hornets. The queen lays eggs that are tended by numerous wingless females called workers.

Antarctica A continent larger than Europe that surrounds the South Pole. It is covered with ice. The only people living there are scientists. Area: 5,400,000 square miles (14,000,000 square kilometers).

Anteater A mammal that has no teeth. The giant anteater lives in South America. It has a long bushy tail and a long thin snout. It rips ant nests open with its claws and licks up the insects with its whiplike tongue.

Antelope Large group of mostly African animals that have hoofs and horns. They look like deer but are in the same family as cattle.

Anthony, Susan Brownell (1820-1906) US champion of women's rights. Throughout her life she worked to give women the right to vote. Fourteen years after Anthony's death, the 19th Amendment to the United States Constitution gave women this right.

Antibiotic A substance that destroys bacteria and microbes that cause disease. Most antibiotics are made from harmless bacteria or fungi (plural of fungus). Penicillin was the first antibiotic. It was discovered in 1928 by Sir Alexander Fleming.

Antibody A substance produced by the body to fight infection by harmful bacteria or viruses. An antibody can also protect a person against a future attack. Antibodies are produced by certain white blood cells.

Gibbon

Orangutan

Gorilla

Chimpanzee

Ape The four mammals most closely related to humans: the chimpanzee, gorilla, orangutan, and gibbon. Apes live in tropical forests in Africa and Asia. They can stand upright and walk on two legs. Unlike most monkeys, none of the apes has a tail.

Apollo program The United States space program to put people on the moon. Twelve astronauts landed on the Moon between July 1969 and December 1972. They were launched into space in the three-man Apollo command module. Two astronauts then transferred to the lunar module to make the Moon landing.

Apostles The twelve men chosen by Jesus Christ to preach his message. They included Simon, Peter, James and John, Matthew, and Judas Iscariot.

Appalachian Mountains Mountain range in eastern North America. It runs from Quebec province in Canada to Alabama, parallel to the Atlantic coast. Highest peak: Mount Mitchell, 6,684 feet (2,037 meters).

Apple The most widely eaten of all fruits. Thousands of different varieties of apples are grown all over the world.

Appleseed, Johnny Nickname of **John Chapman** (1774-1845) US pioneer and folk hero. He collected apple seeds and planted them along the path of pioneers who were traveling west. Johnny Appleseed tended his orchards for many years.

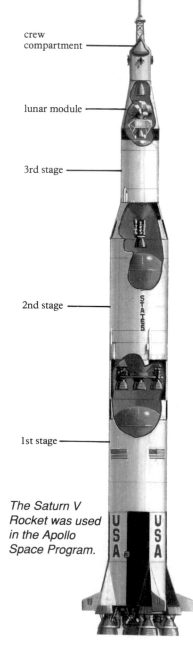

crew compartment

lunar module

3rd stage

2nd stage

1st stage

The Saturn V Rocket was used in the Apollo Space Program.

Arab A person who lives on the Arabian peninsula, another country in the Middle East, or in North Africa.

Arachnid A group containing spiders, daddy longlegs, scorpions, and mites. Arachnids are distinguished from insects by their four pairs of walking legs (an insect has three pairs). They have no wings.

Archaeology The scientific study of ancient civilizations. Archaeologists dig up the remains of past civilizations.

Archaeopteryx Prehistoric bird that lived 150 million years ago. Descended from the dinosaurs, it had teeth, and claws on its wings. Although it had feathers, it was probably a weak flier.

Archaeopteryx

Archimedes (287?-212 BC) Greek mathematician and inventor who discovered the principles of the lever and specific gravity.

Architecture The science of designing buildings. An architect produces the plans and designs that a builder works from. Most societies and ages in history have had their own special styles of architecture.

Arctic The area around the North Pole. It includes the Arctic Ocean, thousands of islands, and the surrounding lands of North America, Asia, and Europe.

Argentina Second largest nation in South America. A major farming nation, agricultural products make up 70 to 90 percent of its exports. Area: 1,073,400 square miles (2,780,092 square kilometers). Capital: Buenos Aires.

Aristotle (384-322 BC) Greek teacher and philosopher. A pupil of Plato, he then taught the young Alexander the Great.

Arithmetic A branch of mathematics dealing with counting and calculating, using numbers. The four main operations in arithmetic are addition, subtraction, multiplication, and division.

Arizona Located in the southwestern United States, Arizona became the 48th state in 1912. Irrigation has turned desert areas into farmland. Livestock is grazed on higher ground. Manufacturing in Tucson and Phoenix is the mainstay of the economy. The Grand Canyon attracts many tourists. Area: 113,909 square miles (295,023 square kilometers). Capital: Phoenix.

Arkansas Arkansas, in the south central United States, became a state in 1836. Manufacturing and the farming of soybeans, rice, and cotton are important. Hot Springs National Park is a major tourist attraction. Area: 53,104 square miles (137,539 square kilometers). Capital: Little Rock.

Armadillo A mammal with hard bony plates covering most of its body. Some are able to roll into a ball for protection. With its sharp claws, it burrows in the ground for insects to eat. Armadillos live in parts of the southern United States, Mexico, and Central and South America.

Armor Protective clothing, usually metal, worn to prevent injury in battle. Though guns and explosives made armor less useful, soldiers still wear helmets today. Warships and tanks have armor plating.

Army, United States The branch of the US military whose soldiers are armed and trained for land warfare.

Arnold, Benedict (1741-1801) US Revolutionary War soldier and traitor. He fought bravely in the American Revolution. In 1780 Arnold plotted to surrender West Point to the British. The plot was discovered. Arnold fled to the British side and fought for them. From 1781 until his death he lived in England.

Arsenic A silvery-white, very poisonous chemical element. Chemical symbol: As.

Art Work created by an artist such as a painter, sculptor, musician, actor, or writer.

Arthur, Chester Alan (1829-1886) Twenty-first president of the United States. He became an outstanding lawyer and head of the Republican Party in New York State. Arthur was elected vice-president of the United States in 1880. He became president in 1881 following the assassination of President Garfield.

Ash A deciduous (leaf-shedding) tree of the olive family, which grows up to 130 feet (40 meters) high. Its winged seeds hang in bunches called keys.

Asia The largest and most populated continent. It occupies 30 percent of the world's total land area, with 60 percent of the world's population. Area: 16,989,000 square miles (44,002,000 square kilometers).

Asp The name for several types of small, poisonous snakes.

Assyrians An ancient people of the Middle East. The Assyrians created a powerful empire between the 19th and 7th centuries BC, from their homeland in northern Mesopotamia.

Asteroids A swarm of small solid objects orbiting the sun between the orbits of Mars and Jupiter. They are also called minor planets or planetoids. The largest asteroid is almost 620 miles (1,000 kilometers) in diameter.

Astrology The study of the movement of the moon, sun, planets, and stars, and their supposed influence on people's lives.

Astronaut A person who is trained in spaceflight or who travels in a spacecraft.

Astronomy The study of the sun, the planets, stars, and other objects in the universe. The astronomer's most important instrument is the telescope. Many astronomers work in an observatory, a kind of laboratory that has a telescope and other instruments.

Common ash tree

Athens Capital city of Greece and center of the ancient Greek civilization. It is famous for its ancient ruins.

Atlanta State capital of Georgia. It has become a major commercial center.

Atlantic Ocean Second largest ocean in the world, after the Pacific. It is bordered by Europe and Africa in the east, and North and South America in the west. Area: 31,814,640 square miles (82,700,000 square kilometers).

Atmosphere The blanket of air around the Earth. It is 21 percent oxygen, 78 percent nitrogen, and 1 percent other gases. It is held in place by Earth's gravity. The atmosphere extends about 300 miles (500 kilometers) above the Earth.

Atom A tiny particle that combines with others to make all forms of matter. At the center of each atom is a nucleus. It is made up of particles called protons and neutrons. Other tiny particles called electrons spin around the nucleus, much as the planets spin around the sun.

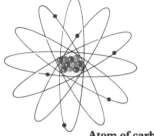

Atom of carbon

Atomic energy Also called nuclear energy. Energy can be released from the nucleus of an atom through fission (breaking it apart) or fusion (joining nuclei together).

Audubon, John James (1785-1851) US painter and ornithologist (one who studies birds). He painted the many birds he studied from life. His 435 life-size colored drawings were published in England under the title *The Birds of America*.

Austen, Jane (1775-1817) English novelist. Daughter of a clergyman, her works include *Pride and Prejudice* (1813) and *Emma* (1816).

Austin State capital of Texas, on the Colorado River. Administrative and commercial center.

Australia A continent and a country in the Southern Hemisphere, between the Indian and southern Pacific oceans. Australia produces almost one fourth of the world's wool and is an important exporter of wheat and other grains. Because most of the interior of Australia is desert, 65 percent of the people live in five large cities along the coast. Area: 2,967,909 square miles (7,686,000 square kilometers). Capital: Canberra.

Austria Mountainous republic in central Europe. Area: 32,375 square miles (83,851 square kilometers). Capital: Vienna.

Automation The use of machines to do work that was once done by people. Once turned on by a person, such machines operate themselves or are controlled by other machines.

Automobile A vehicle for traveling on land. It usually has four wheels and is powered by a gasoline engine. The first automobiles were made in the late 1800s. Today more than 30,000,000 automobiles are produced each year.

1915 Model T Ford

Automobile racing A competitive sport that began in France in 1895. The first Grand Prix (Big Prize) race was held at Le Mans in 1906. Today's racing cars can go as fast as 200 miles (320 kilometers) per hour.

Aztec A member of a native people of central Mexico who had an advanced civilization. They were conquered by the forces of Spain.

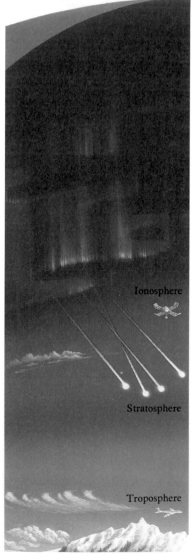

The Atmosphere

Ionosphere

Stratosphere

Troposphere

B

Baboon A large, fierce monkey. Baboons live in troops and are found in Africa and Arabia.

Babylon An ancient city on the Euphrates River. It was the capital center of the kingdom of Babylonia. Its Hanging Gardens were one of the seven wonders of the ancient world. The ruins of Babylon are near the city of Baghdad in Iraq.

Bach, Johann Sebastian (1685-1750) German composer, organist, and choirmaster. He wrote mostly church music, particularly for the organ.

Bacteria Single-celled organisms usually classed as plants, bacteria can be seen only through a microscope. Millions of bacteria are on everything we touch, including our own skin. Some cause disease, while others are useful in medicine.

Baghdad Capital city of Iraq, on the Tigris River. It was founded in 762.

Bahamas A country made up of a group of islands in the Atlantic Ocean, southeast of Florida. About 20 islands are inhabited. Area: 5,380 square miles (13,933 square kilometers). Capital: Nassau.

Bahrain An island country in the Persian Gulf off the Arabian Peninsula. It was the site of the first oil discovery in the Middle East in 1932. Area: 264 square miles (685 square kilometers). Capital: Manama.

Balboa, Vasco Nunez de (1475?-1519) Spanish explorer who discovered the Pacific Ocean.

Bald Eagle A large, North American bird with a

The five positions are the foundations of ballet. Each gives perfect balance.

white-feathered head and neck. It is the national bird of the United States and is often called the American eagle. Bald eagles are an endangered species.

Ballet A popular entertainment with dancing, music, scenery, and costumes.

Balloon A bag filled with heated air or gas so that it floats in the air. The first manned balloon was built by the French Montgolfier brothers in 1783 and was filled with hot air. Ballooning is a popular sport today. Unmanned balloons are used to study the atmosphere.

Bamboo Giant plants of the grass family, which grow very fast. Bamboo grows in tropical areas and is used for building boats, houses, baskets, and boxes. Its shoots provide food for people and panda bears.

Banana A large tropical fruit grown in Africa, South and Central America, and the West Indies.

Bangkok Capital city and port of Thailand.

Bangladesh A country in southern Asia, at the head of the Bay of Bengal. Area: 55,598 square miles (143,998 square kilometers). Capital: Dhaka.

Barbados A small, densely populated island country in the Caribbean Sea. Area: 166 square miles (430 square kilometers). Capital: Bridgetown.

Barber, Samuel (1910-1981) US composer. He was awarded two Pulitzer prizes for his opera *Vanessa* and for his *First Piano Concerto*.

Barium A soft, silvery metallic element. Barium compounds are used in the manufacture of ceramics, paints, and some kinds of glass. Because barium absorbs X rays, doctors use one of its compounds to X-ray patients' digestive systems. Chemical symbol: Ba.

Bark The hard outer covering of the trunk, branches, and roots of trees and shrubs. The surface layer is made of a dead corklike tissue that protects the inner living layers.

Barley The first cereal to be grown by people. It is still an important crop, used for food by people and animals and for brewing malt beverages.

Barnum, P.T. (Full name **Phineas Taylor**) (1810-1891) US showman who formed the Barnum and Bailey Circus. His circus exhibited the dwarf Tom Thumb and Jumbo, a huge African elephant.

Barometer An instrument for measuring air pressure. There are two kinds of barometers, the mercury barometer and the aneroid barometer. In the mercury barometer, air pressure makes the mercury rise or fall inside a long glass tube with numbers on it or next to it. The numbers are read in the same way that numbers on a thermometer are read. The aneroid barometer is an airtight box with most of the air taken out. An increase or decrease in air pressure makes the walls of the box move in or out. This motion waves a pointer over a dial.

Barton, Clara (1821-1912) Founder of the American Red Cross. Because of her devoted care for wounded soldiers during the US Civil War, Barton was called the Angel of the Battlefield. In 1881 Barton organized the American Red Cross. She was its president until 1904.

Base A chemical substance that combines with an acid to form a salt. Some bases are used to make soap and bleaches.

Baseball The national game and most popular sport in the United States. Two teams of nine players try to score by hitting a ball with a bat and completing a run around four bases. The main baseball event is the annual World Series.

Basketball A game usually played indoors by two teams of five players each. Bottomless nets, or baskets, hang 10 feet (3 meters) high at each end of the court. Points are scored by throwing the ball into the net.

Bass A type of freshwater and saltwater fish. Some saltwater bass can weigh as much as 500 pounds (230 kilograms).

Bat The only mammal able to fly. Bats are furry and look somewhat like mice. Their wings are large folds of skin stretched across their fingers. Bats leave their caves and other roosts only at night. Most bats can see

Common long-eared bat

well, but they navigate by using echoes to locate their exact positions.

Battery Plates or cells suspended in chemicals that react to make electricity. Batteries power many things, from watches to cars to spacecraft.

Plates of lead and lead dioxide, surrounded by sulfuric acid, generate electricity in a car battery.

Bean A plant of the pea family that produces nutritious seeds and pods. Beans are an important source of protein for humans and other animals.

Bear Large, shaggy animal

with powerful limbs and claws. American bears include the brown bear, the black bear, and the fierce grizzly bear. Polar bears live in the Arctic.

Bearing The part of a machine that supports a rotating shaft, axle, wheel, or sliding surface. Bearings reduce wear and friction, making the machine work better and last longer.

Beatles, The British rock and roll group of the 1960s. John Lennon, Paul McCartney, George Harrison, and Ringo Starr formed one of the most popular groups in modern music history.

Beaver A large North American rodent. Beavers have broad, flat tails and strong teeth, which they use to cut down trees. They live in rivers, streams and lakes. There they build dams to make pools in which to construct their wooden lodges or homes.

Becket, Thomas à (1118?-1170) English churchman who became the Archbishop of Canterbury and head of the Roman Catholic Church in England. When he refused to do what King Henry II wanted, Becket was murdered by Henry's men. Becket was made a saint in 1173.

Cross section of a beaver lodge, showing the underwater entrance and the snug living quarters.

Bee A flying insect related to wasps and ants. There are two kinds of bees. Solitary bees live alone. Social bees live in colonies. Honeybees are the best-known social bees. They make honey from nectar to feed their egg-laying queen and the young. Beekeepers keep honeybees in specially made hives so that they can collect the honey.

Beech A large deciduous (leaf-shedding) tree growing up to about 80 feet (24 meters) tall. Its nuts are good to eat. The wood is used to make furniture.

Beethoven, Ludwig van (1770-1827) German composer of orchestral, choral, and chamber music. His major works include nine great symphonies, many compositions for violin and piano (called concertos and sonatas), and the opera *Fidelio*.

Beetle A group of insects with hard wing covers. Although they can fly, most live on the ground, burrowing for food. They eat almost anything, from other insects to carrion and dung.

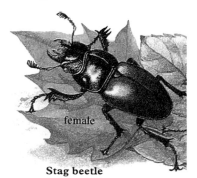

female

Stag beetle

Beijing (Peking) The capital city of China and, for centuries, the home of Chinese rulers. The inner city contains the old imperial palace, formerly called the "Forbidden City." It is now a museum and tourist attraction.

Beirut Port and capital city of Lebanon. Since 1975, much of Beirut has been destroyed in the civil war between Lebanon's Muslims and Christians.

Belgium A small kingdom in western Europe. Dutch-speaking Flemish people live in the north. French-speaking people called Walloons live in the south. Area: 11,781 square miles (31,000 square kilometers). Capital: Brussels.

Belgrade Port and capital city of Yugoslavia, on the Danube River.

Belize A small country on the Caribbean coast of Central America. Sugar, garments, and citrus products are its main exports. Area: 8,867 square miles (23,000 square kilometers). Capital: Belmopan.

Bell, Alexander Graham (1847-1922) Scottish-born US scientist. He invented the telephone in 1876 and organized the Bell Telephone Company in 1877.

Benin A small country in western Africa. Palm oil, raw cotton, and cacao beans are its major exports. Area: 43,483 square miles (113,000 square kilometers). Capital: Porto-Novo.

Berlin, Irving (1888-1989) Writer of popular US songs. His most famous songs include "Always," "Alexander's Ragtime Band," and "God Bless America."

Berlin City in what was the German Democratic Republic (East Germany). After World War II, the city was divided. East Berlin became the capital of East Germany. West Berlin formed close ties to what was the Federal Republic of Germany (West Germany). The Berlin Wall was built in 1961 because of conflicts between the two sides. In 1989 steps were taken to remove the wall. In 1990, Germany became a united country with Berlin as its capital.

Bermuda Group of islands in the western Atlantic Ocean.

Bernstein, Leonard (1918-1990) US music conductor, composer, pianist, and author. He wrote symphonies, operas, and ballets. He also wrote the music for the play *West Side Story* (1957). It is a musical version of Shakespeare's play *Romeo and Juliet*, updated to a 1950s New York City setting.

Bible The book containing the sacred texts of Judaism and Christianity.

Bicycle A vehicle with two wheels, one behind the other, plus a seat, handlebars, and pedals, mounted on a frame. The rider moves the bicycle by pushing the pedals around in a circle, which turns the rear wheel. Today's bicycle has a chain-driven rear wheel, air-filled rubber tires, and gears.

Billy the Kid Nickname of **William H. Bonney** (1859-1881) US outlaw. Billy the Kid led gangs of cattle rustlers. He killed more than 20 people. He was sentenced to death in 1881, but he escaped from prison. Three months later, Sheriff Pat Garrett tracked him down and killed him.

Binary System A numeral system using only two symbols, 0 and 1, instead of the ten symbols, 0 through 9, in the decimal system. The binary system is used in computers because it is easier and cheaper to build a machine that uses two numbers instead of ten.

Biochemistry The study of the chemical processes that take place inside plants and animals.

Biology The study of living things, including their structure, chemical activity, habits, distribution, and origin. Its two branches are zoology, the study of animal life, and botany, the study of plant life.

Birch A family of slender, deciduous (leaf-shedding) trees found in northern lands. They have thin, white, peeling bark, small leaves, and durable wood. The bark was once used by Indians to make canoes.

Bird A warm-blooded vertebrate with wings, a feathered body, and a beak. Most birds can fly, but there are several flightless species, such as the ostrich and penguin.

Bison The large, shaggy-haired, wild, cow-like animal, or buffalo, of North America. It once roamed the plains in vast herds.

Bivalve A sea-dwelling mollusk that has two hinged shells. Mussels, clams, and oysters are bivalves.

Blackbird A bird of North America. The two most common types are the red-winged blackbird and the yellow-headed blackbird. The European blackbird belongs to the thrush family.

Black Death A deadly disease, also known as the bubonic plague. It is carried by rats that have fleas. The disease swept through Europe and parts of Asia in the 1300s, killing almost half of the population.

Black hole A region in space where gravity is so strong that nothing can escape, not even light. Black holes may result from the collapse of a giant star, or supernova.

Black Sea A sea bordered by Turkey, Bulgaria, Romania, and the USSR. It is connected to the Mediterranean Sea. Area: 175,000 square miles (453,000 square kilometers).

Black widow A poisonous North American spider. It is believed that only the female is dangerous to people. It is shiny black with a red patch on its underside.

Red blood cells (left) are disk shaped. Phagocytes (right) are white blood cells that engulf, or eat, bacteria.

Blood The liquid pumped by the heart to all parts of the body. It is necessary for life. Red blood cells carry oxygen from the lungs to the tissues. White blood cells help protect the body against infection and disease.

Blues A form of popular vocal or instrumental music that seems to reflect sad feelings.

Boa constrictor A large snake of tropical America that kills its prey by squeezing it. Some boa constrictors are 14 feet (4 meters) long.

Boar, wild A wild hog found in the forests of North Africa and Asia.

Wild boar

Bobcat A small North American wildcat. It has a short tail and a rust-colored coat with black spots.

Bolivia Mountainous, landlocked republic in South America. Its most important exports are natural gas and tin. Area: 424,162 square miles (1,089,000 square kilometers). Capitals: Sucre (legal) and La Paz (administrative).

Bone One of the parts of a vertebrate skeleton.

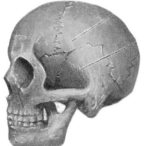

The human skull is made of bone, which protects the soft brain inside.

Bonn City in western Germany, on the Rhine River.

Book A set of written, printed, or blank papers that are fastened together between two covers.

Boone, Daniel (1734-1820) US pioneer and frontiersman. He explored the region that is now the state of Kentucky and helped to settle it. He founded the town of Boonesboro, Kentucky. Boone was captured several times by Indians, but he always escaped.

Booth, John Wilkes (1838-1865) The man who assassinated US President Abraham Lincoln. Booth supported the South during the Civil War. When the South surrendered, he plotted with a group a men to kill Northern leaders. He shot President Lincoln on April 14, 1865, at Ford's Theater in Washington, D.C. He fled the theater but was tracked down and killed.

Boron A non-metallic chemical element. Its best known compound is borax, which is used in soap, washing powder, water softeners, and antiseptics. Chemical symbol: B.

Boston Port and capital city of Massachusetts. It is the commercial center of New England.

Boston Tea Party An attack by American colonists on British ships in Boston Harbor on December 16, 1773. Dressed as Indians, they dumped the contents of 342 chests of tea into the harbor to protest against the British tax on tea. The Boston Tea Party was one of the events that led to the Revolutionary War.

Botany The scientific study of plants.

Botswana An independent, landlocked republic in southern Africa. Area: 224,607 square miles (581,730 square kilometers). Capital: Gaborone.

Boxing A sport in which two contestants fight each other with their fists. They wear padded gloves and fight in a "ring." They may strike only at certain parts of the body (the head and torso).

Brahms, Johannes (1833-1897) German composer. His works include more than 200 songs, concertos for the violin and piano, four great symphonies, and choral music.

Braille, Louis (1809-1852) Frenchman who invented a system of reading and writing for the blind. He himself was blind.

Brain The control center of the body. It receives messages and gives out instructions to all parts of the body by way of nerves. Information is stored in the brain. The brain and spinal cord together form the central nervous system.

Brasilia Capital city of Brazil. It was built between 1956 and 1960 to be the nation's new capital.

Brazil The fifth largest country in the world. Brazil occupies almost half the area of South America. Rapid industrialization has taken place during the past decade. Area: 3,286,487 square miles (8,511,965 square kilometers). Capital: Brasilia.

British Columbia Province of Canada on the country's west coast. Natural resources include timber, copper, oil, coal, and fish. The largest city and main seaport is Vancouver. Area: 366,255 square miles (947,000 square kilometers). Capital: Victoria.

British Isles A group of islands off the western coast of Europe consisting of Great Britain, Ireland, and nearby islands.

Bromine A liquid chemical element that unites easily with many other elements to form bromides. It is used in making dyes and in photography. Chemical symbol: Br.

Brontë, Charlotte (1816-1855) English novelist whose best-known novel was *Jane Eyre* (1847). Her sister Emily (1818-48) wrote *Wuthering Heights* (1847), and her sister Anne (1820-49) wrote *Agnes Grey* (1847) and *The Tenant of Wildfell Hall* (1848).

Brontosaurus The popular name of a huge plant-eating dinosaur that lived 150 million years ago. Apatosaurus is its correct scientific name. It was 75-80 feet (24 meters) long and weighed 30 tons.

Bronze Age The prehistoric period between about 3000 and 1800 BC when people learned to make tools and weapons out of metal. At first they used copper, but then they found that bronze (an alloy of copper and tin) was stronger and easier to use.

Brown, John (1800-1859) US anti-slavery campaigner. Brown wanted to use force to free the slaves. In 1859, he and 18 followers seized the United States arsenal at Harpers Ferry, Virginia (now West Virginia). They were captured by Colonel Robert E. Lee's marines. Brown was hanged as a traitor.

Brunei A small, oil-rich nation on the northern coast of Borneo in the western Pacific Ocean. Many people are farmers and rice is the main crop. Area: 2,226 square miles (5,800 square kilometers). Capital: Bandar Seri Begawan.

Brussels Port and capital city of Belgium, on the Senne River.

Buchanan, James (1791-1868) Fifteenth president of the United States. He became a successful lawyer and later a United States congressman and senator from

The correct name for the Brontosaurus is Apatosaurus.

Pennsylvania. He was a Federalist and, later, a Democrat. Buchanan was president from 1857 to 1861. During his presidency, seven Southern states seceded from the Union. The Civil War began soon after he left office.

Bucharest Capital city of Romania, on the Dimbovita River.

Budapest Capital city of Hungary, on the Danube River.

Buddha (563?-about 480 BC) Original name **Prince Siddhartha**. Indian religious leader and founder of the Buddhist religion.

Buddhists believe that special ways of sitting help them to meditate.

Buddhism A religion founded in India more than 2,500 years ago by Siddhartha Gautama. He is known as the Buddha, or wise one. He taught that the way to find inner peace is to give up selfish desires.

Buenos Aires Capital city and leading port of Argentina, on the estuary of Rio de la Plata.

Buffalo A hoofed mammal of Asia and Africa. It is a member of the cattle family, along with cows, oxen, and bison. The buffalo has large curved horns and is very strong. The American bison is often called a buffalo.

Buffalo Bill Nickname of **William Frederick Cody** (1846-1917) United States cavalry scout who gained fame for his Wild West show.

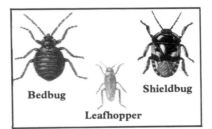

Bedbug   Shieldbug

Leafhopper

Bug An insect that looks like a beetle. Unlike a beetle, it does not have jaws. The mouths of bugs are "beaks" used to pierce plants and suck up their juices.

Bulb A thick underground plant stem that stores food from one growing season to the next. Tulips, onions, and other plants grow from bulbs.

Bulgaria A country of southeastern Europe bordering the Black Sea. Machinery and industrial equipment are its most important exports. Area: 42,823 square miles (111,000 square kilometers). Capital: Sofia.

Bunyan, Paul A US folk hero who was a giant lumberjack. Stories called "tall tales" tell of his adventures in logging with his huge companion, Babe, the Blue Ox.

Buoyancy The ability of an object to float in water. Buoyancy depends on the object's density. Objects like wood, which are less dense than water, will float, while steel, which is more dense than water, will sink.

Burkina Faso A landlocked country in West Africa, long called Upper Volta. Most of the people are farmers. Area: 105,869 square miles (274,179 square kilometers). Capital: Ouagadougou.

Burma Nation in southeastern Asia. Rice, sugar cane, tobacco, and oilseeds are important products. Rice and forest products such as teakwood are the main exports. Area: 261,218 square miles (676,552 square kilometers). Capital: Rangoon.

Burundi A small nation in the heart of Africa. Area: 10,759 square miles (28,000 square kilometers). Capital: Bujumbura.

Bush, George (1924-) Forty-first president of the United States. He joined the Navy during World War II and became its youngest fighter pilot. He was head of the CIA (Central Intelligence Agency) from 1976 to 1977. A Republican, Bush was vice-president under Ronald Reagan from 1981 to 1989. He was elected president in 1988 and took office in 1989.

Bushman One of the oldest peoples of Africa. They are also called the San or Kung. There are now only about 50,000. They are nomadic hunters and gatherers who live in family groups in the Kalahari Desert.

Butter Food made by churning (stirring) cream or whole milk. It is used in cooking and as a spread for bread. It takes over 17 pints (8 liters) of milk to make 2 pounds (1 kilogram) of butter.

Buttercup A bright yellow wildflower that grows in fields, woods and damp areas. Its juice is so bitter that grazing animals will not eat it.

Butterfly An insect with four large, often beautifully

colored, wings. They are related to moths. Butterflies feed on flowers. Butterfly eggs hatch into larva called caterpillars, which eat leaves and turn into a chrysalis, or pupa. It leaves this stage as an adult butterfly with wings.

Buzzard A large, hawklike bird of prey with broad wings. Buzzards eat rabbits, mice, and other small animals.

Byrd, Richard Evelyn (1888-1957) US naval officer, explorer, and aviator. With Floyd Bennett, he made the first flight over the North Pole. He later led five expeditions to Antarctica.

Byzantine Empire A Christian empire located in the Middle East during the Middle Ages. In 330 AD, the emperor Constantine moved the capital of the Roman Empire from Rome to Byzantium. In 395, the empire was divided in two. The eastern half remained the Byzantine Empire until 1453. Its capital, renamed Constantinople in honor of the emperor, is now Istanbul, Turkey.

C

Cactus A family of plants that live in dry places in the southwestern United States and Mexico. The stems store water and the roots spread out to catch any rain. Prickly spines protect the plants from thirsty animals.

Cadmium A metallic element. It is used to make alloys and as a protective coating on other metals. Chemical symbol: Cd.

Caesar Augustus (63 BC - 14 AD) Called Octavian when he was young. First emperor of ancient Rome. His great-uncle was Julius Caesar, who adopted Octavian as his son and heir. "Augustus" is a title that means "sacred" or "of high rank."

Cairo Capital city of Egypt, at the head of the Nile delta. It is Africa's largest city.

Calamity Jane Nickname of **Martha Jane Canary Burke** (1852-1903) US frontier character. She became famous for her skill at horseback riding and shooting.

Calcium A metallic element whose compounds make up a large part of the Earth's crust. It is necessary for life and is found in great quantities in teeth and bones. Chemical symbol: Ca.

Calculator A machine that can be used to find the answer to many kinds of mathematical problems.

Calculus A branch of mathematics that deals with calculating changing quantities.

Calendar A system of organizing time in days, months, and years. The calendar we use today was invented by the Romans.

California The third largest state of the United States, located on the Pacific coast. Area: 158,693 square miles (411,103 square kilometers). Capital: Sacramento.

Camel A hoofed mammal that is used for transportation and food. The Arabian camel, or dromedary, has one hump. The Bactrian camel of Asia has two humps. Fat stored in the humps helps camels to survive in deserts. Alpacas, guanacos, llamas, and vicuñas are members of the camel family.

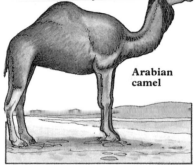
Arabian camel

Camera A device used in photography. When the shutter opens for a fraction of a second, light rays from the object enter the camera. The rays cause an image of the object to be formed on the film.

Cameroon A country in western Africa on the Gulf of Guinea. Coffee and cocoa are major crops, but oil is

Giant redwood trees grow in California. Their huge size is shown by the person near the base of the left-hand tree.

now Cameroon's most important export. Area: 183,591 square miles (475,000 square kilometers). Capital: Yaounde.

Canada The second largest country in the world, situated in North America. Originally French, it was ruled by the British after 1763 and became an independent country in 1867. Area: 3,849,674 square miles (9,970,610 square kilometers). Capital: Ottawa.

Canals Waterways built for the movement of barges and ships. They are sometimes used for irrigation.

Cancer A disease. Cells in the body grow and spread in an uncontrolled way. They form a growing mass of tissue called a tumor, and they destroy normal cells. Cancer may cause death.

Cape Canaveral The main site used by the United States for space launches. Located in eastern Florida, it was known as Cape Kennedy from 1963 to 1973.

Cape Cod A hook-shaped peninsula on the coast of Massachusetts. It reaches 65 miles (105 kilometers) east and north into the Atlantic Ocean. It is a popular vacation spot.

Capitol, United States A building in Washington, D.C., where the US Senate and the House of Representatives hold their sessions. The site was chosen by George Washington, and Congress first met there in 1800. The British set fire to the Capitol during the War of 1812.

Carbohydrate One of the main foods essential to the body, along with protein and fat. Sugar and starch are carbohydrates.

Carbon A nonmetallic element present in all living things. Pure carbon appears in nature as coal, as the soft graphite used to make pencil leads, and as the diamond, the hardest of all known substances. Chemical symbol: C.

Carbon dioxide An odorless and colorless gas made up of carbon and oxygen. It is produced when a substance containing carbon, such as wood or coal, is burned. It is also breathed out by animals, and used by plants when they make food by photosynthesis. Chemical symbol: CO_2.

Carbon monoxide A colorless, poisonous gas with no taste or smell. It is formed when carbon does not burn completely because there is too little air. Car exhaust fumes contain carbon monoxide. Chemical symbol: CO.

Caribbean Sea Part of the Atlantic Ocean. It is bounded by the West Indies, Central America, and northern South America.

Caribou A deer of North America that stands up to 5 feet (1½ meters) tall at the shoulders. Both sexes grow antlers. Caribou graze on the arctic tundra during the summer and move south to the shelter of the forest in the winter.

A selection of foods rich in carbohydrates. They provide energy quickly but if eaten to excess may lead to fatness.

Carnivore Any meat-eating animal. A carnivore is also an order, or group, of mammals called Carnivora. Foxes, bears, cats, weasels, otters, and seals are carnivores.

Carp A family of freshwater fishes that includes minnows and goldfish.

Carson, Kit (Christopher) (1809-1868) US frontier scout, trapper, and Indian agent.

Carter, Jimmy (James Earl, Jr.) (1924-) Thirty-ninth president of the United States. Carter served in the Navy. He later ran the family peanut business before he entered politics. A Democrat, he was elected governor of Georgia in 1970. Carter, a strong supporter of human rights, was president from 1977 to 1981. He helped bring about a peace treaty between Egypt and Israel.

Cartier, Jacques (1491-1557) The French explorer who discovered and explored the Saint Lawrence River in Canada.

Cartoon A humorous drawing. Comic strips in newspapers are a series of cartoons that tell a simple story or joke. An animated cartoon is made of many still cartoons that seem to move when quickly shown one after another.

Carver, George Washington (1864-1943) US agricultural chemist. He was head of agricultural research at Tuskegee Institute in Alabama for almost 50 years. There he made hundreds of products from the peanut, the sweet potato and the soybean. He worked hard to help poor farmers in the South make more money from their crops.

Cascade Range A mountain

range in North America. It stretches from northern California through western Oregon and Washington into southern British Columbia. Mount St. Helens, a volcanic peak in this range, erupted in 1980. The highest peak is Mount Rainier (14,410 feet; 4,392 meters).

Caspian Sea A salt lake situated between Europe and Asia, in the USSR and Iran. It is the world's largest inland body of water, but it has been shrinking in recent years. Area: 143,630 square miles (372,000 square kilometers).

Cassatt, Mary (1844-1926) US impressionist painter, born in Pittsburgh, Pennsylvania. She studied and worked mostly in France. Her paintings often show a mother and child.

Cassowary A large, flightless bird related to the emu. It lives in New Guinea and North Australia.

Castle A military stronghold that was also usually the home of a great noble or ruler. Many stone castles were built in Europe during the Middle Ages.

Castro, Fidel (1927-) Prime minister (1959-1976) and president of Cuba (1976 -). He came to power following a successful revolution against the previous leader.

Cat Any member of the carnivorous cat family which includes the lion, leopard, cheetah, tiger, wildcat, and domestic cat.

Catalyst A substance that speeds up a chemical reaction but is not changed itself in the process.

Caterpillar The larva of a moth or butterfly. A larva is the young of some insects that has just hatched out of an egg. As the caterpillar

eats and grows, it sheds its skin several times. In a few weeks it spins a cocoon around itself. At this stage in its development, it is called a pupa. After several weeks, the cocoon splits open, and a butterfly or moth emerges. (See metamorphosis.)

Catfish A group of about 2,000 species of fish. Catfish have no scales but all have long barbels, or whiskers, around the mouth.

Cathedral A Christian church that is important as the seat, or office, of a bishop. Cathedrals are often noted for their great size and fine architecture.

Cathode-ray tube A glass vacuum tube through which streams of electrons

Domestic cats

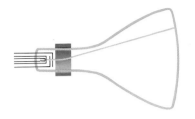

Diagram of cathode-ray tube, showing the electron beam which scans the screen.

are made to strike a screen, forming a bright spot. They are used in computer terminals as well as television and radar sets.

Cattail A plant that grows in swamps and marshes. Some can grow to 6 feet (1.8 meters) high. The plant has reedlike leaves and long, brown, fuzzy flower spikes.

Cattle Members of the ox family along with their wild relatives, the bison and buffalo. They are important farm animals that provide milk, butter, cream, cheese, beef, and leather.

Caucasus Mountain range in the southern USSR, located between the Black Sea and the Caspian Sea.

Cedar A cone-bearing evergreen tree related to the pine tree. The elegant cedar of Lebanon grows up to 132 feet (40 meters) tall and may live for thousands of years.

Cell, biological The basic unit of all living things. The cell's nucleus contains chromosomes, which carry all the genetic information of the cell.

Cell, electric A device that produces electricity from chemicals. A simple electric cell is made up of two different electrodes. These are bathed in a solution of water and acid called an electrolyte, which conducts electricity. When the electrolyte reacts with the electrodes, electricity is formed. A battery is made up of a group of cells.

Cellulose A substance found in most plants, forming the main part of cell walls. Tough and fibrous, it is used to make paper, explosives, plastic, and textiles.

Celts An ancient people who lived over much of central and western Europe during the Iron Age (about 700 BC). They had iron weapons earlier than other peoples, which gave them an advantage in war. Celtic languages such as Irish, Scottish, and Welsh are still spoken in parts of the British Isles.

Centipede One of a group of small animals called arthropods that have between 15 and 170 pairs of legs. The first pair form poisonous fangs. Centipedes live in damp places, under stones or in houses. One tropical species may grow to 12 inches (30 centimeters) in length.

Central African Republic Landlocked country in central Africa with few resources. Cotton, coffee, timber, and diamonds are its main exports. Area: 240,535 square miles (622,984 square kilometers). Capital: Bangui.

Central America The area of North America located south of Mexico and north of South America. It is a thin strip of land made up of the countries of Belize, Costa Rica, El Salvador, Guatemala, Honduras, Nicaragua, and Panama. Area: 227,933 square miles (590,346 square kilometers).

Ceramics Pottery of all kinds, including china, porcelain, and earthenware. These are made of clay mixed with water and baked, or fired, in a hot oven called a kiln to harden them.

Cerberus In Greek mythology, a three-headed dog who guarded the gates of Hades. One of the Labors of Heracles (Hercules) was to capture this dog.

Cereals Plants of the grass family cultivated for their seeds (grain). Rice is one of the world's most important cereals. It is the staple diet of Asia. Wheat is the most important crop in the Americas and Europe. It is made into flour, bread, and breakfast foods.

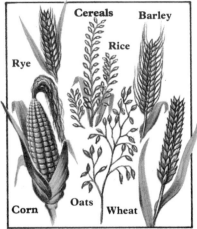

Cereals — Barley, Rice, Rye, Corn, Oats, Wheat

Chad Large, landlocked country in north-central Africa. It is one of the least developed countries in the world. Area: 495,752 square miles (1,283,901 square kilometers). Capital: N'Djamena.

Chalk A soft limestone made up mostly of the remains of tiny marine creatures. It is used in the manufacture of rubber goods, putty, portland cement, and other products.

Chameleon A lizard found in Africa and Asia that has the ability to change its skin color to match its surroundings.

Chamois A small, agile hoofed mammal that lives in small flocks in the mountains of Europe and western Asia. It has horns and looks like a goat.

Champlain, Samuel de (1567-1635) French explorer who founded the French colony of Quebec, Canada, in 1608. Lake Champlain is named for him.

Chaplin, Charlie (1889-1977) English comedian, film actor, and director. He became famous as "the Little Tramp," a comic character who wore baggy pants and a derby hat. His many films include *The Gold Rush* (1925), *City Lights* (1931), *Modern Times* (1936), and *The Great Dictator* (1940).

Chariot A light, two-wheeled, horse-drawn vehicle. In ancient times, the chariot was used in wars because of its speed. Chariot racing was a popular sport in the Roman Empire.

Charlemagne (742-814) King of the Franks (a people who lived mainly in what is now France). He also became emperor of the Holy Roman Empire. His name means Charles the Great.

Chaucer, Geoffrey (1340?-1400) English author of the Middle Ages. He is most famous for *The Canterbury Tales*, a collection of stories told by a group of people traveling to a religious shrine.

Cheetah A member of the cat family that is the world's fastest land animal. The cheetah is capable of run-

Chamois

ning 70 miles (110 kilometers) per hour. It lives on open plains in Africa and India.

Chemical formula A way of showing the chemical makeup of a molecule by using symbols. The chemical formula of water, for example, is H_2O. This means that a water molecule contains two atoms of hydrogen (H_2) and one of oxygen (O).

Chemical reaction A process involving two or more substances that results in chemical changes in those substances. The formation of rust on iron when it is exposed to air is a chemical reaction.

Chemistry The study of substances and the changes that occur when they combine with other substances.

Cherry The small, round fruit of the cherry tree, a member of the rose family. There are hundreds of varieties, ranging in color from red to black and in taste from sweet to sour.

Chesapeake Bay A large inlet of the Atlantic Ocean. It stretches 200 miles (320 kilometers) from southern Maryland to northern Virginia.

Chess A board game for two players. Each player has 16 pieces. One set is white, and the other is black. A player tries to move his or her pieces across the board, capturing the other player's pieces while trying to avoid losing his or her own pieces.

Chestnut A deciduous (leaf-shedding) tree of the beech family. Its wood is long-lasting, and its nuts are good to eat. Most North American chestnut trees have been killed by a disease.

Chicago One of the largest cities in the United States, on the shores of Lake Michigan, in Illinois. It has the largest railroad yard in the world and one of the busiest airports.

Chile Country on the southwest coast of South America. The majority of people live in the central region, which is suitable for agriculture. Area: 292,135 square miles (756,626 square kilometers). Capital: Santiago.

Chimpanzee An African ape that lives in forests in small family groups, eating fruit and leaves. It is noted for its intelligence.

China The third largest country in the world, located in eastern Asia. About twenty percent of the people in the world live in China. Communist rule was established in 1949. Area: 3,678,470 square miles (9,527,200 square kilometers). Capital: Beijing (also called Peking).

Chipmunk A North American and Asian rodent related to the squirrel. It lives in underground burrows. Chipmunks eat nuts and berries and can store them in pouches in their cheeks.

Chlorine A poisonous gas that irritates the eyes, throat, and lungs. It was the first poison gas to be used in warfare (World War I). Its compounds (chlorides) are used in bleaches, explosives, drugs, dyes, disinfectants, and other products. Chemical symbol: Cl.

Chlorophyll The green coloring matter, or pigment, in most plants. Chlorophyll absorbs energy from sunlight. In a process called photosynthesis, the plant uses the absorbed energy, along with carbon dioxide and water, to make its own food.

Chocolate A food made from beans of the cacao plant. The beans are roasted and ground up. Chocolate is often sweetened and flavored. It is used to make candy and desserts.

Chokecherry A wild cherry tree of North America. It belongs to the rose family. Its sour fruit is sometimes used for jam.

Cholera A contagious disease. It is caused by bacteria that enter the intestines and produce toxins, or poisons. The disease causes vomiting and diarrhea and the loss of body fluids. Treatment consists of the replacement of these fluids. It occurs chiefly in those Asian countries where sanitation is poor.

The ancient Chinese built fine chariots drawn by trotting horses.

Christianity A major world religion, based on the life and teachings of Jesus Christ. Christians believe that Jesus was the Messiah (savior), as foretold in the Old Testament, who died to save all people.

Christmas (December 25th) The day on which Christians celebrate the birth of Jesus Christ. It is one of the most important festivals of the Christian church. Members of the Eastern Orthodox churches, mostly Greek and Russian, celebrate Christmas on January 7 because they use a different calendar.

Chromium A hard, metallic element that resists corrosion. It is used to give a shiny plating to other metals. Chemical symbol: Cr.

Chromosome A tiny body in the nucleus of a cell. Chromosomes carry the genes that determine the features a living thing inherits.

Chrysanthemum A plant of the daisy family, grown for its blossoms. Chrysanthemums flower in the fall.

Churchill, Sir Winston Leonard Spencer (1874-1965) British statesman, soldier, and author. Elected Prime Minister in 1940, he led Britain through World War II. His writings include *The Second World War* (1948-54), and *History of the English-Speaking Peoples* (1956-58).

Winston Churchill

CIA (Stands for the **Central Intelligence Agency**) An agency of the United States government. The CIA gathers information about people and other nations. It has also engaged in undercover operations in other countries. It was established in 1947.

Circus An entertainment held in a circular arena, or ring. Modern circuses began in the 1700s. A typical show features clowns, jugglers, acrobats, and sometimes performing animals. Circuses are sometimes shown in a large tent, the Big Top.

Citrus fruit The fruit of citrus trees including oranges, lemons, limes, grapefruits, and tangerines. They contain citric acid, which tastes like lemon juice, and vitamin C.

Civil rights Privileges that belong to everyone in a free country. These include freedom of speech, religion, and the press; freedom from racial and sexual discrimination; and the right to vote.

Civil Service All government workers except members of the armed forces, elected officials, and judges. They carry out the everyday business of running a country, state, or city. Teachers, police officers, and diplomats are examples of people in the civil service. They are called civil servants.

Civil War, American A war fought between the northern US states (Union) and the southern states (Confederacy) from 1861 to 1865. It was fought over two issues, slavery and states' rights. The South feared that newly elected President Abraham Lincoln would abolish slavery. It also believed that states had the right to secede, or withdraw, from the Union. After Lincoln's election, southern states began to secede. Eventually 11 of them tried to form a new nation, the Confederate States of America. The war began when southern troops attacked Fort Sumter in South Carolina in April 1861. It ended when Confederate General Robert E. Lee surrendered to Union General Ulysses S. Grant in April 1865. During this bitterly fought war, more than 620,000 soldiers died, more than in any other US war. But slavery was abolished in the United States, and the Union was preserved.

Clam A mollusk with two shells. There are more than 12,000 saltwater and freshwater species. Most lie buried in the mud of shallow water. Clams are a popular food.

Clay A kind of earth made of very fine particles. When it is wet, it can be easily shaped. When heated and dried, clay becomes very hard. It is used to make bricks, pottery, tiles, and pipes.

Cleopatra (69-30 BC) Queen of Egypt. She ruled Egypt first with her brother, Ptolemy XIII and then with another brother Ptolemy XIV. She met the Roman leader, Mark Antony, in 41 BC. In 31 BC Antony was defeated at the Battle of Actium by Octavian, a rival for the leadership of Rome. Cleopatra let a snake bite her after Antony died.

Cleveland, Grover (1837-1908) Twenty-second and twenty-fourth president of the United States. A Democrat, he was governor of New York from 1883 to 1885. Cleveland was president of the US from 1885 to 1889. He lost the 1888 election to Benjamin Harrison but he came back to win the 1892 election. He served his second term from 1893 to 1897.

Climate The average weather conditions of a place over a period of time. Those weather conditions include temperature, rainfall, winds, and humidity. The climate tends to be warmer near the equator, and cooler toward the poles.

Clock A machine that shows and measures the time. Time is measured in hours, minutes, and sometimes seconds. The face, or front, of a clock has changing numbers or a marked dial over which two hands pass to show the correct time.

Cloud A visible mass of tiny drops of water or ice crystals that floats in the sky. Clouds are usually found at altitudes between 1/2 mile and 7 miles.

Coal A valuable fossil fuel found in layers, or seams, underground. It is called a fossil fuel because it was formed over a period of millions of years from dead plants. Coal is mostly carbon.

Cobalt A silvery white, hard metallic element used in alloys. Chemical symbol: Co.

Cobra A poisonous snake from Africa and Asia. When a cobra is excited, the neck expands and looks like a hood. The cobra bites or spits venom at its victims. The bite is deadly, and venom in the eyes can cause blindness.

Cockatoo A member of the parrot family with a crest of head feathers and loud screech. Cockatoos live in Australia, New Guinea and the Pacific islands.

Cockroach One of the most widespread insect pests. Most species live in hot countries. In cooler places, they often seek warmth in kitchens and restaurants.

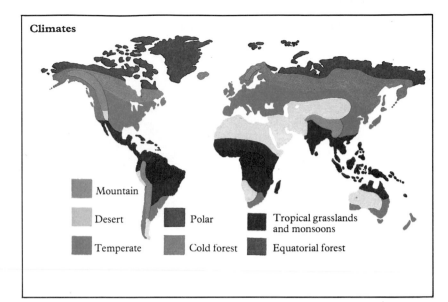

Climates

Mountain, Desert, Temperate, Polar, Cold forest, Tropical grasslands and monsoons, Equatorial forest

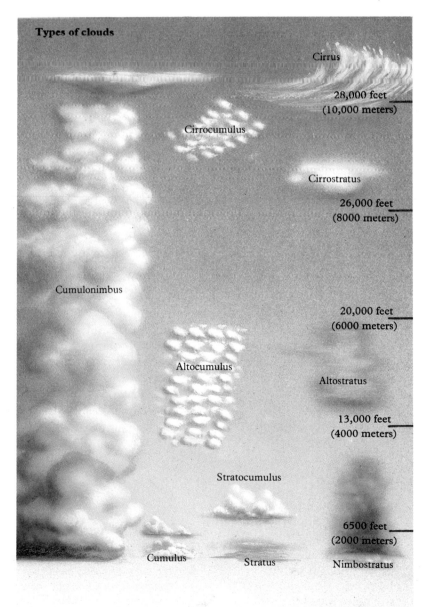

Types of clouds

Cocoa A brown powder made from the beans of the cacao tree. It is used to make chocolate. The trees grow in South America and western Africa.

Coconut The fruit of the coconut palm, a tropical tree that stands up to 100 feet (30 meters) high. The coconut's hard, brown shell, or husk, is lined with a sweet white meat. It has a hollow center filled with a sweet liquid called coconut milk. Dried coconut meat, called copra, contains coconut oil, which is used for cooking. The husk of the coconut is used to make matting, the wood of the tree is used in building, and the leaves are used for roofing.

Cod One of the most important food fishes. Nearly 25 species are found in the northern Atlantic and northern Pacific oceans.

Coffee A drink made from the roasted and ground seeds of a small evergreen tree. These trees grow best where the climate is hot and moist.

College A school that a person may attend after graduating from high school. Colleges offer two or four years of general studies or training for a profession. College graduates are given a certificate called a degree.

Colombia Republic in northwestern South America with coastlines on both the Pacific Ocean and the Caribbean Sea. It produces coffee, sugar, oil, and coal. Gold, emeralds, and platinum are also mined. Area: 439,735 square miles (1,138,825 square kilometers). Capital: Bogotá.

Color A quality of light. An object appears to have a certain color because its surface reflects light of that

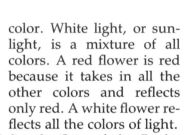

The Rocky Mountains–a view in Colorado.

color. White light, or sunlight, is a mixture of all colors. A red flower is red because it takes in all the other colors and reflects only red. A white flower reflects all the colors of light.

Colorado One of the Rocky Mountain states. Colorado became a state in 1876. On the eastern Great Plains, irrigated farms produce cereals, potatoes, and sugar beets. Colorado also has large herds of cattle and sheep. Mining helped to make Colorado prosperous, but manufacturing is now the chief activity. Tourism and skiing are also important. Area: 104,247 square miles (269,998

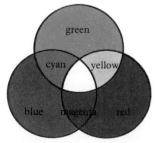

Some results of mixing blue, green, and red light. Equal amounts of all three make white, the color of sunlight.

square kilometers). Capital: Denver.

Colorado potato beetle (Also known as the potato bug) An insect pest that can destroy entire potato crops. It is native to North America but has spread to Europe where it does great damage.

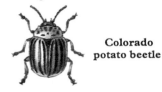

Colorado potato beetle

Colosseum A building in Rome, Italy, where the ancient Romans held their entertainments. It is an oval amphitheater, or stadium, which was built in the 1st century AD. Nearly 650 feet (200 meters) wide, it could hold 50,000 people on its marble benches.

Colt, Samuel (1814-1862) US inventor and arms manufacturer. He patented the pistol that became known as the Colt revolver, or six-shooter. With it, a person could fire six shots without reloading. The pistol was used in the Mexican War and the Civil War and was also popular with settlers in the West. It was used by the US Army and other armies for many years.

Columbus State capital of Ohio, on the Scioto River.

Columbus, Christopher (1451-1506) The Italian-born explorer who was supported by King Ferdinand and Queen Isabella of Spain in his quest to reach Asia by sailing west. He never reached Asia, but he did discover the New World in 1492.

Combustion The process of burning. Substances combine with oxygen when they burn, causing a chemical reaction that produces heat and light.

Comet An object in outer space made of dust, frozen gases, and water. It circles the sun in a long, looping orbit. As a comet approaches the sun, it heats up and begins to glow. Gas and dust are released to form a tail stretching millions of miles through space.

Communism An economic and social system in which property and goods are owned by the community as a whole. There is no private ownership. The first country to have a Communist government was the USSR, after the 1917 revolution. China became a Communist country in 1949.

Compass An instrument showing geographical direction. A magnetic compass has a magnetic needle that points to the Earth's north magnetic pole.

Compound A substance made up of two or more elements. Compounds are formed when elements join together and make a new substance that is com-

pletely different from the elements it contains. Water is a compound of hydrogen and oxygen.

Computer An electronic device that accepts data (information), works on the data as instructed, and gives out the results of its calculation. Computers can work out problems very quickly. They can also store vast amounts of information.

Condensation The process by which vapor (a gas) turns to a liquid. The condensation of water vapor in the atmosphere produces clouds, rain, and snow. At ground level it produces fog, dew, and frost.

The effects of condensation at ground level.

Confederate States of America (Also known as the Confederacy) The name taken by the 11 southern states that tried to form a separate nation from the United States around the start of the Civil War in 1861. These states were South Carolina, Mississippi, Florida, Alabama, Georgia, Louisiana, Texas, Virginia, Arkansas, North Carolina, and Tennessee. Jefferson Davis was elected president.

Confucius (551?-479 BC) Chinese reformer and philosopher. He preached justice, moderation, and loving other people. The *Analects* is a record of his sayings.

Congo Country in west-central Africa straddling the equator, with a short Atlantic coastline. Area: 132,047 square miles (342,000 square kilometers). Capital: Brazzaville.

Congress The lawmaking assembly of the United States. The modern Congress has two elected houses, the Senate and the House of Representatives. The first Congress was the Continental Congress of 1774 in Philadelphia. A second Congress created the historic Declaration of Independence in 1776.

Conifer A tree or shrub that bears cones. The cones hold the plant's seeds. The pines, firs, spruce, and cedar are conifers.

Connecticut One of the original 13 states in the United States. Connecticut ratified the Constitution on January 9, 1788, to become the fifth state. It is a major manufacturing state. Products include transport equipment, machinery, and metal goods. Farmers produce milk, eggs and poultry, tobacco, and other items. Its coastline has popular summer resorts. Area: 5,009 square miles (12,973 square kilometers). Capital: Hartford.

Conrad, Joseph (1857-1924) English novelist. Born in Poland, he became a captain in the British Merchant Navy. He voyaged in the Pacific and the South Seas. Conrad gave up the sea in 1894 and began to write. Most of his novels and stories are about the sea. They include *Lord Jim* and "Heart of Darkness."

Conservation The careful use and protection of forests, water, minerals, and other natural resources.

Constellations A group of stars in a pattern that is often named after a legendary figure or animal. There are 88 constellations. The best known is probably Ursa Major (Great Bear), which contains the group of stars known as the Big Dipper. Some constellations are visible only from the Northern Hemisphere, others only from the Southern Hemisphere.

Constitution The written laws and rules for governing a country and protecting the rights of the people who live in it. The United States Constitution was written in Philadelphia in 1787. It went into effect in 1789. Only 26 amendments were added to the US Constitution in the first 200 years. The first 10 amendments deal mainly with individual rights. They are known as the Bill of Rights.

Continental shelf The edge of a continent, located in shallow ocean water. A shelf usually ends in a steep slope that drops off into deep ocean water.

Continents The great land masses of the world. The continents, in order of size, are Asia, Africa, North America, South America, Antarctica, Europe, and Australia. Because Europe is actually an extension of Asia, together they form a giant continent called Eurasia.

Cook, James (1728-1779) English explorer of the South Pacific and Antarctic oceans. He was the first English sailor to reach Australia.

Coolidge, Calvin (1872-1933) Thirtieth president of the United States. A Republican, he was governor of Massachussetts and later vice-president of the United States. When President Harding died in office in 1923, Coolidge became president. He then won the election of 1924 and remained president until 1929. During his presidency, Coolidge strongly supported business.

Cooper, James Fenimore (1789-1851) US novelist. He is best known for his adventure tale *The Last of the Mohicans*.

Copper Reddish brown metallic element that is an excellent conductor of electricity and heat. It is widely used in electrical equipment and wires, plumbing, and coins. Chemical symbol: Cu.

Coral Sea creatures related to jellyfish. They range in size from less than 1 inch (1 centimeter) to 1 foot (30 centimeters) across. Most live in colonies (groups). When they die, they leave behind their limestone skeletons. These form coral reefs and sometimes entire islands, called atolls, in warm, tropical waters.

Cork Light, springy substance obtained from the bark of the cork oak tree. It is waterproof and is used to cover floors, for shoe soles, and as bottle stoppers.

Cormorant A large sea bird related to the pelican. It is black, with short legs and a long neck. Its bill is hook-shaped for catching fish.

Corn A tall plant whose seeds are used as food. These seeds are called kernels. They grow in rows on ears of the corn plant.

Corrosion The eating away of metals by water, air, or chemicals such as acids. Rust on iron and steel is the most common kind of corrosion.

Cortes, Hernando (1485-1547) Spanish conquistador (conqueror). With only 550 men, he crushed the Aztec empire of Montezuma in Mexico between 1519 and 1521.

Cortes

Costa Rica Central American republic with coastlines on both the Caribbean Sea and Pacific Ocean. Area: 19,652 square miles (50,000 square kilometers). Capital: San Jose.

Cotton Natural fiber made from the fluffy, white seed hairs of cotton plants. Cotton is used to make fabric for clothing and other uses. It has been cultivated, spun, and woven since prehistoric times. The seeds are used for oil and cattle food. It is widely grown and manufactured in the United States, USSR, China, and India.

Covered wagon A large wagon covered by canvas stretched over an arched, wooden frame. It was pulled by horses or oxen. The American pioneers carried their families and belongings across the prairies in covered wagons when they settled the American West.

Cow The adult female of cattle or some other large animals, such as elephants, moose, and whales.

Cowboy A man who works on a ranch, especially in the western United States. Cowboys used to ride horses to herd cattle or horses. Today they often drive trucks to do their work.

Coyote Wild North American relative of the dog, sometimes called the prairie wolf. It preys on small rodents and occasionally sheep. It has an eerie howl.

Crab A crustacean (shellfish) with five pairs of jointed legs and a flat, hard cover protecting the body. The first pair of legs usually ends in grasping claws that the crab uses to catch prey. Most crabs live in water. Some live on land.

Crane A wading bird with a long neck and long legs. Cranes are elegant birds, often resting on one leg with their heads laid on their backs. The whooping crane of the United States is an endangered species.

Crete An island in the eastern Mediterranean Sea. Largest of the Greek islands, it was the center of the ancient Minoan civilization.

Bush cricket

Cricket An insect that is similar to the grasshopper but with much longer antennas. Male crickets "sing" to the females by rubbing their wing cases together.

Crimean War (1853-1856) A war fought between Russia and the allied powers of Great Britain, France, Turkey, and Sardinia (now part of Italy). It began when the Turks refused to allow the Russians to protect Christians living in the Turkish Empire. A deeper cause was Britain's fear of an expanding Russia.

Crockett, Davy (Real name **David Crockett**) (1786-1836) US frontiersman. He fought against the Creek Indians under Andrew Jackson and later was a United States congressman from Tennessee. In 1835 Crockett went to Texas, which was fighting for its independence from Mexico. He was killed at the Alamo by Mexican troops in 1836.

Crocodile A large, scaly reptile related to the alligator. Crocodiles live in rivers and swamps in tropical areas of the world. Fearsome predators able to kill a person, some grow to more than 19 feet (6 meters) long.

Cro-Magnon Cave-dwelling people who lived in Europe, Asia, and North Africa during the Stone Age, over 10,000 years ago. They used tools and weapons made of flint or bone to gather wild plants or hunt wild animals. They

painted pictures of the animals they hunted on the walls of their caves.

Cromwell, Oliver (1599-1658) English general and statesman. During the English Civil War, he overthrew King Charles I and became England's leader from 1653 to 1658.

Crow A family of mainly black birds. They are active and aggressive, with harsh, noisy voices.

Crusades Religious wars or expeditions that set out from Europe in the Middle Ages to recapture Jerusalem and the Holy Land from Muslim rule. Another purpose of the Crusades was to increase the land and wealth of French barons.

Christians fight Muslims during one of many unsuccessful Crusades.

Crustacean An animal with many jointed legs and two pairs of feelers. Most crustaceans live in the sea. Crabs, lobsters, shrimps, and barnacles are crustaceans. They have an external skeleton, or shell, that may be thin and transparent or thick and tough, as in the shell of a crab.

Crystal A solid that has flat surfaces and a definite geometric shape. Most substances are made up of tiny crystals. Among the most familiar crystals are diamonds, salt, sugar, and snowflakes.

Cuba Island republic in the Caribbean Sea. Area: 44,218 square miles (115,000 square kilometers). Capital: Havana.

Curie, Marie (1867-1934) and **Pierre** (1859-1906) Scientists who were husband and wife. They discovered radium, a very radioactive metal.

Cyclone A region of low atmospheric pressure with very strong winds that spiral toward the center. Most cyclones are accompanied by storms. Tropical cyclones create powerful storms known as hurricanes or typhoons.

Cypress A tree of the conifer family. It is found in cooler parts of the Northern Hemisphere and on mountains in warmer lands. Cypress trees have overlapping, scale-like leaves and small, woody cones.

Cyprus Island country in the Mediterranean Sea, off the coast of Turkey. Crops include grapes, wheat, barley, and citrus fruits. Area: 3,572 square miles (9,250 square kilometers). Capital: Nicosia.

Czechoslovakia A republic in central Europe. Its living standards are among the highest in Eastern Europe. Area: 49,371 square miles (127,900 square kilometers). Capital: Prague.

D

Dairy farming Raising cattle for milk, butter, cheese, and other milk (dairy) products.

Dallas City in Texas. It is a major center for industry, commerce, and finance. It was the scene of the assassination of US President John F. Kennedy in 1963.

Dam A thick wall of concrete, rock, or earth built across a river to hold water back. Dams create reservoirs – lakes that store water for drinking and for use in irrigation and industry. At many dams, falling water turns machines called turbines, which produce electric power.

Damascus Capital city of Syria, on the Barada River. It is one of the oldest cities in the world.

Dance A certain pattern of steps and body movements that are usually done in time to music. Ballet, the waltz, and square dancing are kinds of dancing.

Dandelion A bright yellow wildflower related to the daisy. It is often considered to be a weed. The seeds are topped by feathery white "parachutes" that can float through the air.

Danube Second largest river in Europe, after the Volga. It flows from the Black Forest in Germany through Eastern Europe to the Black Sea. Length: 1,770 miles (2,850 kilometers).

Dark Ages The name sometimes used for the period of European history from the 5th century (the fall of the Roman Empire) to the 10th century. It was called the Dark Ages because it was once thought, incorrectly, that little or no learning went on.

Darwin, Charles Robert (1809-1882) English naturalist. He developed the theory of evolution, which states that all living things have developed, or evolved, from earlier forms of life. Darwin wrote about

Charles Darwin

his theory in his book *On the Origin of Species* (1859). His theory of evolution was criticized by many people who believed that each species had been created individually.

Date palm Tree grown in North Africa, the Middle East, and more recently in the United States. It grows to between 30 and 90 feet (10 to 30 meters) in height and yields as many as 200 sweet, highly nutritious dates.

da Vinci, Leonardo (1452-1519) Italian artist, scientist, and engineer. His most famous paintings are the *Mona Lisa* and *The Last Supper*. He also conducted research into hydraulics and the principles of flight.

Davis, Jefferson (1808-1889) President of the Confederate States of America during the US Civil War. After the Union victory he was sent to prison for treason. Davis was never brought to trial, but he spent two years in prison.

Day The time taken for the Earth to spin once on its axis. The average solar day is 24 hours.

D-Day June 6, 1944, the day on which the Allied forces invaded Normandy, France, during World War II. D-Day was the beginning of a campaign that ended with the surrender of Germany, almost one year later.

Dead Sea Salt lake on the border of Israel and Jordan. At 1,292 feet (394 meters) below sea level, this sea is the lowest point on the Earth's surface. It is also the saltiest body of water in the world. Area: 394 square miles (1,020 square kilometers).

Declaration of Independence Document adopted by representatives of the 13 original American colonies on July 4, 1776. It declared that the colonies were no longer subject to British rule. They were now free and independent. Independence Day, the birthday of the United States, is celebrated every year on July 4th.

Decorations Awards, usually medals, given for bravery in war or for outstanding achievement in peacetime.

Victoria Cross

Legion of Honor

Congressional Medal of Honor

George Cross

Deer Hoofed mammals. The males have bony, branched antlers that are shed and re-grown every year. Only in caribou and reindeer do the females have antlers. The largest deer is the moose of North America and its counterpart, the elk of northern Europe and Asia.

Delaware The first of the original 13 states. Delaware is the second smallest state in the United States. Manufacturing is the main activity. The chief products are chemicals, processed foods, and paper products. Area: 2,044 square miles (5,295 square kilometers). Capital: Dover.

Democracy A form of government. "Democracy" comes from a Greek word that means "government by the people." In a democracy, the people take part in the government by electing representatives to make the laws.

Democratic Party One of the two major political parties in the United States. The other is the Republican Party. Andrew Jackson was the first candidate of the Democratic party to be elected president.

Denmark Kingdom in northern Europe. One of the Scandinavian countries, it consists of the peninsula of Jutland and more than 400 islands. Greenland, the world's largest island, is a self-governing dependency of Denmark. Long known for its dairy and meat products, Denmark is fast becoming an important manufacturing country. Area: 16,615 square miles (43,000 square kilometers). Capital: Copenhagen.

Denver State capital of Colorado, on the South Platte River. It is a popular skiing and tourist center.

Depression, Great The period of hard times that lasted from 1929 through the 1930s. It began in the United States when the stock market crashed in October 1929. In the worst year of the Great Depression, 1933, one out of every three workers in the US was unemployed. Full prosperity did not return until the 1940s, when the government began to spend large sums of money on defense.

Desert A dry, hot, barren region that is often sandy. Deserts cover over 15 per cent of the world's land surface. The largest desert is the Sahara in Africa. The driest is the Atacama desert in South America which has no rainfall for many years at a time.

Detergent A chemical substance used for cleaning.

Dew point The temperature at which air can hold no more water vapor. If the air is cooled below this temperature, the water vapor condenses. It becomes water droplets and forms clouds, fog, dew, and frost.

Diamond A crystalline form of pure carbon. It is the hardest substance known and a highly prized gemstone. South Africa is the world's leading diamond producer.

Diatom A microscopic plant found in fresh water and salt water. Diatoms are a kind of algae and have only one cell.

Dickens, Charles (1812-1870) English novelist. His books include *The Pickwick Papers* (1837), *Oliver Twist* (1839), *David Copperfield* (1850), *A Tale of Two Cities* (1859), and *Great Expectations* (1861). Ebenezer Scrooge in Dickens' *A Christmas Carol* (1843) is one of the best-known characters in literature.

Dickinson, Emily (1830-1886) US poet. She lived a very quiet life in Amherst, Massachusetts, writing nearly 1,800 poems. Only seven of

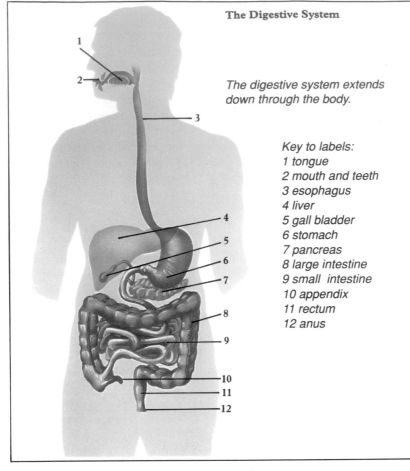

The Digestive System

The digestive system extends down through the body.

Key to labels:
1 tongue
2 mouth and teeth
3 esophagus
4 liver
5 gall bladder
6 stomach
7 pancreas
8 large intestine
9 small intestine
10 appendix
11 rectum
12 anus

mixture of oil and air is compressed in the cylinders of the engine and ignites without the need for spark plugs. Diesel engines are used in locomotives, large trucks and buses, submarines, and ships.

Digestion The process by which food is broken down into small particles and absorbed into the bloodstream.

Dinosaurs Extinct land animals that lived 200 million years ago during the Mesozoic Era. Their name means "terrible lizard," and some of them were fearsome. Tyrannosaurus, a carnivore almost 20 feet (6 meters) tall, had huge jaws and teeth. The plant-eating apatosaurus, also called brontosaurus, was probably very gentle.

Dickinson's poems were published while she lived. She did not sign her name to these. Her sister Lavinia had collections of the poems published after Dickinson's death.

Dictator A person who has complete authority over others. It usually refers to the leader of a country who allows its people very little freedom.

Dictionary An alphabetical listing of many or all of the words in a language, usually in a book. Dictionaries tell word spellings, pronunciations, meanings, and sometimes their histories.

Diesel engine A type of internal combustion engine. It is similar to the gasoline engine, but it burns heavy oil instead of gasoline. The

Diplodocus

Brachiosaurus

Disease A condition in which the body or some part of it is not working properly. There are many kinds of diseases. Infectious diseases are caused by bacteria or viruses. They can spread from one person to another, as does the common cold, chicken pox, and measles. Noninfectious diseases cannot be transmitted to other people. Cancer, heart diseases, and mental illness are examples of diseases that are not infectious. Many diseases can be treated with drugs. In some parts of the world, diseases such as typhoid have been eliminated.

Disney, Walt (1901-1966) US film producer who created Mickey Mouse and Donald Duck. Disney's *Snow White and the Seven Dwarfs* (1937) was the first full-length animated cartoon film. His other films include *Pinocchio* (1940), *Fantasia* (1940), *Bambi* (1942), and *Cinderella* (1950).

Distillation Separating or purifying liquids by boiling them, and then cooling the vapor so that it becomes a liquid again. Distillation is used in making alcoholic beverages and to produce gasoline from petroleum.

Diving machines such as bathyscaphes and submarines can plumb the ocean depths.

Diving, underwater To swim underwater for a period of time, a person must be supplied with air to breathe. A deep-sea diver can receive air through a flexible pipe from the surface. Scuba divers use tanks filled with compressed air strapped to their backs. Air is sent through a valve system to the diver's nose or mouth. Diving machines such as submarines and bathyscaphes can plumb the ocean deeps.

Division The act of separating into parts, groups, or pieces.

Djibouti A small country on the eastern coast of Africa. The country's capital, also called Djibouti, is a port city near the southern entrance to the Red Sea. Area: 8,410 square miles (21,783 square kilometers). Capital: Djibouti.

DNA (Stands for **deoxyribonucleic acid**) A material found in chromosomes inside a cell nucleus. It holds all the information required by a cell in the form of a code. Each piece of information is called a gene. The code is commonly referred to as the genetic code.

Dog A four-legged, meat-eating mammal. Many domestic dogs are kept as pets, but some are used to round up cattle and sheep. Some

Dogs

Kerry blue terrier

Golden retriever

Chow chow

Basset hound

Afghan hound

Beagle

Cavalier King Charles spaniel

Corgi

breeds such as the German Shepherd and the Doberman Pinscher are trained as guard dogs. The domestic dog is related to the wolf, fox, and coyote.

Doll A child's toy that looks like a baby, child, or an adult.

Dolphin A small toothed whale. Like other whales, it is a mammal and lives in the sea. The common dolphin is the best known. In the wild, it roams the oceans in "schools." It is a playful, natural acrobat that is intelligent and friendly toward people.

Dominican Republic A Caribbean country occupying the eastern two thirds of the mountainous island of Hispaniola. Area: 18,704 square miles (49,000 square kilometers). Capital: Santo Domingo.

Donkey A relative of the horse, descended from the wild ass of North Africa. Donkeys are used for riding, to pull carts, and as pack animals.

Dragon An imaginary animal that looks like a huge lizard with wings and sharp claws. Stories tell of dragons that fly and breathe smoke and fire.

Dragonfly An insect that is able to fly forward or backward and hover in the air. Dragonflies have excellent eyesight. Many species are brightly colored.

Drake, Sir Francis (1540?-1596) English explorer, military commander, and pirate. He was the first Englishman to sail around the world.

Dream A series of thoughts, feelings, or scenes that pass through a person's mind when the person is sleeping.

Drugs Chemicals that change

how the body works. Some drugs are used to treat, cure, or prevent diseases. Penicillin and vaccines are examples of this kind of drug. Other drugs, such as cocaine and heroin, can be addictive and can cause death.

Drum A musical instrument made of a hollow tube with a tight, thin cover on one or both ends. A drum makes a sound when beaten with a hand or a stick.

Dublin Capital and port city of the Republic of Ireland, at the mouth of the Liffey River.

Duck A water bird related to the swan and goose. Ducks have webbed feet and waterproof feathers. In the winter they fly south to find water that is not frozen. The mallard and teal are among the best-known ducks.

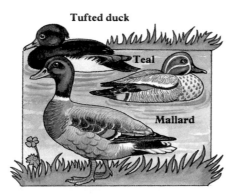

Tufted duck · Teal · Mallard

Dye A substance used to color cloth, hair, or other materials. In the past, dyes were made from berries, flowers, bark, and other parts of plants, as well as from animals and minerals. Today most are synthetic and are made from material extracted from coal tar. Synthetic dyes are cheaper and brighter than natural dyes, and their colors last longer.

E

Eagle A large bird of prey with broad wings. It has sharp eyesight, powerful claws, and a sharp beak. Eagles feed on fish and small animals.

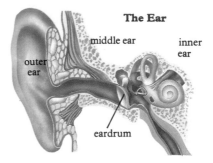

The Ear
middle ear · inner ear · outer ear · eardrum

Ear The organ of the body with which people and animals hear. It has three parts, the outer ear, the middle ear, and the inner ear. The outer ear receives sound waves and funnels them to the middle ear, which amplifies them. The sound waves then travel to the inner ear, where they are changed into nerve impulses. These messages travel through nerves to the brain, which interprets them.

Earhart, Amelia (1897-1937) US aviator. She was the first woman to cross the Atlantic Ocean in an airplane and the first woman to cross the Atlantic solo. She was the first aviator to fly solo from Hawaii to California. In 1937 Earhart tried to fly around the world. She and her plane were lost in the Pacific Ocean.

Earth One of the smaller planets of the solar system, measuring 25,000 miles (40,300 kilometers) around the equator. It is third from the sun at an average distance of 93,000,000 miles

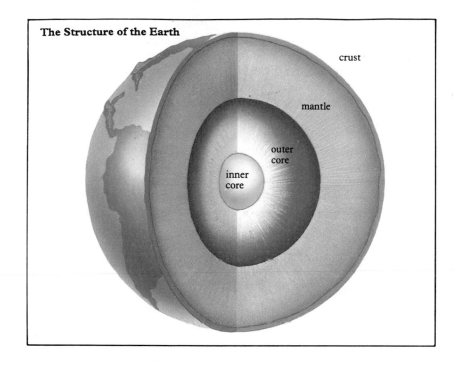

The Structure of the Earth

crust

mantle

outer core

inner core

(150,000,000 kilometers). The Earth was formed, along with other planets in the solar system, about 4.5 billion years ago. The earliest known rocks are about 4 billion years old.

Earthquake A shaking of the Earth's surface. It is caused by movements of the plates that make up the Earth's crust. This usually happens along a fault, a break in the Earth's surface where two plates meet. Movement of rock along the San Andreas Fault nearly demolished San Francisco in 1906. There was another major quake along this fault in 1989.

Earthworm A common worm that burrows in the ground. Earthworms eat their way through the soil, which helps to drain it and supply it with air.

Easter A Christian holiday that celebrates the Resurrection (rising from the dead) of Jesus Christ.

Easter Island A volcanic island in the southern Pacific Ocean. It is about 2,300 miles (3,700 kilo-

meters) west of Chile, to which it belongs. Easter Island is famous for its large, ancient stone statues.

Echo A sound that is bounced back from something. Devices called sonars use echoes to measure the depth of water. Bats, dolphins, and other animals have "built-in" sonars that they use for navigation and to locate prey.

Ecology The study of how plants and animals live in relation to each other and their environment.

Ecuador Republic on the western coast of South America. It is crossed by the equator. Ecuador has large oil fields. Area: 109,484 square miles (283,561 square kilometers). Capital: Quito.

Eddy, Mary Baker (1821-1910) US founder of Christian Science and the Church of Christ, Scientist in 1879. She also founded *The Christian Science Monitor* (1908), a daily newspaper. Christian Scientists believe that the body's ills can be healed by positive thinking.

Edison, Thomas Alva (1847-1931) US inventor who is credited with more than 1,000 inventions. Among his inventions were the phonograph, the transmitter and receiver for the automatic telegraph, the electric light bulb, and the world's first electricity generating station.

Edmonton Capital of the province of Alberta, Canada, on the Saskatchewan River.

Eel A long, slim fish that looks like a snake. Most eels live in the ocean. Even those that live in rivers swim to the ocean to lay their eggs. One kind of eel, the electric eel, produces electricity to stun its prey.

Egypt Country in northeastern corner of Africa. Most people live close to the banks of the Nile River. Area: 386,682 square miles (1,001,710 square kilometers). Capital: Cairo.

Egypt, ancient One of the great civilizations of the ancient world. It was founded on the banks of the Nile River more than 5,000 years ago. The people of ancient Egypt built the pyramids.

Einstein, Albert (1879-1955) German-born US mathematician and physicist. His theory of the relativity of motion, time, and space proved to be the greatest scientific advance since Newton's theory of gravitation. He was awarded the Nobel prize in physics in 1921.

Eisenhower, Dwight David (1890-1969) Thirty-fourth president of the United States. He was an Army general who led the Allied forces that invaded North Africa during World War II. Later, he was the supreme commander of the Allied armies that invaded Europe and defeated the German armies. Eisenhower, a Republican, was president of the United States from 1953 to 1961. He ended the Korean War. He also sent US troops to Little Rock, Arkansas, to enforce the integration of schools.

Elasticity The property of a material that makes it go back to its original shape after it has been pushed or pulled out of shape.

El Dorado Legendary South American kingdom of great wealth. It was sought but never found by numerous Spanish and English explorers.

Electric circuit A path along which electric current flows. An example of a simple circuit is a loop wire connecting the terminals of a battery with a light bulb. The battery makes electrons flow along the wire to light the bulb.

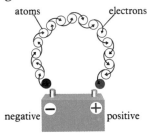

Electricity flows as negative electrons move from atom to atom.

Electricity A form of energy. Most of our electricity comes from the movement of tiny negatively charged particles called electrons. It can power machines or provide light and heat.

Electric motor A machine that turns electricity into movement by turning a shaft. It is the opposite of an electric generator, which turns movement into electricity.

Electrolysis The process of breaking down a chemical compound into its elements by passing an electric current through it. This process has many uses. It is used, for example, to plate objects with silver or other metals.

Electromagnet A magnet produced by passing an electric current through a wire wound around an iron bar. Electromagnets are used in telephones, electric bells, and electric motors. Large electromagnets are used to lift heavy pieces of scrap iron.

An electromagnet. The current-carrying wire turns the iron bar into a magnet.

Electromagnetic radiation Rays given off by the sun and other stars, such as ultraviolet and infra-red light waves. Radio waves, gamma rays, and X rays are also electromagnetic waves.

Electronics The branch of science that deals with the accurate control of electric currents for use in such devices as radios, televisions, and computers.

Electron microscope A device used for seeing very tiny objects. Using beams of light, it can show things that are only one ten-thousandth of a micrometer (one millionth of a meter) across.

Element Any of the basic chemical substances from which everything is made. Each element is made up of tiny particles called atoms. There are more than 100 elements.

Elephant The largest living land animal. Elephants are mammals that may reach 13 feet (4 meters) in height and weigh 6 tons. They have very thick skin. Their long trunks are used for carrying food and water to their mouths, for spraying, and for lifting. They have two long, curved ivory tusks. There are two kinds of elephants, the African elephant and the Asian, or Indian, elephant. Many elephants have been killed for their valuable tusks.

Elevator A small room or platform that can be raised or lowered. Elevators are used most often to carry people or things to different levels in buildings.

Eliot, T. S. (1888-1965) US-born English poet, critic, and dramatist. He won the Nobel prize in literature in 1948. He wrote *The Waste Land* (1922) and *Murder in the Cathedral* (1935).

Elizabeth I (1533-1603) Queen of England whose reign was a time of great achievement. The daughter of Henry VIII, she is known for her love of art and success in economic and foreign affairs.

Ellis Island A small island of 27 acres in Upper New York Bay. It is owned by the United States government. Between 1892 and 1943 it was the center for receiving immigrants to the United States. Today it is part of the Statue of Liberty National Monument.

Elm A family of large deciduous (leaf-shedding) trees. They can grow up to 100 feet (30 meters) tall.

El Salvador Small republic in Central America on the Pacific coast. Area: 8,260 square miles (21,400 square kilometers). Capital: San Salvador.

Emancipation Proclamation The official order that abolished slavery in the Confederate States. It was issued by President Abraham Lincoln on January 1, 1863.

Emerson, Ralph Waldo (1803-1882) US essayist and poet. For many years he lived in Concord, Massachusetts. One of Emerson's best-known poems is "The Concord Hymn." Emerson was the foremost American writer of his day and a close friend of other leading writers. Among them were Nathaniel Hawthorne, Henry David Thoreau, and Herman Melville.

Emu A flightless Australian bird. It is related to the ostrich and cassowary.

Energy The ability to do work. There are two basic kinds of energy, potential energy and kinetic energy. A wound-up spring or the water behind a dam both have stored-up energy, or potential energy. As the spring unwinds or the water flows through turbines, the energy is changed to kinetic energy, or moving energy.

Engineering The use of scientific knowledge for practical things, such as designing and building factories, machines, bridges, dams, airplanes, and spacecraft.

England A country that is part of the United Kingdom of Great Britain and Northern Ireland. It is the most densely populated part, with the largest cities. Area: 50,331 square miles (130,000 square kilometers). Capital: London.

English language A language spoken by almost 450 million people. Only Mandarin Chinese is spoken by more people. English is the principal language in the United States, Canada, Great Britain, Ireland, Aus-

Wind erosion in Oklahoma stripped farms clear of soil overnight and created the famous Dust Bowl in the 1930s.

tralia, and New Zealand. The English language developed through three periods: Old English (700 to 1100), Middle English (1100 to 1500), and Modern English (1500 to the present).

Enzyme A protein that speeds up chemical reactions in animals and plants. The human body contains more than a thousand types of enzymes. Without these we could not digest our food, see, or breathe.

Equator An imaginary line around the Earth, halfway between the North Pole and South Pole. The equator is 0 degrees latitude. Almost 25,000 miles (40,300 kilometers) long, it divides the Earth into the Northern and Southern hemispheres.

Equatorial Guinea Republic in western Africa made up of a small, forested mainland area and a number of islands. Area: 10,832 square miles (28,000 square kilometers). Capital: Malabo.

Equinox Either of the two times in the year when the sun is exactly above the equator. All parts of the

world then have 12 hours of light and 12 hours of darkness. In the Northern Hemisphere, the spring (or vernal) equinox occurs about March 21, marking the beginning of spring. The autumn (or autumnal) equinox occurs about September 23, marking the beginning of fall. In the Southern Hemisphere, the seasons are reversed.

Erosion The wearing away of the land surface by water, wind, and ice.

Eskimos A people of the arctic regions. They call themselves Inuit, which means "people." Originally from Asia, Eskimos today live in Greenland, Canada, Alaska, and northeastern Siberia. They were once nomads who lived by hunting and fishing. Many Eskimos still live using the traditional skills, but more and more live in settlements.

Ethiopia A country in northeastern Africa, with a coastline on the Red Sea. It is a land of hot deserts and cool plateaus. Area: 471,778 square miles (1,221,900 square kilometers). Capital: Addis Ababa.

Eucalyptus Some 600 species of evergreen gum-trees native to Australia. Some grow 300 feet (90 meters) tall. They yield timber, gum, and aromatic oil from the leathery leaves.

Europe The small, densely populated continent between the USSR and the Atlantic Ocean. The farms of Europe are often small but highly efficient. Europe's industrial production ranks among the world's greatest. Area: 4,065,000 square miles (10,528,000 square kilometers).

European Communities (EC; also known as the **Common Market)** A group of 12 Western European nations. Their goal is to remove all trade barriers and unite their economies. A more distant goal is to establish a political union.

Evaporation The changing of a liquid into a gas, or vapor, without boiling it. The rate of evaporation increases with heat. The evaporation of water from the surface of the sea by the heat of the sun is responsible for the water cycle.

Everest, Mount The highest mountain in the world. It is located in the Himalayas on the Nepal-Tibet border. Height: 29,028 feet (8,848 meters).

Everglades A large swampy area in southern Florida. Part of the Everglades has been set aside as a US national park. Area: 2,746 square miles (7,112 square kilometers).

Evergreen A plant that has leaves throughout the year. Leaves are lost and replaced as part of a continual process. The evergreens include the pine, fir, spruce, and cedar.

Evolution Theory of slow, gradual changing in plants or animals over many generations as they adapt to their environment. Eventually the plants or animals produce new species. The theory of evolution was proposed by Charles Darwin in 1859.

Explorer A person who travels to a new place for adventure or discovery.

Explosive A substance that suddenly bursts apart or blows up with great force when struck or ignited. When an explosion takes place, the explosive materials rapidly change into gases and give out great amounts of heat. Explosives include TNT and dynamite.

Eye The organ of the body with which people and animals see. The eye is a tough, fluid-filled ball, with a lens suspended across the front of it. The lens focuses light rays so that they fall onto a region at the back of the eye called the retina. Light-sensitive cells send messages to the brain which interprets them.

F

Falcon A bird of prey, related to the hawk. It has long, pointed wings and can fly so fast it can catch other birds in the air.

Farming The business of growing crops or raising animals on a farm.

Fascism A form of government. A fascist government is opposed to democracy and is usually led by a dictator. It controls the country's economy and is sometimes militarily aggressive. Fascism started in Italy in 1922 under Benito Mussolini. The governments of Nazi Germany under Adolf Hitler (1933-1945) and Spain under Francisco Franco (1939-1975) were fascist.

All these foods contain fat, though in some it is "hidden."

Fats One of the most important foods from animals and plants. A large part of our body energy comes from eating fats.

Faulkner, William (1897-1962) US author. He wrote novels and short stories about life in the American South.

FBI (stands for **Federal Bureau of Investigation)** The chief investigative branch of the United States Department of Justice. It was founded in 1908. The FBI investigates all types of crime.

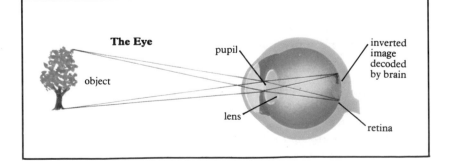

The Eye

pupil

object

lens

inverted image decoded by brain

retina

FCC (Stands for **Federal Communications Commission**) A United States government agency that regulates communications by telephone, telegraph, radio, television, and satellite.

Federalist Party A political party formed by Alexander Hamilton and John Adams. It was active from 1789 to 1816. The party wanted the United States Constitution to be adopted by all the states. It also wanted a strong central government.

Feminist movement A women's rights movement. Feminists believe that women should be able to receive the same jobs, pay, and respect that men do.

Fermentation A chemical change that takes place in animal and vegetable matter. It is usually brought about by yeasts, bacteria, or enzymes. During fermentation, sugar is changed into alcohol. Fermentation causes bread to rise, milk to turn sour, and cider to turn into vinegar.

Fermi, Enrico (1901-1954) Italian-born US nuclear physicist. He was awarded the 1938 Nobel prize in physics for his work on radioactivity. He led the team that built the first nuclear reactor and helped build the atomic bomb.

Fern A flowerless plant with large leaves. Ferns do not have seeds. New ferns grow from tiny spores on the underside of the leaves. Ferns grow best in warm, damp regions, where some species grow to 30 feet (10 meters) tall.

Ferris wheel An entertainment ride at amusement parks, fairs, and carnivals. It is a large, upright revolving wheel with two rims. People ride in the seats that hang between the rims. It was invented in 1893 by George Ferris, a US engineer.

Fertilizer Plant food added to the soil to make plants grow better. There are two types of fertilizers, natural and chemical. Natural fertilizers include decaying leaves and grass, bone meal, and barnyard manure. Chemical fertilizers have nitrogen, phosphorus, and potassium in them.

Fiber A long, thin, flexible strand that can be spun into a yarn. Natural fibers include animal fibers, such as wool and silk, and vegetable fibers, such as cotton. Artificial, or man-made, fibers include nylon, rayon, and polyester. Fibers are used to make rope, nets, rugs, and thousands of other products. Their main use is in making textiles.

Fiber optics Hair-thin glass or plastic fibers that allow the passage of light. The light can carry large amounts of data. Fiber-optic devices are used to carry television programs and telephone conversations.

Fifth Amendment An important part of the Bill of Rights, the first ten amendments to the United States Constitution. It guarantees that people cannot be made to give evidence against themselves.

Fiji Republic in the southwestern Pacific Ocean, consisting of over 800 islands. Approximately 100 are inhabited. Area: 7,000 square miles (18,000 square kilometers). Capital: Suva.

Fillmore, Millard (1800-1874) Thirteenth president of the United States. He learned law while working in a law office. Fillmore, a member of the Whig Party, entered politics and was elected to Congress in 1832. He became vice-president in 1849. When President Zachary Taylor died in office, Fillmore became president. He served from 1850 to 1853.

Finch Any of a large family of seed-eating birds. There are more finches than any other kind of bird. The finch family includes the goldfinch, bullfinch, canary, sparrow, and cardinal. They have strong, heavy beaks. Many of these birds are very colorful.

Fingerprints The pattern of ridges on a person's finger pads. The pattern is unchanging and unique to each person. The prints provide an almost fool-proof method of identifying people and are useful in criminal investigations.

Finland A republic in northern Europe. It is one of the world's leading wood pulp and paper producers. Shipbuilding, textiles, and glassware are other major industries. Area: 130,119 square miles (337,000 square kilometers). Capital: Helsinki.

Fir

Fir An evergreen tree belonging to the pine family. Firs have flattened needles and woody, upright cones.

Fire The light, heat, and flame caused by burning something.

Firefly One of several kinds of beetles that glow in the dark. Fireflies are also known as lightning bugs or lightning beetles. The light is caused by certain chemicals in the firefly's abdomen. It flashes on and off at intervals and serves as a courtship signal. The glowworm is a wingless firefly.

Fireworks Devices that are exploded or burned to make colored light shows, noise, and smoke. Most fireworks are made of paper tubes stuffed with gunpowder, which ignites easily and burns very rapidly. Small amounts of other chemicals are added to create colors.

Fish An aquatic animal with a streamlined body and fins. It is well adapted to a life under water. Fish take in oxygen from the water through their gills. Most have scales, and all are cold-blooded.

Fishing The business or sport of catching fish.

Fission, nuclear The splitting of the nucleus of an atom of heavy elements, such as uranium and plutonium, by bombarding them with other atomic particles. Fission produces heat, which is used by nuclear power stations to make electricity.

Flag Day June 14. It marks the anniversary of the day in 1777 when the Stars and Stripes was adopted as the United States flag.

Flags Pieces of cloth, usually colored, with designs or emblems on them. They are used as symbols of countries or organizations, or to give signals. Flags were originally used as battle emblems for identifying kings and knights.

Flamingo A water bird that lives near shallow water in warm areas of the world. It has bright pink or red feathers, a curved beak, and webbed feet. Flamingos have long, thin necks and legs.

Flatfish A member of a group of fish that lives at the bottom of the sea. The group includes sole, halibut, and flounder, which all are important food fish.

Flea A small, wingless, bloodsucking insect. Fleas are parasites. They feed on the blood of mammals and birds. Fleas sometimes carry diseases.

Fleming, Sir Alexander (1881-1955) Scottish scientist who discovered penicillin in 1928. He shared the Nobel prize in medicine in 1945.

Flint A variety of quartz. Flint can be chipped to produce

Examples of different marine fish: (1) garfish; (2) herring; (3) shark; (4) John Dory ; (5) lamprey; (6) cod; (7) ray; (8) lumpsucker; (9) eel; (10) plaice. Both the eel and the lamprey spend part of their lives in fresh water.

very sharp edges. In the Stone Age people used it to make tools and weapons.

Flood A great flow of water over land that is usually dry. Floods occur when heavy rain or melting snow causes rivers to overflow their banks. Near coastlines, storms and underwater earthquakes may send high seas over low-lying land, especially in the tropics. Floods can cause great damage and loss of life.

Florence City in central Italy on the Arno River. It was home of the artists Leonardo da Vinci and Michelangelo.

Florida The southeasternmost state of the United States mainland. Florida contains Miami Beach, Disney World, the Everglades National Park, and the John F. Kennedy Space Center at Cape Canaveral. Area: 58,560 square miles (151,670 square kilometers). Capital: Tallahassee.

Flower The seed-producing part of a plant. Inside the brightly colored petals are the male and female parts of the flower. The male part, the stamen, produces grains of pollen. The female part, the pistil, produces eggs. When the pollen joins with the eggs in the ovary at the bottom of the pistil, seeds are formed.

Fluorine A light yellow, poisonous gas. It is found in nature only in combination with other elements. Fluorine compounds added to drinking water help prevent tooth decay. Chemical symbol: F.

Fly One of a group of insects with only a single pair of wings. There are many species, including the horsefly, housefly, and mosquito.

Flying squirrel A small squirrel that glides, not flies, from tree to tree. Various species live in the forests of North America, Europe, Asia, and Africa.

Fog A cloud of water vapor at ground level. It is caused by air cooling at night, or warm air passing over a cold sea. A light fog is called a mist.

Food preservation Techniques used to keep food from spoiling and to last longer. These techniques include heat treatment, chilling, freezing, drying, curing, pickling, and the use of chemicals. Sterilization and pasteurization raise the temperature of food to kill germs.

Football A game played between two teams of eleven players, using an inflated oval ball, on a rectangular field 120 yards long and 53½ yards wide. The object of the game is to score points by moving the ball across the opponent's goal line, or by kicking it over a crossbar between the goal posts.

Ford, Gerald R. (1913-) Thirty-eighth president of the United States. He served in the US Navy during World War II. A Republican, he was a member of the US House of Representatives from Michigan from 1949 to 1973. He was appointed vice-president by Richard Nixon after Spiro T. Agnew resigned in 1973. He became president the following year when Nixon resigned during a political scandal. Ford was president until 1977.

Ford, Henry (1863-1947) US automobile manufacturer who used mass production to build inexpensive cars. He founded the Ford Motor Company in 1903.

Forest A thick growth of trees and underbrush covering a large area. Forests are home to a great variety of animal life. In many parts of the world, forests have been cut down to make room for farms, communities, and industry.

Fort Knox A stronghold and military reservation in northern Kentucky. Most of the United States' gold bars, or bullion deposits, are stored here.

Fort Worth City in Texas on the Trinity River.

Fossil The remains or imprint of an animal or plant that died millions of years ago. A fossil may be an entire animal or as little as a single bone.

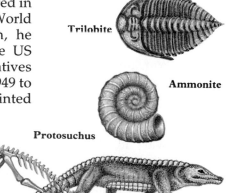

Fossils can be dated from the rocks in which they are found. Trilobites crawled across the sea floor over 500 million years ago. Ammonites, mollusks with a coiled shell up to 6 1/2 feet (2 meters) across in some species, died out 65 million years ago. Protosuchus was a crocodile-like reptile living 225 million years ago. Fossilized bones enable scientists to reconstruct the original animal.

Foster, Stephen (1826-1864) US songwriter. He wrote more than 200 songs. Among the best known are "O Susanna" and "My Old Kentucky Home."

Founding Father A delegate to the Constitutional Convention in Philadelphia in 1787. The delegates at the Convention drew up the United States Constitution.

Fox A bushy-tailed mammal related to the dog. The red fox of North America, Asia, and Europe lives in forests and open areas.

Foxglove A tall woodland plant with tube-shaped blooms arranged in long spikes. Though poisonous, they bear a valuable heart drug, digitalis.

Fraction A part, portion, or section of a whole thing.

France The largest country in western Europe. Long a center of world culture, France is also a major industrial nation. Its automobiles, aircraft, and machinery are sold all over the world. Area: 211,208 square miles (547,026 square kilometers). Capital: Paris.

Franklin, Benjamin (1706-1790) US scientist, writer, and statesman. He proved that lightning is electricity. One of the Founding Fathers during the Revolutionary War period, he was also a successful diplomat in both England and France.

French and Indian War (1754-1763) A war in North America in which French soldiers and Indian tribes that were friendly to France fought against English soldiers and colonists.

French Revolution (1789-1799) A rebellion of the people against the monarchy (king) and nobility in France. Its motto was "liberty, equality, and fraternity." After 10 years, its first republic ended when Napoleon became emperor.

Frequency The number of complete cycles of a wave motion (for example, radio waves) that take place in a second. The higher the frequency, the shorter the length of each wave.

Freud, Sigmund (1856-1939) Austrian psychiatrist. He believed that mental illness could be traced back to childhood events. If a person could be helped to remember an unhappy childhood experience, the person could understand a present problem and thus get better. Freud's method of treating people is called psychoanalysis.

Common frog

Frog A small animal that has no tail. Frogs have long back legs and webbed feet for jumping and swimming. They develop from tadpoles. Like other amphibians, most frogs live part of their life in water and part on land. Some live in trees.

Front In meteorology (the science of weather), the boundary between air masses with different temperatures and humidity. A warm front usually brings light rain followed by warmer weather. A cold front can bring showers and stormy winds. It is followed by colder weather.

Frost, Robert (1874-1963) US poet. His poems about simple things in nature often contain a more complicated meaning.

Frost Frozen moisture that forms on solid objects when the temperature falls to 32 degrees Fahrenheit (0 degrees Celsius) or below. The term is also used for air temperature at or below the freezing point of water.

Fruit The part of flowering plants that contains the seeds. There are many different types of fruit. Some are dry, such as nuts or the ripe pods of peas. Others are fleshy, like plums and berries.

FTC (Stands for **Federal Trade Commission**) A United States government agency that investigates unfair competition in business. It also protects consumers from unfair business practices.

Fuel cell A device that turns chemical energy into electrical energy. Fuel cells provided the electrical onboard power for the Apollo space program.

Fulbright, James William (1905-) United States Senator from Arkansas from 1945-1975. A Democrat, he sponsored the Fulbright Act that provides for the exchange of students and teachers between the United States and other countries.

Fulton, Robert (1765-1815) US engineer and inventor. He build the first practical steamboat, the *Clermont*. He also built the world's first steam-powered warship for the United States government.

Fungus A simple plant. Fungi do not have stems, flowers, roots, or leaves. Nor do they have the green coloring matter called chloro-

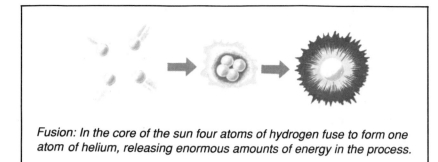

Fusion: In the core of the sun four atoms of hydrogen fuse to form one atom of helium, releasing enormous amounts of energy in the process.

phyll. Mushrooms, molds, and yeasts are examples of fungi.

Fuse, electric A safety device in an electric circuit. The main part of a fuse is usually a piece of wire that melts easily. If the current rises too high and the circuit gets too hot, the fuse melts and breaks the circuit.

Fusion, nuclear A process in which different kinds of hydrogen atoms are fused, or joined together, releasing huge amounts of energy. The sun's energy comes from fusion.

G

Gabon A republic on the west coast of Africa. Forest covers much of the country, and forestry is an important industry. Oil, however, is the main export. Area: 103,347 square miles (267,667 square kilometers). Capital: Libreville.

Galapagos Islands A group of islands in the Pacific Ocean, less than 700 miles (1,130 kilometers) west of Ecuador. This Ecuadorean territory's unique forms of plant and animal life include the giant tortoise.

Galaxy A collection of stars held together by gravity. The sun and its family of planets are in the Milky Way galaxy, together with about 100 billion other stars.

Galileo (1564-1642) Italian astronomer and physicist. He built the first astronomical telescope and discovered the moons of Jupiter. He also confirmed the theory that the earth and other planets circle the sun.

Gallup Poll A survey to find out what people think about current issues. It is a public opinion poll. Only a small number of people are asked questions, but they are chosen carefully so that they represent the entire population. This method was developed by George Gallup. The news media, politicians, businesses, and others use public opinion polls.

Gama, Vasco da (1460?-1524) Portuguese explorer. He was the first to sail from western Europe around the Cape of Good Hope at the southernmost tip of Africa. He continued to sail on to India.

Gambia A small country in western Africa located on both sides of the Gambia River. Area: 4,361 square miles (11,295 square kilometers). Capital: Banjul.

Gandhi, Indira (1917-1984) Political leader in India. She was prime minister from 1966 to 1977 and from 1980 to 1984. She was shot to death by people who opposed her rule.

Gandhi, Mohandas (1869-1948) Indian leader, known as the Mahatma or "great soul." He worked to win Indian independence from Britain by using nonviolent resistance. He also preached that Hindus, Muslims, and others should live peacefully together. But in 1948, the year following India's independence, Gandhi was assassinated by a Hindu fanatic.

Ganges A river in Asia flowing from the Himalayas through India and Bangladesh into the Bay of Bengal. The Ganges is sacred to the Hindus. Length: 1,557 miles (2,400 kilometers).

Garfield, James A. (1831-1881) Twentieth president of the United States. He fought in the Union Army during the Civil War. A Republican from Ohio, he was a member of the US House of Representatives. He was elected president in 1880 and inaugurated in March 1881. He was assassinated only four months later.

Garvey, Marcus (Moziah) (1887-1940) Civil rights leader. He was born in Jamaica and came to the United States in 1916. He believed that black Americans should leave the United States to live in Africa.

Gas One of the three states of matter, the others being liquid and solid. Gas expands to fill a container, taking on the container's shape. Some types of gas are used as fuels.

Gastropods A class of mollusks that includes slugs, snails, and limpets. Many live in the sea, although there are freshwater and

Gas turbine

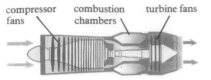

compressor fans   combustion chambers   turbine fans

land forms. Many have a single, coiled shell.

Gas turbine Also called a **jet engine**. A rotary engine. Air is sucked in by fans and compressed. Then it is mixed with fuel and ignited, releasing hot gases that escape at high speed and create the thrust.

Gauguin, Paul (1848-1903) French artist. He moved to the island of Tahiti in the Pacific Ocean where he did colorful paintings of the people and scenery there.

Gazelle A small antelope with round horns. It is found in Africa and Asia.

Geiger counter An instrument for detecting and measuring radioactivity. Radioactive particles pass through gas-filled tubes, knocking electrons from the gas atoms. These electrons give a signal, which is recorded on a meter or heard as a series of clicks from a loudspeaker.

Gem A jewel. A gem is a valuable or costly stone that is cut and polished, such as a diamond, ruby, or emerald. Pearls are also called gems.

Generator, electric A machine that produces electricity. Generators have many coils of wire around shafts that are between huge magnets. Engines or turbines powered by coal, oil, or falling water make the shafts rotate. When a coil of wire rotates in a magnetic field, electricity is produced.

Genetics The study of genes and the role they play in heredity. Genes are found in the nucleus of cells. They determine the characteristics that are passed on from parent to offspring.

Genghis Khan (1162-1227) Great Mongol leader whose vast empire stretched from the Pacific coast of China to southwestern Russia. A ruthless conqueror, his armies left a trail of destruction wherever they went.

Geography The study of the Earth's surface and how it is used by people, animals, and plants. Geography includes the study of landforms, climates, resources, and the way people live in different parts of the world.

Geology The study of the structure of the Earth, its rocks, and surface features.

Geometry The branch of mathematics that deals with lines, angles, points, shapes, and surfaces.

George III (1738-1820) King of England from 1760 to 1820. His political policies led to the American Revolution (1775-1783).

Georgia The fourth state to adopt the US Constitution in 1788, Georgia suffered greatly during the Civil War. A southeastern state, the economy is based on textiles, food products, transport equipment, and timber products. Farming is also important. Area: 58,876 square miles (152,488 square kilometers). Capital: Atlanta.

Germany Country in Europe. In 1949, it was divided into two nations, East and West Germany. In 1989, steps were taken to reunify the country. The reunification became official on October 3, 1990. Manufacturing is important to the economy. The Ruhr and other industrial areas produce iron, steel, and other metal goods, precision instruments, chemicals, and electronics. Germany is among the world leaders in automobile making. Crops and livestock are raised on small farms, but Germany still has to import food. The Bavarian Alps are a popular tourist attraction. Area: 137,773 square miles (358,210 square kilometers). Capital: Berlin.

Germination The early growth of a seed, when a root emerges and grows into the soil. The young shoot then begins to grow upward toward the light.

Geronimo (1829-1909) Apache Indian leader. With his tribe, he fought against settlers and soldiers to defend their homeland in the Southwest. He finally surrendered in 1886.

Gershwin, George (1898-1937) US composer. He wrote popular songs, musical comedies, and music for symphony orchestras. He also wrote the music for the American folk opera *Porgy and Bess*. Gershwin's best-known orchestral music is *Rhapsody in Blue*.

Geyser An underground spring that shoots steam and hot water into the air from an opening in the ground. Geysers are like safety valves, releasing pressure from volcanic regions in the earth where water is heated up in underground chambers. The most famous geyser in the United States is Old Faithful in Yellowstone National Park.

Ghana A country in Africa. Cocoa and gold are its main exports. Area: 92,100 square miles (238,598 square kilometers). Capital: Accra.

Gibraltar A rocky peninsula

jutting out from Spain at the entrance to the Mediterranean Sea. Both Britain and Spain have claimed possession of Gibraltar. Area: 2.25 square miles (6 square kilometers).

Gila monster A large lizard that lives in deserts in northern Mexico and the southwestern United States. It is poisonous but so rare that it is protected by law.

Gill The breathing organ of most fish and of many other animals that live in the water. The gills of fish are located on each side of the body just behind the head. Water comes in through the mouth and passes over the gills, which then pass the oxygen from the water into the blood. This water, with carbon dioxide waste, is forced out through the gill covers.

water in
mouth
gills
water out

Giraffe A hoofed African mammal. The tallest animal in the world, its long neck makes it able to browse on the savannah treetops that no other animal can reach. Males may grow to 18 feet (5.5 meters) in height.

Glacier A large mass of ice that flows slowly down a valley. Glaciers are formed when large amounts of snow turn into ice in the polar regions or high in some mountains.

Gland An organ that produces a chemical substance that is useful to the body. The salivary glands, for example, produce saliva, and the lacrimal glands produce tears. Many glands

produce hormones. The liver, the body's largest gland, aids digestion.

Glass A hard material made by melting sand with lime and soda. Molten glass can be made into almost any shape before it cools. Glass can usually be seen through and breaks easily.

Glenn, John (1921-) US astronaut and senator. He was the first American and the third man to orbit the Earth.

Glue A substance used to stick things together. It is made from bones, skin, and other parts of animals. Other adhesives, often called glues, are gums, cements, and epoxies.

Gnu A large antelope of eastern and southern Africa. It is also known as the wildebeest.

Gnu

Goat A horned animal related to sheep. All are expert climbers and feed on almost any vegetable matter, from grass to the bark and leaves of trees. There are wild goats and domestic goats. People raise goats in all parts of the world for their milk and skins.

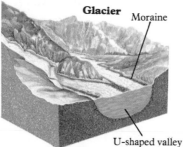

Glacier Moraine

U-shaped valley

Valley glaciers in mountain regions transport moraine (loose rock). U-shaped valleys testify to glaciation in the past.

Gobi A vast desert in Mongolia and China. Area: about 500,000 square miles (1,300,000 square kilometers).

Goddard, Robert Hutchings (1882-1945) US physicist and inventor. His experiments with rockets laid the groundwork for space travel. He is considered the father of rocketry and space flight. He tested the first liquid-fuel rocket and launched the first rocket to fly at the speed of sound.

Gold A precious yellow metal. It has been used since ancient times to make jewelry and coins. Gold is also used in different industrial processes because it resists corrosion, and in some electronic circuits because it is a good conductor of electricity. South Africa is the world's largest producer of gold. Chemical symbol: Au.

Golden eagle A large eagle of North America. It has golden-brown feathers on its neck and on the back of its head.

Golden Gate A strait (narrow passage of water) in western California. It is 2 miles (3.2 kilometers) wide. It connects San Francisco Bay and the Pacific Ocean. The Golden Gate bridge over this strait is a tourist attraction.

Goldfish A small fish of the carp family. A great many varieties are bred and kept in aquariums or pools. Some goldfish can live for over 25 years.

Golf A game played by hitting a small ball with a stick called a club. The object is to hit the ball around a course of up to 18 holes. The ball must go into a cup on each hole before the player can start the next hole. The score is the total number of shots needed for all 18 holes.

Goose A large bird related to ducks and swans. Geese have webbed feet and swim well. They often live in large flocks. Geese make long migratory flights in V-shaped formations.

Gorilla The largest of the apes, weighing about 450 pounds (200 kilograms). Gorillas grow up to 6 feet (1.8 meters) tall. Family groups lead a peaceful nomadic life in the rain forests of central Africa, feeding on fruit and leaves.

Government A system for running a country, state, city, or other geographical area. Governments provide services and make and enforce laws. There are many kinds of government. In a democracy, the people govern themselves by electing other people to represent them in the government. In a dictatorship, a single leader rules, often disregarding the desires of the people.

Grammar The rules of language, telling how it is organized for writing and speaking. Grammar describes things such as sentence structure and parts of speech (noun, verb, adjective, adverb) and the correct way to use them.

Grand Canyon A spectacular gorge in northwest Arizona. Cut by the Colorado River, the gorge is over a mile (1.5 kilometers) deep, up to 18 miles (30 kilometers) wide, and over 200 miles (349 kilometers) long. Some of the exposed rocks in the Grand Canyon are about 2 billion years old.

Granite A hard, igneous rock made up of quartz, feldspar, and other minerals. It

Grant, Ulysses S. (1822-1885) Eighteenth president of the United States. Grant fought in the Civil War. He rose in rank to become commander-in-chief of the Union Army. His defeat of Confederate General Robert E. Lee ended the war in April 1865. A Republican, Grant was president from 1869 to 1877.

Grape A small, smooth skinned, juicy fruit that hangs in bunches from vines. Grapes are eaten fresh or are dried to make raisins. They are also fermented to make wine.

Graph A drawing that shows the relationship between quantities. There are many kinds of graphs, including line graphs, bar graphs, and circle graphs.

Grass One of the largest families of the flowering plants. It has long thin leaves and tiny green flowers that grow in spikes without petals. Grasses grow almost everywhere. They include cereals such as wheat, barley, oats, and rice.

Grasshopper A jumping insect related to crickets and locusts. Grasshoppers have long, powerful hind legs. They live in meadows and fields, eating the plants there. Each year, grasshoppers cause millions of dollars worth of damage to crops.

Grasshopper

Gravity The force that attracts any two bodies toward each other. Newton's law of

gravitation says that the larger the objects are and the closer together they are, the more they will be attracted to each other. Gravity holds the planets in their orbits. It is the force that makes things fall when they are dropped.

Great Barrier Reef The largest coral reef in the world. It extends some 1,250 miles (2,000 kilometers) along the northeast coast of Australia.

Great Britain Island country in northwestern Europe. It contains England, Scotland, and Wales. Great Britain and Northern Ireland together form the United Kingdom. (Sometimes "Great Britain" and "United Kingdom" are loosely used for each other.) Area: 88,789 square miles (230,875 square kilometers). Capital: London.

Great Lakes A group of five lakes in North America: Superior, Michigan, Ontario, Huron, and Erie. They are interconnected and are linked to the Atlantic Ocean via the Saint Lawrence Seaway. Together they form the world's largest body of fresh water.

Great Wall of China A wall 4,000 miles (6,400 kilometers) long in China. It was built in the 3rd century to keep out invading tribes from the north. The wall is from 20 to 50 feet (6 to 15 meters) high and 15 to 25 feet (4.5 to 7.5 meters) thick.

Greece A country on the Mediterranean coast of Europe. It is made up of the southern part of the Balkan Peninsula and many islands in the Aegean Sea. Area: 50,944 square miles (131,979 square kilometers). Capital: Athens.

Greece, ancient An early civilization in the Mediterranean region. It reached its peak during the 5th and 4th centuries BC. Ruins of its fine temples can still be seen in Athens and elsewhere.

Greek mythology A set of stories and beliefs of the people of ancient Greece. These myths told about their many gods and heroes. Zeus was the king of the gods, and Hera was his queen. Apollo was the god of the sun. Aphrodite was the goddess of love. Achilles and Odysseus were legendary heroes.

Greenland The world's largest island. It lies northeast of the North American continent. Most of the island is above the Arctic Circle. Greenland is a self-governing part of Denmark. Most of the people are of Eskimo and Danish ancestry and live in coastal settlements. Area: 839,999 square miles (2,175,600 square kilometers). Capital: Godthab.

Grizzly bear A very large, powerful bear of western North America. It has grayish brown fur and long claws. There are not many now living in the wild.

Guatemala A republic in Central America with coasts on both the Pacific Ocean and the Caribbean Sea. Coffee is the main export. Area: 42,042 square miles (109,000 square kilometers). Capital: Guatemala City.

Guinea A republic in West Africa on the Atlantic coast. Bauxite, which is used to make aluminum, and other minerals are the main exports. Area: 94,925 square miles (246,000 square kilometers). Capital: Conakry.

Guinea-Bissau A republic on the Atlantic coast of West Africa. The economy is based on agriculture. There are very few factories. Area: 13,948 square miles (36,000 square kilometers). Capital: Bissau.

Guinea pig A domesticated South American rodent. Guinea pigs are kept as pets by many people. They are also used in scientific research experiments.

Guitar A six-stringed musical instrument played by plucking the strings with the fingers or a plectrum (pick). Some folk guitars have 12 strings.

Gulf States The US states on the Gulf of Mexico. They are: Florida, Alabama, Mississippi, Louisiana, and Texas.

Gulf Stream A warm ocean current flowing from the Gulf of Mexico along the Atlantic coast of North America. Part of the Gulf Stream reaches the shores of Europe, warming the climate.

Gull A medium-to-large seabird with black, gray, and white feathers. Gulls are scavengers and are commonly found near human habitation in search of food.

Gun A weapon that shoots bullets, shot, or shells. Pistols and giant artillery are guns. They have a barrel that is closed at one end. A cartridge filled with gunpowder or other explosive is placed in the barrel and fired by pressing a trigger.

Gunpowder An explosive made from saltpeter (potassium nitrate), sulfur, and carbon. Invented by the ancient Chinese, gunpowder was unknown in the western world until the 13th century.

Gutenberg, Johannes (1400?-1468) German printer. He invented a printing press that used movable type (letters). It was used to publish the first large printed book, the Bible.

Guyana A republic in South America. Bauxite, a mineral used to make aluminum, and sugar are the main exports. Area: 83,000 square miles (215,000 square kilometers). Capital: Georgetown.

Gymnastics A sport. Competitors perform acrobatic movements on the floor and on various pieces of equipment such as the bars, rings, and vaulting horses.

Some gymnastic positions

Gyroscope An instrument that consists of a wheel that spins on an axle inside a frame. Once the wheel is spinning, the axle always points in the same direction. Gyro compasses are used to steer aircraft, ships, rockets, and torpedos.

H

Haddock An important food fish belonging to the cod family. Large schools of haddock are found in the northern Atlantic Ocean. The fish weighs about 3 pounds (1.4 kilograms).

Hades God of the underworld in Greek mythology. He ruled over the souls of the dead. The Romans called him Pluto.

Hair One of many of the threadlike growths on the skin of people and animals.

Halloween Festival celebrated on October 31, the eve of All Saints' Day. Once a pagan celebration before the beginning of winter, it is still associated with ghosts and witches.

Hamilton, Alexander (1757-1804) US statesman and first secretary of the treasury. He was killed in a duel with Aaron Burr.

Hamster A short-tailed rodent. It is considered a pest in the wild but is popular as a pet.

Hancock, John (1737-1793) US statesman. He was one of the leaders of the American Revolution and the first to sign the Declaration of Independence. He became the first governor of Massachusetts.

Handel, George Frideric (1685-1759) German-born British composer. He wrote more than 40 operas and over 30 musical compositions called oratorios. His most famous oratorio is *The Messiah* (1742). Handel also wrote organ and orchestral music, including the popular *Water Music* (1717).

Hannibal (247-183 BC) General of Carthage, an ancient city in northern Africa. He conquered southern Spain, then led his army and elephants across the Alps into Italy. Hannibal won a series of brilliant victories against the Romans. He was later defeated by the Romans in 202 BC.

Hanoi Port and capital city of Vietnam, on the Red River.

Harding, Warren G. (1865-1923) Twenty-ninth president of the United States. A Republican, he was a senator from Ohio. As president from 1921 to 1923, his administration was marked by political scandals. Harding died of pneumonia before completing his term of office.

Brown hare

Hare An animal with long ears and long legs. It is related to the rabbit. It can run very fast and lives in open fields. The jackrabbit is actually a hare, not a rabbit.

Harrison, Benjamin (1833-1901) Twenty-third president of the United States. He was the grandson of William Henry Harrison, the ninth president. Harrison was a lawyer. He served in the Union Army during the Civil War. After the war, he returned to his law practice and later was a senator from Indiana. A Republican, he was president from 1889 to 1893.

Harrison, William Henry (1773-1841) Ninth president of the United States. He had a distinguished army career. From 1800 to 1812 he was governor of the Indiana Territory. He was a member of the House of Representatives and the Senate from Ohio. A member of the Whig Party, Harrison died of pneumonia one month after he was inaugurated as president in 1841.

Hawaii The 50th state to join the United States. It is a group of about 130 volcanic islands in the central Pacific Ocean. Area: 6,450 square miles (16,705 square kilometers). Capital: Honolulu.

Hawthorne, Nathaniel (1804-1864) US writer. He wrote many children's stories, as well as short stories and novels. The novels include *The Scarlet Letter* and *The House of the Seven Gables*.

Haydn, Franz Joseph (1732-1809) Austrian composer. He wrote over 100 symphonies, over 80 string quartets, 20 operas, and a number of other musical works.

Hayes, Rutherford B. (1822-1893) Nineteenth president of the United States. He was a general in the Union Army during the Civil War. A Republican, Hayes entered politics after the war. He served three terms as governor of Ohio. He was president of the United States from 1877 to 1881. During his presidency, federal troops were withdrawn from the South.

Heart A muscular organ that

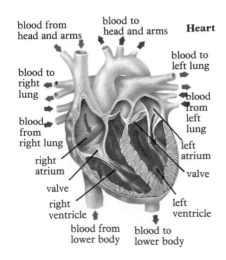

Heart

blood from head and arms

blood to head and arms

blood to left lung

blood to right lung

blood from left lung

blood from right lung

right atrium

left atrium

valve

valve

right ventricle

left ventricle

blood from lower body

blood to lower body

pumps blood through the body. It is actually like two pumps working closely together. The right side receives blood from the body and pumps it out to the lungs, where it collects oxygen. The left side receives blood from the lungs and pumps it out to the body.

Heat A form of energy. A substance will heat up when its molecules start moving faster and bumping into each other. When an object is heated, its temperature rises. When heat is removed, the object's temperature goes down. Our main source of heat is the sun. Heat also comes from the burning of fuels.

SH-60B Sea Hawk helicopter

Helicopter An aircraft with one or more horizontal propellers called rotors. A rotor acts as a wing as well as a propeller. Helicopters with only one main rotor have a small rotor on the tail which keeps the helicopter from spinning around. Helicopters can fly forward, backward, sideways, straight up, and straight down. They can also hover in one spot.

Helium The second lightest element after hydrogen. It is one of the inert (inactive) gases. It will not burn, so it is safe for use in filling balloons and airships. Chemical symbol: He.

Hemingway, Ernest (1899-1961) US writer. Two of his novels, *A Farewell to Arms* and *For Whom the Bell Tolls*, draw on his experiences of war in Italy and Spain. Other books by Hemingway are *The Sun Also Rises* and *The Old Man and the Sea*, which won a Pulitzer prize. He was awarded the Nobel prize for literature in 1954.

Henry VIII (1491-1547) King of England from 1509 to 1547. He was married six times. Because the Roman Catholic Church would not give him a divorce from his first wife, Henry left the Church to create a separate Church of England. He made himself the head of that church.

Henry, Patrick (1736-1799) US Revolutionary leader. He was a brilliant speaker. He is best remembered for a speech in 1775. To urge the arming of the Virginia militia, he said, "Give me liberty or give me death." Henry also served as governor of Virginia.

Heracles (Roman Hercules) In Greek legend, a hero who was famous for his courage and strength. He was the son of Zeus. Because he murdered his wife and children in a fit of insanity, Heracles had to perform 12 labors as a form of penitence, including capturing Cerberus, the three-headed

dog that guarded Hades.

Heraldry The study of family emblems, called coats-of-arms, and family trees, or genealogies. The knights of the Middle Ages were the first to wear coats-of-arms on their shields and banners.

Herb A flowering aromatic plant. Herbs are used to flavor food, give scents to perfume, and are sometimes used in medicines.

Heron A large water bird with a long neck and legs. Herons stand in shallow water waiting to grab fish with their long, pointed bills.

Herring One of the most abundant fish of the northern Atlantic and northern Pacific oceans. It is related to the sardine. A herring is about 8 inches (20 centimeters) long.

Hibernation A sleeplike condition in which some animals spend the winter. By hibernating in a safe place, the animals avoid harsh weather and lack of food during the winter. Ground squirrels, woodchucks, and gophers are some of the animals that hibernate.

Hickok, Wild Bill Nickname of **James Butler Hickok** (1837-1876) US frontiersman and peace officer. Hickok was a stagecoach driver on the Santa Fe and Oregon trails. During the Civil War, he was a scout and a spy for the Union Army. After the war Hickok became a United States marshal in Kansas frontier towns. He also was an Indian fighter and a member of Buffalo Bill Cody's Wild West Show. He was murdered in Deadwood, in the Dakota Territory.

Hieroglyphic A kind of writing in which pictures or symbols represent words, ideas, and sounds. The ancient Egyptians used this type of writing.

Himalayas Massive mountain system in central Asia. It contains the world's highest mountain, Everest – height: 29,028 feet (8,850 meters).

Hinduism The main religion of India. It is several thousand years old, one of the oldest existing religions. Hindus worship many gods but believe there is one unifying, pure spirit called Brahman. They have many sacred texts including the *Vedas*, the *Ramayana* and the *Puranas*.

A Hindu goddess.

Hippopotamus A large African mammal that can weigh as much as 5,800 pounds (2,600 kilograms). The elephant is the only land animal that is as large. The hippopotamus spends most of its time wallowing in rivers and lakes. The smaller pygmy hippopotamus also lives in Africa.

History Everything that has happened in the past, and what people have written about the past.

Hitler, Adolf (1889-1945) The Austrian-born dictator of Nazi Germany from 1934 to

Adolf Hitler

1945. He ordered the murder of millions of Jews, as well as other people, and led Germany into World War II. Defeated in 1945, he died in Berlin soon after.

Ho Chi Minh (1890-1969) Vietnamese revolutionary leader. He won independence from France for North Vietnam. As president from 1954, he led the guerrilla war against South Vietnam.

Ho Chi Minh City Port and largest city in Vietnam. Its name was Saigon before North Vietnam took over South Vietnam in 1975.

Hockey, ice A game played by two six-man teams on ice. The players wear ice skates. They use long sticks with flat blades to hit a hard rubber disk, called a puck, into the opponent's net. A similar game, field hockey, is played on foot in a field. Field hockey teams have 11 players, and a ball is used instead of a puck.

Hollywood An area in Los Angeles, California, that is considered the movie capital of the world. It is the site of large film studios, and home to many film stars. Today most of the studios produce television programs.

Holmes, Oliver Wendell (1841-1935) US lawyer and judge. He was the son of the writer Oliver Wendell Holmes. After serving in the Union Army during the Civil War, he practiced and taught law. He was appointed to the Massachusetts Supreme Court and then to the United States Supreme Court. He often disagreed, or dissented, with the other Supreme Court justices. As a result he came to be called the Great Dissenter.

The Hollywood Bowl–a popular place for concerts and other entertainments.

Holography The production of a three-dimensional picture called a hologram. It is produced by splitting a laser beam. One part of the beam is aimed at an object and is reflected from the object onto a photographic plate. The other part of the beam is shined directly on the plate. The hologram can be viewed by shining a light or laser beam on the developed plate.

Homer Greek poet of the 8th century BC. Although no one knows for sure, he is credited with writing the *Iliad* and the *Odyssey*, narrative (story) poems that were the models for all later epics, or heroic tales.

Honduras Republic in Central America, on the Caribbean Sea. The economy is based on agriculture. Area: 43,277 square miles (112,000 square kilometers). Capital: Tegucigalpa.

Hong Kong A British colony on the southern coast of China. One of the busiest ports in the world, it is made up of Hong Kong Island, Kowloon peninsula, and the New Territories. In 1984, Britain agreed to return Hong Kong to China in 1997. Area: 400 square miles (1,000 square kilometers).

Hood, Mount A mountain in the Cascade Range in northern Oregon. It was once an active volcano. At 11,239 feet (3,426 meters), it is the highest mountain in Oregon.

Hoover, Herbert Clark (1874-1964) Thirty-first president of the United States. He was a mining engineer and traveled widely throughout the world. After World War I, he worked for European relief. A Republican, he was a president of the United States from 1929 to 1933. The stock market crash of October 1929 and the start of the Great Depression took place during his presidency.

Hoover Dam A dam on the Colorado River, at the Arizona-Nevada border. Named after President Hoover, it is 726 feet (221 meters) high.

Hormone A chemical "messenger" produced by certain glands in the body and carried by the blood. Each hormone regulates a specific activity in the body.

Hornet A large stinging wasp. It has a dark body and white or yellow markings. Hornets build large, community nests in trees and around houses.

Horse A hoofed mammal that lived in Europe and Asia in prehistoric times. Horses were brought to North America by the Spanish. Domesticated over 4,000 years ago, there are now more than 150 breeds and types worldwide.

Horse racing A sport known since early times. One of the most famous American horse races is the Kentucky Derby, first run in 1875.

Hospital A place where sick or injured people are cared for by doctors and nurses.

House A building in which people live.

House of Representatives One of the two groups of people who make laws in the United States Congress. Members of the House are elected from each state. The number of representatives from each state is based upon the state's population.

Houston, Sam (Real name **Samuel Houston**) (1793-1863) US soldier and statesman. While in his teens, he lived with the Cherokee Indians in Tennessee. He later entered politics. He served in the House of Representatives and was governor of Tennessee. Houston then returned to the Cherokee, who had settled in Oklahoma. He went to Texas in 1832. In 1836 Texas became the Republic of Texas, and Houston was elected its president. The city of Houston, Texas, is named for him. When Texas became a state, Houston became a senator and governor.

Hovercraft

Hovercraft A vehicle that travels over land or sea on a cushion of air produced by jets from its engines. Large propellers provide the speed.

Howe, Julia Ward (1819-1910) US writer and social reformer. She campaigned for women's rights, world peace, and the abolition of slavery. She is probably best known today as the writer of "The Battle Hymn of the Republic."

Hubble, Edwin Powell (1889-1953) US astronomer. He worked at the Mount Wilson and Mount Palomar observatories in California. Hubble is known for his studies of galaxies. He discovered that the galaxies are moving away from our own galaxy, the Milky Way. This means that the universe is expanding.

Hudson, Henry (died 1611) English explorer and navigator. On voyages to North America, he discovered the Hudson River and Hudson Bay while seeking a Northwest Passage to China. During Hudson's last expedition, his crew mutinied and cast him adrift to die near the bay that is named after him.

Hudson's Bay Company A trading company formed by the British in 1670. The purpose of the company was to get furs from the Indians in the Hudson Bay area of North America. The furs were sold in Europe. The company also promoted settlements in the area. It played a major part in opening up Canada. It became the world's leading fur-trading company.

Humidity The level of water vapor in the air. High humidity makes the air feel moist or damp.

Hummingbird A tiny, brightly colored bird that feeds on nectar. It is named for the hum of its rapid wing beats, which can be as many as 70 per second. The bee hummingbird is only 2 inches (5 centimeters) long and is the smallest bird in the world. Hummingbirds are the only birds that can fly backwards.

Hungary Landlocked republic in east-central Europe. In 1949 a communist state was proclaimed. This led to an anticommunist uprising in 1956 that was put down by Soviet troops. In 1989, like other communist countries in eastern Europe, Hungary made plans to hold free elections. Area: 35,921 square miles (93,000 square kilometers). Capital: Budapest.

Hybrid The offspring of two animals or plants of different species or varieties. The mule is a hybrid of a male donkey and a female horse.

Hydra A tiny freshwater animal with a tube-like body. They are related to jellyfish. Hydras catch worms and insect larvae with their stinging tentacles.

Hydraulics The study of the behavior of liquids in motion. Hydraulic engineers work with machines like turbines and pumps. They build dams, canals, and irrigation and water supply systems.

Hydrocarbon A substance that contains only hydrogen and carbon. Hydrocarbons are obtained from oil and natural gas. They are used to make plastics and synthetic fibers.

Hydrofoil A craft that rises up out of the water when it reaches a certain speed. It is supported on wing-shaped foils, or fins, under the hull. Only the foils touch the water, reducing friction and allowing the craft to reach high speeds using very little power.

Hydrogen The simplest and lightest of the elements. Hydrogen gas catches fire very easily. Combined with oxygen, it forms water and is therefore essential to life. Combined with carbon, it forms a vast number of organic compounds known as hydrocarbons. Chemical symbol: H.

Hyena A doglike mammal of Africa and Asia. Hyenas have large, powerful jaws and hunt in packs. There are three species: brown, striped, and spotted. The spotted hyena has a cry that sounds like human laughter, so it is sometimes called the laughing hyena.

I

Ibex A wild mountain goat found in Europe and Asia. The Alpine ibex (male) has backward-sweeping horns about 29 inches (75 centimeters) long.

Alpine ibex

Ibsen, Henrik Johan (1828-1906) Norwegian playwright and poet. His plays, often about psychological and social problems, include: *A Doll's House*, *Ghosts*, *The Wild Duck*, and *Hedda Gabler*.

Ice The solid form of water. Pure water forms ice at 32° Fahrenheit (0° Celsius), when the movement of the water molecules becomes so slow that it crystallizes into ice. When frozen its volume increases by one-eleventh. Ice is therefore lighter and less dense than water, so it floats.

Ice Age Scientists have found that ice ages have occurred several times, when the Earth's distance from the Sun has increased. The last ice age began about 2 million years ago and ended about 10,000 years ago. Glaciers covered the United States and Canada.

Iceberg A huge lump of floating ice that breaks off the edge of polar ice fields. Icebergs drift in the sea with about 90 per cent of their mass underwater. They are a shipping hazard in the Atlantic Ocean.

Iceland An island republic in the North Atlantic. The landscape consists largely of barren plains and mountains, with large ice fields. Area: 39,769 square miles (103,000 square kilometers). Capital: Reykjavik.

Idaho In the far western United States, Idaho became the 43rd state in 1890. The leading industry today is farming, with potatoes as the best known product. Idaho produces silver and manufactures food products and machinery. Area: 83,557 square miles (216,412 square kilometers). Capital: Boise.

Igloo A type of Eskimo house. It is shaped like a dome and is made of blocks of ice and snow.

Iguana A large, long-tailed lizard of tropical America and the Galapagos Islands. Some are 5 feet (1.5 meters) long.

Illinois A midwestern state. In 1818 it became the 21st state. Fertile prairies make farming important. A leading activity is manufacturing, especially around Chicago, the largest city. Area: 56,400 square miles (146,075 square kilometers). Capital: Springfield.

Immunity The defense system in the body that fights off infection from bacteria and viruses. White blood cells "recognize" foreign substances and release antibodies to fight them. Vaccinations boost the immune system.

Impala A graceful African antelope with long, curving horns. It has remarkable leaping abilities.

Inauguration Day January 20 of the year following a United States presidential election. It is the day on which the new president takes office. The inauguration is a ceremony in Washington, D.C. in which the president takes the oath of office and swears to uphold and defend the US Constitution.

Incas A civilization of South American Indians based in Cuzco, Peru. It reached its height at the end of the 1400s. The Inca civilization was conquered by the Spanish under Francisco Pizarro in 1532.

Independence Day July 4. It celebrates the signing of the US Declaration of Independence. It is a legal holiday in the United States.

India A country in south-central Asia, with the second largest population in the world. Area: 1,269,219 square miles (3,287,263 square kilometers). Capital: New Delhi.

Indiana Located in the east central United States, Indiana became the 19th state in 1816. Manufacturing dominates the economy. Metals and transport equipment are major products. Grain, soybeans, fruits, and mint are grown. Area: 36,291 square miles (93,993 square kilometers). Capital: Indianapolis.

Indianapolis State capital of Indiana, on the White River.

Magnificently clad elephants are a feature of Indian ceremonial processions.

Indians, American The first people to live in the Americas. They are known as Native Americans. The first Indians came to the Americas more than 20,000 years ago from Asia. At that

Map of the Indian Nations in 1880. Inset: Sitting Bull, the famous Indian warrior who led the Sioux at the battle of Little Bighorn (1876) in which General Custer and his troops perished.

time there was a land bridge that connected Siberia and Alaska. From there, the Indians made their way to all parts of North, Central, and South America.

Indonesia A republic in Southeast Asia comprising more than 13,000 islands, among them Sumatra and Java. Area: 741,101 square miles (1,919,443 square kilometers). Capital: Jakarta (on Java).

Indus A river in Asia, flowing from Tibet through India and Pakistan into the Arabian Sea. Length: 1,800 miles (2,897 kilometers).

Industrial Revolution The transformation of Britain, Europe, and North America from agricultural to mainly urban, industrial societies between 1760 and 1900. This was caused by technological developments in agriculture, transportation, and production.

Inert gases A group of gases including argon, helium, krypton, neon, radon, and xenon. They are called inert because of their lack of reaction with other elements.

Inertia The tendency for anything to resist change in its motion. Inertia has to be overcome to start an object moving, and again to stop it. The more mass an object has, the greater its inertia.

Inoculation A medical technique to safeguard a person against infection by a disease. By injecting the person with a mild dose of the disease itself, antibodies are stimulated to kill off the disease, leaving the body resistant to any future attack by the disease.

Inquisition A system of courts set up by the Roman Catholic Church from the 13th to the 17th centuries.

Its goal was to discover and punish people of different beliefs. People who were found guilty were often put in prison or even killed.

Insect Any creature belonging to the largest group of animals (about 800,000 species). Insect bodies are divided into three sections: head (with antennae), thorax (with three pairs of legs), and abdomen. Most insects have wings. All true insects have six legs.

Instinct Any animal behavior that is hereditary rather than learned. Examples of instinctive behavior are shown in animal courtships, care of young, and migration.

Intelligence The ability to assemble facts learned from past experiences and use them to overcome new problems. The ability of a person or an animal to understand a situation is a measure of its intelligence.

Internal combustion engine An engine that works by burning fuel, such as gasoline or diesel oil, in its cylinders. The hot gas produced by the fuel pushes the pistons up and down to drive the crankshaft around.

International Date Line An imaginary line that for the most part follows the 180° meridian of longitude, opposite the Greenwich meridian (0°) in England. There is a 12-hour time difference (one hour for every 15 degrees) between Greenwich and the date line. Crossing the date line going west means losing a day, while going east means gaining one.

Interpol (International Criminal Police Organization) An organization of police forces from more than 140

countries. Based in a suburb of Paris, France, Interpol was established in 1923. It helps police forces in countries throughout the world by storing and giving out information about criminals and crimes.

Invertebrate Any animal without an internal skeleton of bones. Protozoans, crabs, worms, and insects are all invertebrates.

Iodine A bluish-black, nonmetallic element. It is used in photography. Dissolved in alcohol, it forms the antiseptic tincture of iodine. Chemical symbol: I.

Iowa In the central United States, Iowa became the 29th state in 1846. Nearly all of Iowa is farmed. Its chief crops are soybeans and grain. Cattle and pigs are raised. Manufacturing and

The stages of the internal combustion cycle.

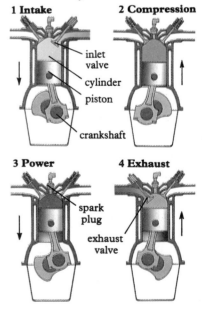

In the intake stage, air and gasoline are sucked into the cylinder. They are squeezed together in the compression stage. In the power stage, a spark from the spark plug ignites the mixture, which propels the piston down the cylinder. In the final stage, the hot gases are exhausted, or pushed out of the cylinder.

food processing are also important. Area: 56,290 square miles (145,790 square kilometers). Capital: Des Moines.

Iran An Islamic republic in Asia. Iran was a kingdom until 1979 when its ruler was overthrown and the republic proclaimed. Area: 636,372 square miles (1,648,000 square kilometers). Capital: Tehran.

Iraq A republic in Asia, center of the ancient civilizations of Mesopotamia. Area: 169,235 square miles (438,317 square kilometers). Capital: Baghdad.

Ireland An island in the Atlantic Ocean. It is separated from Great Britain by the Irish Sea. It is politically divided into Northern Ireland (part of the United Kingdom) and the Republic of Ireland. Area: 32,595 square miles (84,420 square kilometers).

Ireland, Republic of An independent republic in Europe occupying over 80 per cent of the island of Ireland. Area: 27,137 square miles (70,000 square kilometers). Capital: Dublin.

Iron The most important metallic element and the second most common metal in the Earth's crust after aluminum. Iron is extracted from its ores by a process known as smelting in a blast furnace. Chemical symbol: Fe.

Iron Age The period in history following the Bronze Age, when people learned how to make tools and weapons of iron.

Irrigation The artificial watering of land in order to grow crops. It is generally used where rainfall is less than 20 inches (500 millimeters) per year.

Irving, Washington (1783-

Muslims at prayer in a mosque. The walls are not decorated with pictures and statues but with abstract patterns.

1859) US writer. He wrote humorous stories and essays. His best-known stories are "Rip Van Winkle" (1820), and "The Legend of Sleepy Hollow" (1820). From 1842 to 1846, he was the United States minister to Spain.

Islam The religion of Muslims. Mohammed is the main prophet, and Allah is believed to be the supreme being. The holy book of Islam is the Koran.

Island A piece of land completely surrounded by water. It is smaller than a continent.

Isotope An element that has had neutrons added or taken away from the nuclei of its atoms. Some isotopes are radioactive and are very useful in various industries as well as in medicine.

Israel A republic in Asia on the east Mediterranean coast. Israel became an independent Jewish state in 1948. It has been in continuous conflict with its Arab neighbors and has fought four major wars. Area: 7,992 square miles (20,770 square kilometers). Capital: Jerusalem.

Italy A republic in Europe consisting of a peninsula in the Mediterranean and the two principal islands of Sicily and Sardinia. Area: 116,324 square miles (301,000 square kilometers). Capital: Rome.

Ivory Coast A republic on the Gulf of Guinea, West Africa. Area: 124,504 square miles (322,463 square kilometers). Capital: Abidjan.

Ivy A woody plant with glossy leaves. Ivy grows over trees, rocks, and walls by means of small roots that grow from the stem and take hold in the tiniest cracks.

Ivy League A group of seven universities and one college in the northeastern United States. Brown, Columbia, Cornell, Harvard, Pennsylvania, Princeton, and Yale are the universities. The one college is Dartmouth. These schools form a league for intercollegiate sports. Their college buildings are often covered with ivy.

Iwo Jima A small island in the northwestern Pacific Ocean. During World War II, United States troops captured it from the Japanese. The island was returned to Japan in 1968.

J

Jackal A wild member of the dog family, found in Africa and southern Asia. Jackals are scavengers, feeding on animals that are already dead. But they also hunt in packs at night, preying on small mammals.

Jack-in-the-pulpit An American plant of the arum family. It has spiky flowers that are partly covered with arched hoods.

Jackson, Andrew (1767-1845) Seventh president of the United States. He was a prominent judge, lawyer, and soldier. He led campaigns against the British and the Creek Indians in the War of 1812. He became a popular hero after defeating the British at New Orleans. Jackson served two terms as president from 1829 to 1837. He was the first Democrat to be elected president.

Jackson, Jesse (1941-) US Baptist minister and civil-rights and political activist. In 1988, he was the first black person to run for president of the United States.

Jackson, Michael (1958-) US pop music singer, songwriter, and dancer. He is also known for his unique music videos. "Thriller," "Beat It," and "Billie Jean" were popular both as songs and as music videos.

Jackson, Stonewall (Real name **Thomas**) (1824-1863) Confederate general in the American Civil War (1861-1865). He was given the nickname Stonewall because he made it so difficult for others to get past the Southern troops under his command.

Jaguar Largest cat of the Americas. It is found from the southwestern United States to the southern tip of South America. It weighs up to 500 pounds (136 kilograms) and has a spotted coat.

Jamaica Mountainous island country in the Caribbean Sea. Area: 4,244 square miles (10,964 square kilometers). Capital: Kingston.

James, Henry (1843-1916) US author. He wrote biographies, autobiographies, and many novels, including *The Portrait of a Lady* (1881) and *The Turn of the Screw* (1898).

James, Jesse (1847-1882) US outlaw. He lived mostly in Missouri. With his gang, he robbed many banks and trains before he was killed by one of his own men.

Japan Country in eastern Asia, made up of four large islands and 3,000 smaller ones. In World War II, Japanese troops conquered much of Asia but were then defeated in 1945 by the United States and its allies. In recent years, Japan has become one of the world's most important industrial countries. Area: 145,870 square miles (377,708 square kilometers). Capital: Tokyo.

Jazz A musical form developed by black Americans in the southern United States, especially New Orleans, around 1900. Like some African music, it has strong rhythms. There are many different kinds of jazz, including blues, ragtime, swing, and Dixieland jazz.

Jefferson, Thomas (1743-1826) Third president of the United States. He was responsible for drafting the Declaration of Independence. He was elected president in 1800 and again in 1804. Under Jefferson's administration, Louisiana was purchased from France in 1803.

Jellyfish A sea creature with a transparent, umbrella-shaped body and long, hanging tentacles. Some species grow up to 6 feet (2 meters) across. Jellyfish paralyze small fish by releasing poison from stinging cells in their tentacles.

Common jellyfish

Jerusalem Ancient and historic city in central Palestine. It is the capital of Israel. It is a holy city for Jews, Muslims, and Christians.

Jesus Christ (about 6 BC-30 AD) Founder of Christianity. Christians believe Jesus is the son of God who performed many miracles during his life on Earth. The Pharisees saw him as a revolutionary and persuaded Pontius Pilate, the Roman governor, to have him crucified (put to death by nailing to a cross).

Jet engine An engine that moves a vehicle in one direction by shooting out a stream of heated air and gases in the opposite direction. Jet engines are used in airplanes, rockets, and other vehicles.

Joan of Arc, Saint (1412-1431) French heroine who believed she had been chosen by God to save France. She led the French army in a series of victories against the English. Later she was captured, and the English burned her at the stake as a witch.

Johnson, Andrew (1808-1875) Seventeenth president of

the United States. A Republican, he was governor of Tennessee and a senator. In 1864 he was elected vice-president. When Abraham Lincoln was assassinated in 1865, Johnson became president. His political enemies tried to remove him from office in a process called impeachment. He was tried by the Senate, but was acquitted by one vote. Johnson held office until 1869.

Johnson, Lyndon Baines (1908-1973) Thirty-sixth president of the United States. A Texas Democrat, he was a member of the House of Representatives and of the Senate. He was elected vice-president in 1960 and became president in 1963 following the assassination of John F. Kennedy. Johnson held office until 1969. During his presidency, Johnson worked for social and economic reforms, but he also increased American involvement in the Vietnam War.

John the Baptist, Saint (died about AD 29) A Hebrew prophet who is considered by Christians to be the forerunner of Jesus. He foretold the coming of the Messiah. He was beheaded by Herod Antipas, the son of Herod the Great, king of Judea.

Joint Chiefs of Staff An agency in the United States Department of Defense. It advises the president, the secretary of defense, and the National Security Council on military policy. Its permanent members are its chairman, the chiefs of staff of the Army and the Air Force, the chief of Naval Operations, and the commandant of the Marine Corps.

Jordan Kingdom in the Middle East. During the Arab-Israeli war of 1967, Jordan lost its land (Palestine) on the West Bank of the Jordan River. Area: 35,738 square miles (97,740 square kilometers). Capital: Amman.

Judaism The religion of the Jews, and the first religion to teach the belief in one God. It is based on the teachings and laws of the Old Testament of the Bible.

Julius Caesar (about 101-44 BC) Roman general, statesman, and writer. As a general, he conquered Gaul (France), defeated the German tribes, and invaded Britain. He then ruled Rome as a dictator but introduced social reforms and was popular with many of the people. He was murdered by his enemies in the Roman Senate.

Jupiter The largest planet in the solar system. Its diameter is nearly 88,700 miles (142,700 kilometers), 11 times the diameter of the Earth. It orbits the sun at a mean distance of over 480 million miles (772 million kilometers). Jupiter may be composed largely of liquid hydrogen. The surface, however, is hidden by swirling clouds. Jupiter has 16 known moons.

Jute An important natural fiber. It is also the name of the plant from which it comes. The fiber is soft but can be spun into tough, strong threads suitable for rope, sacks, and mats. It is grown in India and Bangladesh.

K

Kalahari Desert Semi-desert region in southern Africa, lying mainly in Botswana. It is inhabited by Bushmen. Area: 200,000 square miles (520,000 square kilometers).

Kampuchea (formerly Cambodia) Communist country of southeast Asia. Communist forces (Khmer Rouge) killed more than 1 million people in the 1970s. In 1978 Vietnamese forces invaded the country and set up a new government. The Vietnamese left in 1989. Area: 69,898 square miles (181,000 square kilometers). Capital: Phnom Penh.

Kangaroo A long-legged Australian marsupial. Large kangaroos are able to leap 6 feet (1.8 meters) high and travel at over 40 miles (64 kilometers) per hour. Gray kangaroos live in the eastern forests, and red ones dwell on the plains. Babies, called *joeys*, remain in their mother's pouch for six months.

Kansas Kansas became a United States territory in

Settlers in Kansas in the 1850s did their plowing with oxen.

1803 and the 34th state in 1861. Located in the center of the country, Kansas is a major beef and wheat producer. It also produces oil and natural gas. Its manufactured goods include transport equipment, machinery, and food products. Area: 82,264 square miles (213,063 square kilometers). Capital: Topeka.

Kayak A boat shaped like a canoe. Its top is covered except for one to four small openings where people sit to paddle the kayak. Eskimos have used kayaks for thousands of years. Their kayaks were once made of sealskins stretched over a whalebone or wooden frame. Today most kayaks are made of fiberglass.

Keller, Helen (1880-1968) US lecturer and writer. She was blind and deaf from the age of two. She was taught to speak and read by Anne Sullivan Macy. Helen Keller earned a degree from Radcliffe College. She spent her life working on behalf of the blind.

Kennedy, John F. (1917-1963) Thirty-fifth president of the United States. At 43 he was the youngest man and the first Roman Catholic to be elected president. Elected in 1961, and immensely popular, he opposed racial discrimination and dealt ably with the Cuban Missile Crisis (1962). Kennedy was assassinated by Lee Harvey Oswald in Dallas, Texas, on November 22, 1963.

Kennedy, Robert Francis (1925-1968) US politician. He was attorney general of the United States during the presidency of his brother, John F. Kennedy. Kennedy was an active promoter of civil rights. A

Democrat, he was a senator from New York. He was assassinated in 1968 while campaigning for the Democratic party's nomination for the presidency.

Kentucky Kentucky, in the east central United States, became the 15th state in 1792. Farmland covers over half of the state, and soybeans, grain, and wheat are important crops. Beef cattle, milk, pork, eggs, and poultry are its main products. The state leads all others in coal production. Louisville is the largest city. Area: 40,395 square miles (104,659 square kilometers). Capital: Frankfort.

Kentucky Derby A US horse race that has been run every year since 1875 at Churchill Downs in Louisville, Kentucky.

Kenya Country in Africa bordering the Indian Ocean. The majority of the people live by farming the rich volcanic soil. The chief exports are coffee, tea, and petroleum products. Area: 224,961 square miles (582,800 square kilometers). Capital: Nairobi.

Kepler, Johannes (1571-1630) German astronomer who worked out the laws that

govern the motion of planets. He used arithmetic based on the detailed observations of the Danish astronomer Tycho Brahe.

Key, Francis Scott (1779-1843) US lawyer and poet. During the War of 1812 he wrote a poem, later set to music, that became known as "The Star-Spangled Banner." The song was adopted in 1931 as the national anthem of the United States.

Kidney Either of two organs in the body that clean the blood of waste products. The waste is passed to the bladder as urine, which is then passed from the body.

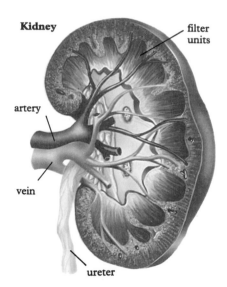

Kidney
filter units
artery
vein
ureter

The grave of President Kennedy, in Arlington National Cemetery.

King, Coretta Scott (1927-) US civil rights leader and wife of Martin Luther King, Jr. She carried on his work after he was assassinated.

King, Martin Luther Jr. (1929-1968) US minister and civil rights leader. He headed the Southern Christian Leadership Conference. It organized the nonviolent demonstrations in the South during the 1960s that won many civil rights for black Americans. King was awarded the Nobel Peace Prize in 1964. He was assassinated in 1968.

Kingfisher

Kingfisher A small, brightly colored bird with a large head. Kingfishers are shy birds that live by streams and ponds and in woodlands. They dive into the water to catch fish. The belted kingfisher, found in the United States, has deep blue-black feathers.

Kipling, Rudyard (1865-1936) English writer who won the Nobel prize for literature in 1907. His works include short stories and poems, some of them for children. Most are set in India. Among his most famous works is *Barrack-Room Ballads* (1892), a collection of poems that includes "Gunga Din" and "The Road to Mandalay." *The Jungle Book* (1894) and *Just So Stories* (1902) were very popular children's books.

Kiribati A country in the Pacific Ocean. It consists of a string of 33 islands that straddle the equator. Area: 281 square miles (728 square kilometers). Capital: Tarawa.

Kissinger, Henry Alfred (1923-) US political scientist and statesman. He was assistant for national security affairs and secretary of state under Presidents Nixon and Ford. He played a major role in making and carrying out American foreign policy.

Kite A bird of prey, about the same size as the buzzard. It is recognized by its forked tail and soaring flight.

Kiwi A chicken-sized bird which cannot fly. It is the emblem of New Zealand. It has hairlike feathers and a long beak with which it searches the forest floor for worms and insects.

Knox, John (about 1515-1572) Scottish clergyman and religious reformer (changer). He was the leader of the Protestant Reformation in his country.

Koala An Australian marsupial that looks like a teddy bear. The mother carries her baby in her pouch for several months. The koala only eats leaves from the eucalyptus tree.

Koran The sacred book of Islam. The Koran is written in classical Arabic and memorized by many Muslims.

Korea, Democratic People's Republic of (Also known as North Korea) A country that occupies the northern part of the Korean Peninsula in East Asia. Area: 46,540 square miles (120,538 square kilometers). Capital: Pyongyang.

Korea, Republic of (Also known as South Korea) A country that occupies the southern part of the Korean Peninsula. South Korea is an important Asian industrial power. Area: 38,025 square miles (98,484 square kilometers). Capital: Seoul.

Kremlin The government of the Soviet Union, especially the part that deals with its relationship with other countries. It takes its name from a famous building in Moscow.

Kublai Khan (1216-1294) Grandson of Genghis Khan. He was one of the greatest Mongol emperors.

Kuwait A small country on the Arabian Peninsula at the head of the Persian Gulf. It is rich in oil. Area: 6,880 square miles (17,824 square kilometers). Capital: Kuwait.

L

Labor day The first Monday in September. It is a legal holiday in the United States and Canada that honors working people.

Lacrosse A game played between two teams of ten or twelve players using sticks that have a net at one end. The aim is to hurl or kick a small rubber ball into the opponent's goal. The game was invented as a war-training exercise by North American Indians.

Lake A large body of fresh or salt water that is surrounded by land.

Language Spoken or written words. There are about 3,000 different spoken languages in the world and many more dialects (local variations).

Laos Country in southeastern Asia. It is a mountainous country mostly covered with forests. Most people are farmers. Area: 91,400 square miles (236,862 square kilometers). Capital: Vientiane.

Lapland The northern areas of Norway, Sweden, Finland, and the Soviet Union where the Lapp people live. It is north of the Arctic Circle. The Lapps fish, herd reindeer, and hunt sea mammals.

Lark A bird known for its sweet song and hovering flight. There are many kinds in Europe, Asia, and northern Africa.

Larva The wormlike, newly hatched form of an insect or other animal. A caterpillar is the larva of a butterfly or moth.

Laser An instrument that produces a thin beam of light. Some lasers are so intense that they can drill holes in steel plates.

Latin The language of the ancient Romans. It was the language of learning and science in Europe until the Middle Ages. Today it is the official language of the Roman Catholic Church.

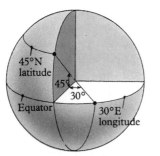

Lines of latitude and longitude.

Latitude and longitude A system of imaginary lines intersecting north-south and east-west used to locate places on the Earth's surface. Latitude is the distance north or south of the equator. Longitude is the distance east or west of Greenwich Observatory,

near London, England. Lines of longitude are called meridians. The meridian that runs through Greenwich is called the prime meridian. Latitude and longitude are measured in circular degrees. The equator is 0° latitude, and Greenwich is 0° longitude.

Laurel The name given to many kinds of trees and shrubs with sweet-smelling bark. The true laurel, or sweet bay, grows in southern Europe. The cinnamon tree, avocado, and sassafras belong to the laurel family.

Law The system of rules of a society. In most societies, the law is enforced by police and courts. In the United States, the basic law of the land is the Constitution.

Lead A heavy, soft, metallic element. It is widely used in alloys and car batteries. Lead compound was commonly put into gasoline to improve the performance. This has proved to increase air pollution, leading to a change back to lead-free gas. Chemical symbol: Pb.

Leaf The main food-making part of a plant. The green color of many leaves is due to chlorophyll, which absorbs the energy of sunlight and uses it to power the food-making process, called photosynthesis.

Leather Animal skin, or hide, that has been treated with chemicals to make it smooth, soft, and strong. It is used for making clothing, shoes, and many other things.

Lebanon Country at the eastern end of the Mediterranean Sea, with Syria to the north and Israel to the south. Its recent history is

one of invasion and civil war. Area: 3,950 square miles (10,400 square kilometers). Capital: Beirut.

Lee, Robert Edward (1807-1870) US soldier. He commanded Confederate armies in the Civil War. He won many important battles and was made general-in-chief. Lee surrendered to General Ulysses S. Grant in April, 1865.

Leech A blood-sucking worm, found mainly in fresh water. Leeches have sucking disks at each end of their bodies which enable them to cling to fishes and other animals and suck their blood.

Wood lemming

Lemming A mouselike rodent of cold climates that lives in underground colonies. Every few years, overpopulation causes food shortages and the lemmings migrate in great numbers. Many die as they try to cross rivers or lakes, or are killed by other animals.

Lemur A primate. It is found in Madagascar. Lemurs grow from 5 inches (13 centimeters) to 28 inches (71 centimeters), not including the tail. Lemurs have large eyes and long, bushy tails. They live in trees.

Lenin, Vladimir Ilyich (1870-1924) Russian revolutionary leader who founded the Communist Party. He led the communist seizure of power in Russia in 1917 and

Vladimir Ilyich Lenin

ruled that country until his death seven years later.

Leningrad Major port and second largest city in the USSR, on the Neva River.

Lens A curved piece of glass that can make light rays bend. Some lenses magnify images by bringing rays of light together. Other lenses can spread out light rays, making an image look smaller. Lenses are used in eyeglasses, cameras, and optical instruments such as microscopes.

Lent The religious period of 40 days before Easter, not including Sundays. It begins on Ash Wednesday and ends on Easter Sunday. Some Christians fast during Lent, but many more spend time in prayer, remember their sins, and resolve to do better.

Leopard A large cat up to 8 feet (2.5 meters) long, with yellow fur and black spots. One kind of leopard, called the black panther, has black fur. Leopards live in Africa and Asia.

Lesotho A mountainous country in southern Africa. Most people work on farms and raise livestock. Wheat, barley, beans, and corn are grown. Area: 11,720 square miles (30,362 square kilometers). Capital: Maseru.

Lewis and Clark Expedition An exploration of the northwestern United States from 1804 to 1806. It opened up the vast new territories of the Louisiana Purchase to settlers. Meriwether Lewis and William Clark led the expedition. Their aim was to find a good land route to the Pacific. They also wanted to collect information about the Indians and the Far West. The expedition left St. Louis, Missouri, crossed the Rockies, and reached the Pacific Ocean. The explorers returned to St. Louis with reports on their discoveries and adventures.

Liberia A country on the west coast of Africa. Liberia was founded in 1822 as a settlement for freed slaves from the United States. Iron ore, rubber, coffee, and logs and timber are the major exports. Area: 43,000 square miles (111,398 square kilometers). Capital: Monrovia.

Liberty Bell The bell that was rung on July 8, 1776, when the Declaration of Independence was formally accepted. It hung in Independence Hall in Philadelphia, Pennsylvania. It became a symbol of freedom. Tradition says that it got its famous crack when it was rung for a funeral in 1835. It can still be visited today.

Library A collection of books. There have probably been libraries since people began to write. Public libraries began in the 19th century in the US. The US Library of Congress is one of the biggest reference libraries in the world. Today libraries may have magazines, newspapers, records, films, videotapes, and compact discs (CDs) as well as books.

Library of Congress The national library of the United States in Washington, D.C. It was established in 1800 by the US Congress for the use of its members. It is now open to the public. With over 20 million books, it is one of the largest libraries in the world.

Libya Country in northern Africa, with a coastline on the Mediterranean Sea. Wealth from oil revenues has been used to finance irrigation of the desert and to start new industries. Area: 679,362 square miles (1,759,540 square kilometers). Capital: Tripoli.

Lichen An unusual plant that consists of a mixture of a fungus and an alga. Most are extremely hardy. Many grow on bare rocks in very hot or cold places.

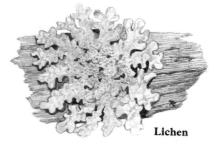

Lichen

Liechtenstein A small European country, on the Rhine River between Switzerland and Austria. Its economy relies heavily on tourism and finance. Area: 62 square miles (158 square kilometers). Capital: Vaduz.

Light That part of electromagnetic radiation that people can see. Radio and X rays are electromagnetic radiation that people cannot see. Light travels at a speed of 186,282 miles (299,792 kilometers) per second.

Lighthouse A tall tower with a bright light on top. It is built near reefs, rocks, and other dangerous spots to warn ships.

Lightning A flash of light in the sky caused by electricity moving from cloud to cloud or cloud to ground. Lightning makes a loud sound called thunder.

Light-year The distance traveled by light in one year. Light travels at a speed of 186,282 miles (299,792 kilometers) per second. In one year, then, light travels almost 6 trillion miles (10 trillion kilometers). Light-years are used in astronomy to measure the distances to and between the stars.

Limestone Rock consisting mainly of calcium carbonate from the remains of shells and coral. It is used for building, to smelt iron ore, and to make lime, a fertilizer. Chalk is a type of limestone.

Lincoln, Abraham (1809-1865) Sixteenth president of the United States. Opposed to slavery, he was elected president in 1860. He led the North during the Civil War. He was reelected in 1864, but was assassinated by the actor John Wilkes Booth in 1865, less than a week after the South surrendered. His leadership through the war preserved the American Union.

Lindbergh, Charles (1902-1974) American aviator who became a national hero when he made the first solo nonstop transatlantic flight in 1927.

Linen Woven fabric made from the fiber of the flax plant. Flax is very strong and is used to make such products as fire hose and fish nets.

Lion A large cat found mostly in Africa south of the Sahara Desert, and in India. Its fur is brownish yellow. The male has a majestic mane and is the center of the family group.

Liquid One of the three states of matter, the others being solid and gas. Molecules in liquid are not firmly attached to each other. As a result, liquid flows easily and takes on the shape of any container into which it is poured. Water and milk are liquids.

Lisbon Port and capital city of Portugal, with a fine natural harbor at the mouth of the Tagus River.

Little Bighorn A river in Wyoming and Montana. The battle of Little Bighorn was fought in Montana in 1876. General George Armstrong Custer and all his men were killed by Sioux and Cheyenne Indians led by their chiefs Crazy Horse, Gall, and Sitting Bull.

Liver A large gland in the body with several important functions. It helps break down fatty foods, produces several blood proteins, and stores sugars in the form of glycogen. It also stores important vitamins.

Livingston, Robert R. (1746-1813) US lawyer and statesman. He helped draft the Declaration of Independence. As the minister to France from the United States, he negotiated the Louisiana Purchase.

Lizard A reptile with a long tail. It is related to snakes. Some species, such as the slowworm, have no legs and look more like snakes. The Komodo dragon, the largest lizard in the world, can grow to 10 feet (3 meters) long. It lives in Indonesia.

Llama South American hoofed mammal of the camel family. It is used as a pack animal in the Andes. It is also valued for its meat and wool. Unlike its relative the camel, the llama has no humps.

Lobster A large crustacean that lives on the sea bed. Lobsters have hard shells, long antennae, eyes on stalks and five pairs of legs. The first pair forms large pincers, or claws. Lobsters are tasty and are an important seafood.

Locomotive An engine that moves on its own power to pull railroad cars. There are

The first steam locomotive was built by Richard Trevithick in 1804.

three main types of locomotives: diesel, electric, and steam. The first locomotive, a steam-powered model, was built in 1804.

Locust A type of grasshopper. Some species destroy crops. They swarm in the millions and rapidly strip fields and trees bare of green vegetation.

London Capital city of the United Kingdom, situated in England on the Thames River.

Longfellow, Henry Wadsworth (1807-1882) The most popular American poet of his time. One of his most famous works is *Ballads and Other Poems* (1841), which includes "The Village Blacksmith." Other well-known poems are "The Song of Hiawatha" (1855), "The Courtship of Miles Standish" (1858), and "Paul Revere's Ride" (1863).

Los Angeles Port and city in California. It is the second largest city in the United States. Hollywood, the film center of the United States, is part of Los Angeles.

Loudspeaker An instrument that turns electric signals into sounds. It then amplifies the sound (makes it louder).

Louis XIV (1638-1715) King of France from 1643 to 1715. He was called "Louis the Great" and "The Sun King." He lived a life of luxury.

Louis XVI (1754-1793) King of France from 1774 to 1792. During his reign, the French people revolted against high taxes and very bad living conditions (French Revolution, 1789-1799). Louis XVI and his wife, Marie Antoinette, were put on trial and found to be criminals. They were both beheaded by a guillotine.

Louisiana A southern state, on the Gulf of Mexico. It was once part of the enormous French colony of Louisiana, which the United States purchased in 1803. It became the 18th state in 1812. Soybeans, sugar cane, and rice are major crops. Leading mineral products are oil and natural gas. Chief manufactured goods are chemicals and foods. The largest city is New Orleans, a major international port. Area: 47,752 square miles (123,677 square kilometers). Capital: Baton Rouge.

Louisiana Purchase The treaty signed in 1803 by which the United States bought all of the Louisiana Territory from the French for 15 million dollars. The territory was much larger than the present state of Louisiana. It stretched from the Mississippi River to the Rocky Mountains and from the Gulf of Mexico into what are now the states of Montana and North Dakota. The purchase nearly doubled the size of the United States.

Lung One of two large organs used for breathing. As we

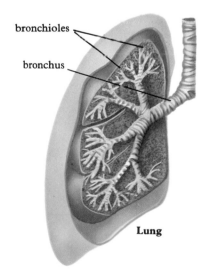

Lung

Each lung has an immense number of tubes inside it. The main tube into each lung is called a bronchus. Each bronchus branches into hundreds of smaller tubes called bronchioles.

A view of Beverly Hills–part of Los Angeles, California and home to many movie stars.

breathe in, our lungs take oxygen from the air and pass it into the blood-stream. When we breathe out, the lungs remove waste carbon dioxide from the body.

Lungfish Freshwater fish found in South America, Africa, and Australia. Unlike other fish, they have a lunglike organ for breathing air. They can live in shallow or stagnant water. Some burrow in the mud when their rivers dry up.

Luther, Martin (1483-1546) German religious leader who spoke out against the corrupt practices of the Roman Catholic Church of his day. He is regarded as the leader of the Protestant Reformation (change) in Germany.

Lynx Bobtailed (with a short tail) member of the cat family, with tufted ears. They live mainly in forests, especially pine, hunting for small animals by night. The Canada lynx is the largest variety.

Lynx

M

Macao A small Portuguese colony on the south coast of China, at the mouth of the Pearl River. Fishing, tourism, and commerce are the major economic activities. In 1987, Portugal agreed to return Macao to China in 1999. Area: 6 square miles (16 square kilometers).

MacArthur, Douglas (1880-1964) US soldier. In World War I he commanded the 42nd Division in France. In World War II he commanded the United States forces in the southwest Pacific. Near the end of the war he was made supreme commander of all Allied forces in the Pacific. After the Japanese surrender, he directed the Allied occupation of Japan. During the Korean War he was in command of the United Nations military force. President Truman removed him from his post for failing to obey the orders of the president.

Macaw A large, colorful, long-tailed parrot of tropical America.

Machine gun An automatic weapon that can fire hundreds of rounds of ammunition in a minute. The ammunition is fed in from a cartridge holder called a magazine, or from a belt.

Mackerel An important food fish found in the North Atlantic Ocean. Mackerel can weigh up to 3 pounds (1.4 kilograms).

MacLeish, Archibald (1892-1982) US poet and public official. His poem "Conquistador" (1932), about Cortes, the Spanish conqueror of Mexico, won a Pulitzer prize. He was also librarian of Congress and assistant secretary of state.

Madison, James (1751-1836) Fourth president of the United States. Because of his work at the Constitutional Convention, he was called "the father of the Constitution." With Alexander Hamilton and John Jay, he wrote a series of papers, *The Federalist*.

These explained the new Constitution to the public and argued for its adoption. Madison was secretary of state under Thomas Jefferson from 1801 to 1809. A Democratic-Republican, he was president of the United States from 1809 to 1817. Madison led the country during the War of 1812 with Great Britain.

Madrid Capital of Spain, situated on the Manzanares River. It is the administrative and financial headquarters of Spain.

Magellan, Ferdinand (1480?-1521) Portuguese commander of the first ships to sail around the world. He discovered the Strait of Magellan, near the southern tip of South America, which connects the Atlantic and Pacific oceans. Magellan died before the voyage was completed.

Maggot The larva of certain types of flies. It has no legs and its head is tiny. Maggots are often found on decaying matter or filth.

Magna Carta A charter granted in 1215 by King John I of England that limited the king's power. It was forced on the king by an alliance of barons. The charter gave certain rights to the barons and to the Roman Catholic Church, but it did little to guarantee liberties for most of the people. In later years, however, the Magna Carta became a model for those who sought to obtain individual rights and liberties.

Magnesium A light, silvery-white metal that burns with a brilliant white flame. It is used in lightweight alloys. Chemical symbol: Mg.

Magnetism The ability to attract iron, steel, and some other things. Magnetism is found in some stones and metals, and in all electric currents.

Magnolia A tree or shrub widely cultivated for its beautiful, fragrant flowers. There are several species, some of which are evergreen.

Magpie A black and white member of the crow family related to jays. It has a long, tapering tail and a habit of noisy chattering.

Mahogany A tall tree with hard wood that is valued for furniture and cabinetwork. The color of the wood varies from light tan to dark reddish-brown. The trees grow in Mexico, tropical South America, and Africa.

Maine Bordering on Canada and the Atlantic Ocean, it is the largest of the New England states. It joined the United States in 1820 as the 23rd state. Tourism, timber, and paper industries form the basis of the economy. The main fishing port and largest city is Portland. Area: 33,265 square miles (86,156 square kilometers). Capital: Augusta.

Malaria A tropical disease caused by a parasite transmitted into the bloodstream by the bite of certain female mosquitoes.

Malawi A landlocked country in southeastern Africa, on the shores of Lake Malawi. Tobacco, tea, and sugar cane are grown for export. Area: 45,747 square miles (118,515 square kilometers). Capital: Lilongwe.

Malaysia A country in Southeast Asia. Crops include rice, pepper, and pineapples. Malaysia is the world's largest producer of rubber and tin. Oil is an important export. Area: 127,317 square miles (329,749 square kilometers). Capital: Kuala Lumpur.

Mali A landlocked country in West Africa. The Sahara Desert covers the northern half of the country. In the south, which is more fertile, the main crops are cotton and cereals. Area: 478,800 square miles (1,240,000 square kilometers). Capital: Bamako.

Mallard A wild duck, common on marshes, coastal mudflats, and lakes. The female is speckled brown. During the mating season, the male has gray and reddish-brown feathers, with a dark green head.

Malta A small island country in the central Mediterranean Sea. The three main islands are Malta, Gozo, and Comino. Tourism and shipbuilding are important industries. Area: 122 square miles (316 square kilometers). Capital: Valletta.

Mammal Any of the large class of backboned animals in which the female feeds her young with milk from her own body. All mammals are warm blooded. With a few exceptions, they are all covered with hair.

Mammoth A large, woolly elephant that roamed the plains of Europe, Asia, and North America during the Ice Age. It probably became extinct about 10,000 years ago. Whole animals have been found perfectly preserved in the icy soils of Siberia and Alaska.

Manatee Bulky aquatic mammals up to 14 feet (4.5 meters) long that live around tropical coasts. Also called sea cows, they are thought to have been the mermaids that sailors once claimed to see basking on the rocks.

Mandrill A large, strong monkey that lives in the forests of West Africa. The male mandrill's face and rump are decorated with blue and scarlet skin patches. Its fur is brown.

Manganese A brittle, grayish metallic element. A form of it is used in making steel. It removes impurities from the steel and strengthens it. Chemical symbol: Mn.

Mangrove A tall, tropical tree that grows in shallow salt water. Its stiltlike roots grow down from the branches.

Manhattan Island An island in New York City bounded by the Hudson, Harlem, and East rivers and upper New York Bay. Area: 22 square miles (57 square kilometers).

Manitoba A Canadian Prairie Province, it became Canada's fifth province in 1870. Nickel, copper, oil, and zinc are mined. Beef, dairy products, and wheat are the chief farm products. Area: 251,000 square miles (649,950 square kilometers). Capital: Winnipeg.

Praying mantis

Mantis A long, thin, winged insect. It is also known as the praying mantis because it strikes a prayerlike pose while waiting for prey.

Mao Zedong (1893-1976) Chinese revolutionary

leader and founder of the People's Republic of China. He was one of the original members of the Chinese Communist party and creator of the Red Army. After a long and bitter campaign against the Chinese Nationalists under Chiang Kai-shek, he became Chairman of the People's Republic of China in 1949.

Map A drawing that shows part or all of the Earth's surface drawn to scale. Maps can show such features as rivers, mountains, roads, cities, and boundaries.

Maple One of a family of more than 100 species of deciduous (leaf-shedding) trees. The sap, which is rich in sugar, is boiled down to make syrup. The maple's hard wood is used to make furniture. The maple leaf is the national symbol of Canada.

Marathon A long-distance foot race. Runners follow a course that is 26 miles, 385 yards (42 kilometers, 53 meters) long. It is an event for men and women in the Summer Olympic Games.

Marble A hard form of limestone. Marble can take a high polish and is used in building and sculpture.

Marconi, Guglielmo (1874-1937) Italian physicist and engineer who shared the Nobel prize for physics in 1909. He contributed to the development of wireless telegraphy. In 1901 Marconi transmitted the first transatlantic radio signals.

Margarine A spread that is similar to butter. It is made from vegetable oil, skim milk, salt, water, and sometimes food coloring and added vitamins.

Marie Antoinette (1755-1793) Queen of France as wife of Louis XVI. She was very unpopular because she spent so much money on herself and did not understand how poor most of the French people were. During the French Revolution (1789-1799), she and Louis XVI were put on trial and found to be criminals. They were both beheaded by a guillotine.

Marine Corps, United States An independent branch of the United States Navy. The Marine Corps was created as a military service in 1798. In 1989, there were nearly 200,000 men and women on active service in the Marines.

Marjoram A fragrant, flowering plant of the mint family. Marjoram is widely cultivated for its leaves, which are used for flavoring food.

Mars The fourth planet from the sun. It is known as the Red Planet because of the color of the rocks on its surface. In 1976, the United States landed two Viking spacecraft on Mars, but found no signs of life. It has two moons. Diameter: 4,200 miles (6,790 kilometers). Mean distance from the sun: 142 million miles (228 million kilometers).

Marsupial A mammal that cares for its newborn babies in a pouch. The babies, less than 2 inches (5 centimeters) long, climb up into the mother's pouch after birth and nurse there. Kangaroos, koalas, and other marsupials live in Australia, New Guinea, and nearby islands. The opossum is the only marsupial that lives in the Americas.

Martial arts Combat sports that include judo, karate, and kung fu. Historians think kung fu was first used for self-defense in China almost 4,000 years ago. Martial arts were later practiced in India, Korea, and Japan. Judo is now an event at the Olympic Games.

Martin A migratory bird in the swallow family. Its appearance is similar to the swallow, but the martin has a shorter forked tail.

Marx, Karl (1818-1883) German philosopher and founder of modern communism. Marx and his friend Friedrich Engels wrote the *Communist Manifesto* (1848). After settling in England he wrote *Das Kapital*. The first volume was published in 1867. The others were published after his death.

The Viking craft that landed on Mars in 1976 was even able to analyze the planet's red soil but it found no trace of life.

Maryland One of the original 13 states in the United States. On the coast of the Atlantic Ocean, the city of Baltimore is a major port. Manufacturing is the leading activity, although farmland covers almost half of Maryland. Poultry, milk, corn, soybeans, and tobacco are the chief farm products. Area: 10,460 square miles (27,092 square kilometers). Capital: Annapolis.

Mason-Dixon Line The boundary line between Pennsylvania to the north and Maryland and West Virginia to the south. It is named after the two English astronomers who surveyed it. In the days before the Civil War, the phrase "Mason-Dixon line" came to mean the dividing line between slave states and free states. It is still used today to mean the dividing line between the South and the North.

Mass The amount of matter in a body. Unlike weight, mass does not vary. An object may become weightless in space, outside Earth's gravity, but its mass remains the same.

Massachusetts A New England state and one of the original 13 states in the US. The economy is based on manufacturing, especially machinery and electronic equipment. Dairy and farm products, as well as fishing, are also important. Area: 8,257 square miles (21,385 square kilometers). Capital: Boston.

Mauritania A hot, dry desert country in western Africa. Minerals, particularly copper and iron ore, are the country's chief resource. Area: 398,000 square miles (1,030,969 square kilo-meters). Capital: Nouak-chott.

Mauritius A small island nation in the Indian Ocean, east of Madagascar. Sugar is its main export. Area: 790 square miles (2,045 square kilometers). Capital: Port Louis.

Maya An Indian people who developed a civilization in the Yucatan peninsula of south Mexico and Central America. The civilization reached its height between the 3rd and 9th centuries AD.

Mayfly An insect related to the dragonfly. It has a long, slender body, delicate wings, and a trailing tail. Mayfly larva sometime survive for years. The adult stage lasts only a few hours or days and then the insect dies.

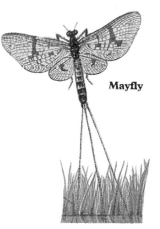

Mayfly

McKinley, Mount The highest summit in North America. Native Americans call it Denali, "The Great One." It lies in central Alaska, in the Alaska Range. Permanent snowfields cover much of the mountain and feed many glaciers. It is named after President William McKinley. Mount McKinley is in Denali National Park. It has a height of 20,320 feet (6,194 meters).

McKinley, William (1843-1901) Twenty-fifth president of the United States. He served in the Civil War, then practiced law before entering politics. A Republican, McKinley was a member of the House of Representatives. He also served as governor of Ohio. McKinley was president of the United States from 1897-1901. He was assassinated in 1901. During McKinley's presidency, the United States fought the Spanish-American War (1898).

Mead, Margaret (1901-1978) US anthropologist (someone who studies people). She studied and wrote about the life and culture of the people of the South Pacific islands of Samoa, Bali, and New Guinea.

Mecca The holiest city of Islam, located in Saudi Arabia. It is the birthplace of Mohammed and a place of pilgrimage for Muslims.

Mechanics The branch of physics that deals with the effects of forces on objects. Engineers use mechanics to find out about stresses on structures like dams and bridges. Astronomers use mechanics to study the motions of stars and planets.

Medici A family of rich, powerful bankers, merchants, and rulers of Florence and Tuscany. They lived in Italy between the 14th and 16th centuries.

Medicine The art and science of detecting, treating, and preventing disease.

Mediterranean Sea A large sea bounded by Europe on the north and west, Asia on the east, and Africa on the south. It is an arm of the Atlantic Ocean.

Melville, Herman (1819-1891) US novelist. His works include *Moby-Dick* (1851), and

Billy Budd (1924), which was published after his death. Both books draw on his experience at sea, in a whaler and later in a man-of-war.

Memorial Day A day in late May set aside to honor the memory of war dead. It is a legal holiday in the United States.

Mendel, Gregor (1822-1884) Austrian monk and botanist. He studied the pea plants that he grew in the monastery garden. He discovered how traits (such as size, color, and flowers) are passed from one crop of peas to the next. Mendel's law also applies to other plants and animals.

Menotti, Gian Carlo (1911-) US composer best known for his operas. Born in Italy, he settled in the United States in 1928. *The Medium* was his first popular success. His best known opera is *Amahl and the Night Visitors*. It is often shown on television at Christmastime. *The Consul* won a Pulitzer prize in 1950 and *The Saint of Bleecker Street* in 1955.

Mercury (metal) The only metal that is liquid at room temperature. Often called quicksilver, mercury is used in thermometers, barometers, and other scientific instruments. Chemical symbol: Hg.

Mercury (planet) One of the smallest planets and the one closest to the sun. Mercury is an almost airless, waterless world scarred by craters. It has no moons. Diameter: 3,031 miles (4,878 kilometers). Mean distance from the sun: 36 million miles (58 million kilometers).

Metal A chemical element, such as gold, silver, iron, copper, and aluminum. Metals are usually shiny. They are good conductors of electricity and heat.

Metamorphic rock Rock that has been changed by heat or pressure in the Earth's crust. Marble and slate are metamorphic rocks.

Metamorphosis A total change of form during the life of an animal. Examples include frogs and toads, which start life as legless tadpoles. Among insects, the butterfly starts life as a caterpillar.

Meteor A fragment of rock from outer space that enters the Earth's atmosphere. Friction makes it glow and burn, causing a streak of light in the sky. Meteors are also called shooting stars or falling stars. Occasionally, larger fragments of rock may reach the Earth. These are known as meteorites. Many thousands of years ago, an enormous meteorite formed a crater nearly a mile (1.2 kilometers) wide in Arizona.

Meteorology The study of the Earth's atmosphere, including weather and weather conditions.

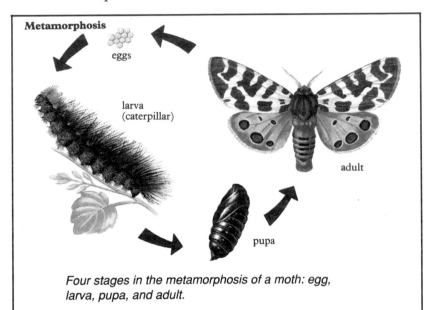

Metamorphosis

eggs

larva (caterpillar)

pupa

adult

Four stages in the metamorphosis of a moth: egg, larva, pupa, and adult.

The impact of an iron meteorite made this vast crater in Arizona about 50,000 years ago.

Metric system A system of weights and measures based on the number 10. The meter is the basic unit of length. The liter is the basic unit of capacity. The kilogram is the basic unit of mass or weight.

Mexico Country in Latin America, south of the United States. Despite large oil reserves, Mexico has economic problems. Area: 758,136 square miles (1,963,564 square kilometers). Capital: Mexico City.

Mexico, Gulf of On the southern coast of North America, the gulf is part of the Atlantic Ocean.

Mexico City Capital and largest city of Mexico. Extensive damage was caused by an earthquake in 1985.

Michelangelo (1475-1564) Italian Renaissance painter, sculptor, architect, and poet. Among his greatest works are the statues of David in Florence and the Pietà in Rome, and his paintings of Biblical scenes on the ceiling of the Sistine Chapel in Rome.

Michigan A state in the midwestern United States. It is bordered by parts of four of the Great Lakes. The scenery attracts many visitors. Michigan became the 26th state to join the Union, in 1837. It is a prosperous industrial state, known for its cars, machinery, and steel. There are farms in the south. The largest city is Detroit. Area: 58,527 square miles (151,586 square kilometers). Capital: Lansing.

Microorganism An organism that is so small it can be seen only through a microscope. Protozoa, viruses, bacteria, and single-celled organisms are microorganisms.

Microphone A device for changing sound waves into electrical signals. The mouthpiece of a telephone is a microphone.

Microscope An instrument for magnifying objects too small to be seen with the naked eye. Ordinary microscopes can magnify objects up to 500 times. Using electron beams, ion microscopes are able to magnify objects two million times.

Middle Ages The period in European history between the fall of the Roman Empire and the Renaissance. The Middle Ages lasted from about the 5th to the 15th century.

Middle East A large area made up of the countries of southwestern Asia, southeastern Europe, and northeastern Africa. Some of the larger countries in the Middle East are Egypt, Turkey, Iraq, Iran, Saudi Arabia, and Sudan.

Migration The regular movement of animals, such as birds, from one area to another and back again. Most animals migrate on a daily or seasonal basis.

Mildew A kind of fungus that grows on the leaves of plants and on cloth, paper, and other materials that are damp. It looks like a thin, furry, whitish coating or discoloration.

Milky Way A galaxy with hundreds of billions of stars. The sun and the planets of the solar system are in the Milky Way.

Millipede A wormlike animal with as many as 115 pairs of legs. Millipedes usually feed on decaying vegetation. Most species are long and slender. Almost every body segment has two pairs of legs.

Mime A form of acting in which the performer never speaks, expressing meaning only by using facial and body movements. Mime was popular in ancient Greece and Rome, and is still practiced today.

Minerals The various chemical combinations that make up rocks and the crust of the Earth. Some minerals, such as copper, are valuable metal ores. Others, such as rubies, are valuable gemstones.

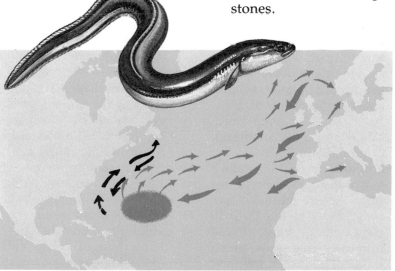

Migration: Eels spawned in the Sargasso Sea travel up to 3,000 miles (4,800 kilometers) across the Atlantic. During the journey they turn from larvae into elvers. They spend their adult lives in North American and European waters. Then they make the return trip to die.

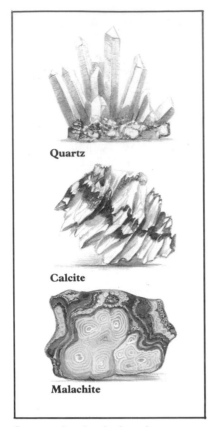

Commonly mined minerals.

Quartz

Calcite

Malachite

Mining Extracting or digging minerals from the Earth. In addition to coal, dozens of different minerals are mined.

Minnesota Located in north central United States, it was the 32nd state to join the Union in 1858. It is a major food producer, as well as a major iron mining state. Manufactured goods include machinery, metal products, and food. Minnesota has thousands of lakes. Area: 84,402 square miles (218,601 square kilometers). Capital: Saint Paul.

Minnow One of the smallest fish of the carp family. Most fully grown minnows are only 2 to 4 inches (5 to 10 centimeters) long. Some minnows can grow much larger. The Indian minnow can reach 9 feet (2.7 meters).

Mint A plant with fragrant leaves which are used to flavor food. There are over 3,000 different types of mint.

Minutemen A group of armed citizens who were ready to fight "at a minute's notice" in the American Revolution.

Mirage An optical illusion caused by the refraction and reflection of light. Light rays are bent when they pass from cool to warm air, causing images of objects to be seen in places where they do not exist.

Mirror A smooth, polished surface that reflects the image of a person or thing in front of it. Most mirrors are made of glass. The back of the glass is sprayed with a thin layer of aluminum or silver. Images are reflected from the metal through the glass.

Mississippi Located in the southern United States, it became the 20th state in 1817. Farming used to dominate the economy, but now manufacturing is the leading activity. Products include transportation and electric equipment, timber, and food products. Mississippi also produces oil and natural gas. Area: 47,716 square miles (123,584 square kilometers). Capital: Jackson.

Mississippi River The chief river in the United States, flowing from northwest Minnesota to Louisiana and into the Gulf of Mexico. The river drains approximately 1,247,300 square miles (3,230,490 square kilometers). It causes considerable flood-control problems. Length: 2,348 miles (3,779 kilometers).

Missouri In the center of the country, Missouri became the 24th state in the United States in 1821. It is a major farming and industrial state. Transport equipment, chemicals, and food products are manufactured. Soybeans, wheat, and corn are leading crops, and livestock is raised. Area: 69,686 square miles (180,486 square kilometers). Capital: Jefferson City.

St. Joseph, Missouri, was the starting place of the Pony Express, which carried mail out west in 1860-61.

Missouri River One of the main tributaries of the Mississippi River. It is extensively used for irrigation and hydroelectric power stations. Length: 2,315 miles (3,726 kilometers).

Mistletoe A woody plant that grows on the trunks and branches of trees, especially those of the apple tree. It produces small white berries in winter and is used as a Christmas decoration.

Mockingbird A small bird of North, South, and Central America. It has gray and white feathers. It can imitate (mock) the songs of other birds.

Mohammed (570?-632) Arabian prophet and founder of Islam. He was born in the holy city of Mecca. Muslims believe he was the last messenger of God, and that the Koran was dictated to him by an angel sent from God.

Mold A fuzzy fungus that grows on decaying matter. The most familiar mold is the bluish-green mold caused by penicillium, from which the first antibiotic, penicillin, was derived.

Mole A small, furry animal that lives underground. Moles have spade-shaped front feet, which are ideal for digging the maze of tunnels in which they live. Moles feed mainly on earthworms and insects.

Molecule The smallest part of a substance that has the characteristics of the substance. A molecule consists of one or more atoms.

Mollusk A soft-bodied animal that has no bones. Most mollusks, such as the octopus, squid, clam, and oyster, live in water. Clams, oysters, and some other mollusks have hard shells. The octopus and squid do not. Snails, slugs, mussels, and scallops are other mollusks.

sea snail   **Mollusks**

mussel

limpet

Molybdenum A hard, silvery-white metallic element chiefly used to harden steel. Chemical symbol: Mo.

Momentum The tendency of a moving object to keep moving. For an object moving in a straight line, the momentum is equal to the velocity of the object multiplied by its mass. A large truck driving at 60 miles (100 kilometers) an hour has a greater momentum than a car driving at the same speed, because the truck has a greater mass.

Monaco One of the smallest countries in the world, on the southeast coast of France. Monaco is a self-governing principality, protected by France. Area: 0.73 square miles (1.9 square kilometers). Capital: Monaco.

Monarchy A government or state headed by one person (king, queen, emperor, or sultan) who inherits or is elected to a throne for life. Several countries still have monarchies, including the United Kingdom, Norway, Sweden, Denmark, Belgium, The Netherlands, and Spain. In most monarchies today, the monarch has little real political power.

Monastery A building housing a community of monks or others. These people withdraw from ordinary ways of living so that they can dedicate themselves to their religion.

Mongolia A country north of China and south of the USSR. Mongolia has been under Russian influence since the 1920s. Area: 604,250 square miles (1,565,000 square kilometers). Capital: Ulan Bator.

Mongols Warlike, nomadic tribes of Asia, united in the 1200s under Genghis Khan. The Mongols ruled an empire that stretched from China to eastern Europe. The empire broke up at the end of the 14th century.

Mongoose A small, fierce carnivore of Africa and southern Asia. These animals can move quickly enough to catch poisonous snakes without harm. They can be tamed and kept for killing snakes.

Monkey A small mammal related to apes. Monkeys live mostly in forests, feeding on fruit, leaves, and some small animals.

Monorail A railroad with only one rail. Monorail trains can be suspended from the rail, or they can be balanced on the rail. Monorails can be built above city streets.

Monroe, James (1758-1831) Fifth president of the United States. After fighting in the American Revolution, he had a distinguished political career as a Democratic-Republican. He was a senator from Virginia and governor of that state. Later he was secretary of state and secretary of war. Monroe was president from 1817 to 1825. His Monroe Doctrine warned the countries of Europe that the United States would not allow any further European intervention or colonization in the Americas.

71

Monsoon A seasonal wind that blows over the northern Indian Ocean and parts of southern Asia. Monsoons usually bring heavy rain.

Montana Located in the northwestern United States, Montana became the 41st state in 1889. Vast areas of grazing land are found in the eastern Great Plains, with the Rocky Mountains in the west. The leading farming activity is raising livestock. Wheat is the chief crop. Oil, coal, and copper are mined. Area: 147,138 square miles (381,086 square kilometers). Capital: Helena.

Montreal Port and city of Quebec, Canada, at the meeting of the Saint Lawrence and Ottawa Rivers. It is Canada's principal port. The population is largely French-speaking.

Moon The natural satellite of the Earth. It orbits Earth every 27⅓ days, always keeping the same face turned toward the planet. Diameter: 2,160 miles (3,476 kilometers). Mean distance from the Earth: 238,857 miles (384,403 kilometers).

Moose The largest animal in the deer family. It can weigh up to 1,800 pounds (816 kilograms) and stand as much as 7.5 feet (2.3 meters) high. Moose are found in the northern parts of North America, Asia, and Europe.

Morgan, John Pierpont (1837-1913) US banker and financier. He was the son of J.S. Morgan, who founded the J.S. Morgan and Company banking firm in London. J.P. Morgan, based in New York, financed governments, railroads, and shipping. He helped organize the United States Steel Corporation. He contributed to many charities and left a large collection of art and rare books to the public.

Mormon A member of the Church of Jesus Christ of Latter-Day Saints. Joseph Smith founded the church in 1830 in the United States. Many Mormons live in Utah.

Morocco Country in the northwestern corner of Africa, with coastlines on the Mediterranean Sea and the Atlantic Ocean. Much of the country is desert, but the northern hills are wooded and more fertile. Area: 177,117 square miles (458,730 square kilometers). Capital: Rabat.

Morse Code A system of dots and dashes that stand for letters and numbers. It was patented by the US inventor Samuel Morse in 1840 for his telegraph machine. It has now been replaced by teleprinters and facsimile machines.

Moscow Capital city of the USSR, on the Moscow River. Originally built mainly of wood, the city was largely burned to the ground during Napoleon's occupation (1812). Today, it is the site of many of the USSR's most famous buildings, including the Kremlin and Lenin's tomb.

Moses, Grandma Nickname of **Anna Mary Moses** (1860-1961) US painter. Grandma Moses farmed for most of her life in Virginia and New York State. She took up painting when she was 76. Her paintings are simple and colorful scenes of the rural life that she knew.

Mosquito A small, flying insect. Some mosquitoes spread diseases such as malaria and yellow fever. Most do not spread disease, but they have painful bites.

Moss A group of green, flowerless plants. Mosses grow in damp places, forming soft mats on the ground. Some mosses grow in lakes, ponds, or rivers.

Moth A flying insect related to the butterfly. Both belong to a large insect group, called *Lepidoptera*, which means "scale wing." Their wings are covered with tiny scales, which give them their color.

Gypsy moth

Peppered moth

Motion The process of moving. When an object changes its position, it is in motion.

Motion picture Also called movies. A series of pictures, on a reel of photographic film, that are shown on a white screen. The film passes through a projector quickly so that the people and things in the pictures appear to be moving.

Motorcycle A vehicle with two or three wheels that is powered by a gasoline engine. The first motorcycle was built by the German engineer Gottlieb Daimler in 1885, using a Benz gasoline engine. European motorcycles dominated the world markets until the 1950s, when highly sophisticated, lightweight Japanese models were introduced.

Fold mountains are formed when two plates are pushed against each other. As one plate slides under the other, it melts. The melted rock may rise to the Earth's surface through volcanoes.

Mountains Areas of land that rise high above their surrounding areas. Mountains are formed by changes in the Earth's crust. Some changes cause rock layers to be squeezed and buckled so that they rise up to form great "fold" mountains. Other changes, such as volcanic eruptions, erosion, and swelling of hot liquid beneath the Earth's crust, also form mountains.

Mountie A member of the Royal Canadian Mounted Police.

Mount Rushmore A mountain in the Black Hills of western South Dakota in the north central United States. The portraits of presidents George Washington, Thomas Jefferson, Abraham Lincoln, and Theodore Roosevelt are carved into the northeast side. The work was begun in 1927 and finished in 1941. Height: 5,600 feet (1,710 meters).

Mount Vernon The home of George Washington. It is located on the Potomac River in northeastern Virginia. Washington is buried on its grounds.

Mouse A small rodent closely related to rats. It has a long snout, a long tail, and large ears.

Mozambique A country in southeastern Africa bordering the Indian Ocean. Most of its people live either on the coastal plain or in the valleys of the Limpopo and Zambezi Rivers. Area: 308,642 square miles (799,380 square kilometers). Capital: Maputo.

Mozart, Wolfgang Amadeus (1756-1791) Austrian composer and child prodigy. He composed over 40 symphonies, more than 20 piano concertos, over 20 operas, and many string quartets. Today, his music is performed regularly throughout the world.

Muir, John (1838-1914) US naturalist and conservationist. Muir helped to found Yosemite National Park.

Multiplication The act of adding a number to itself a certain number of times. The mathematical symbol for multiplication is ×.

Muscle The tissue in the body that enables people and animals to move. Skeletal muscles, such as those of the arms and legs, are attached to the body's bones and are controlled by the individual. Other muscles, such as those in the stomach and the heart, are controlled automatically by the brain.

Mushroom A type of fungus that has a stalk topped by an umbrella-shaped cap. Some mushrooms can be eaten. Many others, called toadstools, can be poisonous.

Music Sounds arranged in patterns of rhythm and melody. The art of making music is a human activity, although some natural sounds, such as birdsong, may be called musical.

Musical instrument There are four kinds of musical instruments. The wind instruments include the woodwinds, such as the flute, clarinet, and the recorder, and brass instruments such as the trumpet, French horn, and trombone. Stringed instruments include the piano, violin, cello, and guitar. Percussion instruments include the drums, cymbals, and tambourine. Electronic instruments include the electronic organ and Moog synthesizer.

Musk ox Animal of the North American Arctic regions and Greenland, related to cattle. They have shaggy hair, short tails, and short legs. When they feel threatened, they form a circle around their calves to protect them.

Muskrat A North American and European rodent. It lives near streams, ponds, and rivers, feeding on water plants. Muskrats are also raised for their fur.

Mussel A mollusk with a two-part shell, found in both fresh and salt water. Marine mussels are found on rocky shores, clinging to rocks. The shells of freshwater mussels are a source of mother-of-pearl.

N

Nairobi Capital city of Kenya, Africa.

Name A word or words used to identify a person, place, or thing.

Namibia Formerly known as **South West Africa**. Large, sparsely populated country in southwestern Africa. Area: 317,818 square miles (823,145 square kilometers). Capital: Windhoek.

Napoleon I Original name **Napoleon Bonaparte** (1769-1821) Soldier and statesman who crowned himself Emperor of France in 1804. He was born on Corsica, a French island. A brilliant general, he conquered most of Europe before being defeated by the British at the battle of Waterloo (in Belgium) in 1815.

Napoleon reviewing his troops in 1804.

Narcotics Any drug that dulls the senses. Narcotics are used as painkillers and sleeping pills and to calm people. Narcotics can become addictive (habit-forming). Large doses can cause death.

Narwhal A small whale of the Arctic Ocean. It is about 18 feet (5.5 meters) long, and males have a straight, twisted tusk that may be up to 8 feet (2.4 meters) long.

NASA (Stands for **National Aeronautics and Space Administration**) A United States government organization in charge of non-military space exploration and research. It was founded by President Dwight Eisenhower in 1958, but its roots go back to 1911. Two of its most famous sites are Cape Canaveral and the Johnson Space Center.

Nashville State capital of Tennessee, on the Cumberland River.

Nassau Port and capital city of the Bahamas, an island nation southeast of Florida.

National Guard Volunteer reserve groups of the United States Army and Air Force. They can be called up by the president in a national emergency or by the governor during a state crisis. Units are found in every state, territory, and the District of Columbia. There are about 500,000 volunteers.

National monument A landmark, site, or structure, such as a fort, canyon, or mountain, that has been chosen as a site of historical interest. It is preserved and maintained by the government for public study or enjoyment.

National park A large area of land set aside as public property by a government for preservation. Such parks have great natural beauty or special scientific or historical value. Yellowstone National Park, the first national park in the United States, was established in 1872.

Natural gas A mixture of flammable gases that have formed naturally from organic matter. Plants and animals that died millions of years ago decayed and became natural gases. Natural gas is often found along with oil.

Natural selection The process in nature by which those organisms best suited to their environment will survive and reproduce. It is part of Charles Darwin's theory of evolution.

Navigation The science of directing or controlling the course of airplanes, ships, or spacecraft on land or sea or through the air.

Navy, United States The branch of the United States military that uses ships and submarines for warfare and protection. Some ships, called aircraft carriers, have airplanes on them.

Nazism (Also known as **National Socialism**) The political theory of the party led by Adolf Hitler in Germany, created in the early 1920s. Nazis believed that the state should control the economy and that the country should expand by waging war.

Nebraska Located in the midwestern United States, it was admitted as the 37th state in 1867. It is a major agricultural state. Beef and dairy cattle are raised on huge ranches. Corn, soybeans, and wheat are the chief crops. Area: 77,355 square miles (200,350 square kilometers). Capital: Lincoln.

The Orion nebula glows from the light of newborn stars at its center.

Nebula A great mass of gases and dust particles in space. Some nebulas are believed to be the birthplace of stars.

Neon One of the inert (inactive) gases present in air in small quantities. It is used in neon lights, the glass tubes used for advertising signs. Neon produces a brilliant reddish-orange glow. Chemical symbol: Ne.

Nepal Mountainous kingdom in Asia, between Tibet (now part of China) and India. The Himalayas, the world's highest mountain range, cover most of Nepal. Mount Everest, the world's highest mountain, is on the Nepal-Tibet border. Nepal exports rice, cereals, and cattle. Area: 56,827 square miles (147,181 square kilometers). Capital: Kathmandu.

Neptune The eighth planet from the Sun. Neptune has an atmosphere containing large amounts of hydrogen and methane gas. The Voyager II spacecraft flew by the planet in 1989 and discovered some new moons and a system of rings. Diameter: 30,200 miles (48,600 kilometers). Mean distance from the sun: 2.8 billion miles (4.5 billion kilometers). Number of moons: 8.

Nero (AD 37-68) Roman emperor from 54 AD, and last of the Caesars. He ordered the murders of his chief rival, his mother, and both his wives. He persecuted (mistreated) the Christians, blaming them for the fire that destroyed Rome.

Nervous system The system of the body that controls all of its actions and reactions. The brain is the main control center, and the spinal cord extends from it. The spinal cord carries nerve impulses to and from the brain and other nerve cells.

Netherlands, The A flat country in Europe sometimes also called Holland. Its flourishing industries include farming and shipping. It also has offshore gas reserves. Area: 14,405 square miles (37,310 square kilometers). Capital: Amsterdam, but the Government actually sits at The Hague.

Nevada The scenery of this Rocky Mountain state in the United States attracts many tourists. The discovery of silver in 1859 attracted many settlers, and Nevada became the 36th state in 1864. Manufacturing is important. Dams, such as the famous Hoover Dam, generate hydroelectric power. Livestock is also raised. Area: 110,540 square miles (286,297 square kilometers). Capital: Carson City.

The immense Hoover Dam, in Nevada.

New Brunswick A province in eastern Canada. Manufacturing, fishing, and farming are important. The province has zinc, lead, coal, and potash. Area: 28,354 square miles (73,440 square kilometers). Capital: Fredericton.

New Deal General name for the economic programs and policies introduced by US President Franklin D. Roosevelt. They were started during the Great Depression of the 1930s to speed up economic recovery and promote social welfare. These included reform, social security, and financial relief on all levels to combat the effects of the Depression.

New England The northeastern US states of Maine, New Hampshire, Vermont, Massachusetts, Connecticut, and Rhode Island. They were named New England by Captain John Smith (1580-1631), an English colonist.

Newfoundland Province in eastern Canada. Fishing, forestry, and mining are important. Area: 156,649 square miles (405,720 square kilometers). Capital: Saint John's.

New Guinea A large island that is located north of Australia. Part of the island belongs to the country of Indonesia. The rest is an independent country called Papua New Guinea. Its capital is Port Moresby. Area: 316,000 square miles (818,000 square kilometers).

New Hampshire A New England state, and one of the original 13 states in the US. Dairy and poultry farming are important, but manufacturing dominates the economy. Machinery, computers, and wood and paper products are produced. Tourism is also important. Area: 9,304 square miles (24,097 square kilometers). Capital: Concord.

New Jersey A Middle Atlantic state, New Jersey became the third state to adopt the US Constitution, in 1787. Small but densely populated, New Jersey is a major manufacturing center. Chemicals, food products, and machinery are produced. New Jersey has a fine climate and many tourist resorts. Area: 7,836 square miles (20,295 square kilometers). Capital: Trenton.

New Mexico The fifth largest state, New Mexico, is located in the southwestern United States. It became the 47th state in 1912. The chief resources are oil and natural gas, uranium, potash, copper, and coal. Tourism and cattle and sheep ranching are important. Area: 121,666 square miles (315,113 square kilometers). Capital: Santa Fe.

New Orleans Port and city in Louisiana, on the Mississippi River near where it flows into the Gulf of Mexico. One of the busiest ports in the world, it is famous as the home of Dixieland jazz and as the site of a large Mardi Gras celebration.

Newspaper A publication that presents news and comments on events of public interest. It is usually published daily or weekly. Newspapers began to appear regularly in the 17th century. The first regularly published American newspaper, *The Boston News-Letter*, appeared in 1704. Almost 1,700 daily newspapers are published in the United States.

Newt A small, lizard-like amphibian. It is a type of salamander.

Newton, Sir Isaac (1642-1727) English mathematician and scientist. He was the first to explain how gravity works. He invented calculus (a branch of mathematics) and the reflecting telescope. He also experimented with and explained much about motion, light, and color.

New York One of the Middle Atlantic states. It is one of the original 13 states and became the 11th US state in 1788. It has the largest city (New York City) in the United States. It is known for its beautiful mountains, rivers, and lakes. Area: 49,108 square miles (127,189 square kilometers). Capital: Albany.

New York City A seaport in southeastern New York State, at the mouth of the Hudson River. It is the largest city in the United States. It is known for its skyscrapers, shopping, theaters, and businesses.

The famous skyscrapers of New York.

New Zealand A country in the Pacific Ocean, consisting of two main islands, North Island and South Island. Industries include timber, paper, and manufacturing. Area: 103,883 square miles (269,057 square kilometers). Capital: Wellington.

Niagara Falls in the nineteenth century—a view painted by Edwin Chenan.

Niagara Falls Two large waterfalls of the Niagara River, on the boundary between Canada and the United States. The two falls are separated by Goat Island. The American Falls are 176 feet (54 meters) high. The Canadian falls, called Horseshoe Falls, are 167 feet (51 meters) high.

Nicaragua Country in Central America, with long Atlantic and Pacific coastlines. From 1936 to 1979 the Somoza family held power as dictators. They were overthrown by a socialist revolution in 1979. Area: 50,200 square miles (130,000 square kilometers). Capital: Managua.

Nickel A white metallic element with great resistance to corrosion. One of its uses is electroplating other metals. Chemical Symbol: Ni.

Niger A landlocked country in western Africa. Four-fifths of the country is desert, so it is a hot, dry land with few trees. Most people live by farming and herding animals. Millet and sorghum are grown. Area: 489,200 square miles (1,267,000 square kilometers). Capital: Niamey.

Nigeria A large country in western Africa, on the Gulf of Guinea. Oil and natural gas provide most of the national income. It is the most populous country in Africa. Area: 356,669 square miles (923,768 square kilometers). Capital: Lagos.

Nightingale A small European bird belonging to the thrush family. It feeds on insects. The bird is known for its beautiful song.

Nightingale, Florence (1820-1910) English founder of modern nursing. She took care of soldiers during the Crimean War. In 1860 she founded a nurses' training school in London.

Nile River in northeastern Africa. It is one of the longest rivers in the world. The White Nile flows north from Lake Victoria. The Blue Nile flows from Ethiopia and joins the White Nile at Khartoum in Sudan. From Khartoum it is known as the Nile, and flows through northern Sudan and Egypt, emptying into the Mediterranean Sea. Length: 4,145 miles (6,671 kilometers).

Nitrogen A colorless, odorless gas that makes up nearly four-fifths of the Earth's atmosphere. Chemical symbol: N.

Nixon, Richard Milhous (1913-) Thirty-seventh president of the United States. He was an officer in the US Navy during World War II. A Californian, he was a member of the House of Representatives for two terms and the Senate for one. He served eight years as vice-president, from 1953 to 1961. Nixon lost the 1960 presidential election by a narrow margin. He ran again in 1968 and won. He was the first president to visit China while in office, and worked with the USSR to limit the production of nuclear weapons. In 1974,

The famous Badlands of North Dakota include this unusual landscape.

during his second term of office, Nixon resigned after a political scandal.

Nobel, Alfred Bernhard (1833-1896) Swedish chemist and engineer who invented dynamite. He established a fund to provide annual prizes in physics, chemistry, physiology or medicine, literature, and the promotion of international peace. In 1969 a sixth prize, in economics, was added in his memory. It is a very great honor to win a Nobel prize.

Nomads People who wander from place to place to make a living. Some travel with their herds of animals, such as cattle, sheep, and goats, in search of pasture. Many nomads are found in the deserts of Africa and Asia.

North America The third largest continent. It occupies about 16 percent of the Earth's land area. North America is a rich continent, blessed with huge mineral resources and fertile farmlands. The people of the United States and Canada, the two largest countries in North America, enjoy some of the highest standards of living in the world. Area: 9,360,000 square miles (24,241,000 square kilometers).

North Atlantic Treaty Organization (NATO) A defensive military alliance formed in 1949. Its members are the United States, Canada, Great Britain, France, Germany, Belgium, The Netherlands, Luxembourg, Denmark, Norway, Iceland, Italy, Spain, Portugal, Greece, and Turkey.

North Carolina A southern state in the United States, it was one of the original 13 states. Manufacturing is the chief source of income. Textiles and chemicals are lead-ing products. Major farm products include soybeans, corn, peanuts, and tobacco, as well as poultry and eggs. Area: 52,669 square miles (136,413 square kilometers). Capital: Raleigh.

North Dakota Located in the north central United States, it became the 39th state in 1889. Farming is the leading economic activity, and wheat is the chief crop. Mining is important, and there are reserves of oil and coal. Food processing is the leading manufacturing industry. Area: 70,665 square miles (183,022 square kilometers). Capital: Bismarck.

Northern Ireland Part of the United Kingdom. It occupies the northern section of the island of Ireland. Conflict exists between the northern Protestants, who wish to remain part of the United Kingdom, and the Roman Catholics, who want to join the Republic of Ireland. Area: 5,462 square miles (14,000 square kilometers). Capital: Belfast.

Northwest Territories Vast northern region acquired by Canada in 1870. Mining is the chief economic activity. Gold, oil, zinc, and other minerals are produced. Area: 1,322,910 square miles (3,426,320 square kilometers). Capital: Yellowknife.

Norway A country in northern Europe. It is part of Scandinavia. It is a rugged, mountainous land with deep lakes and swift rivers. Fishing is important. Norway has a large merchant fleet. Area: 149,405 square miles (386,958 square kilometers). Capital: Oslo.

Noun A word that describes a person, place, or thing.

Nova Scotia An Atlantic province of Canada. Farms produce milk, fruits, meat, poultry, and vegetables. Fishing is important, as well as the manufacturing of food products and paper. Area: 21,425 square miles (55,490 square kilometers). Capital: Halifax.

Nuclear energy The energy that is released from the nucleus of an atom. When the nucleus of an atom is broken apart, a large amount of energy is released as heat. In nuclear power, this heat is used to produce steam to drive turbines that generate electricity.

Nuclear weapons Weapons that use the sudden release of nuclear energy to create great explosions. The first nuclear weapon was exploded on July 16, 1945, by the United States. In August 1945 the United States dropped atomic bombs on Hiroshima and Nagasaki, Japan. Japan surrendered, and World War II ended.

Number A symbol or word that tells how many there are of something. There are 10 different numbers in our counting system: 0, 1, 2, 3, 4, 5, 6, 7, 8, and 9.

Nursing Taking care of sick people. Nurses go to school to learn how to help doctors treat people who are ill.

O

Oak A group of more than 600 species of large, broad-leaved trees. All of them produce acorns as fruit.

Oasis An area in a desert where there is water, and plants can grow. The water usually comes from streams or underground springs.

Observatory

Observatory A place from which astronomers study the sky with telescopes or other instruments. Many observatories are built on tall mountains, where the air is clear.

Ocean The vast body of salt water that covers more than 70 percent of the Earth's surface. The Pacific is the largest ocean, followed by the Atlantic and Indian oceans. The Arctic Ocean, surrounding the North Pole, is frozen over for most of the year.

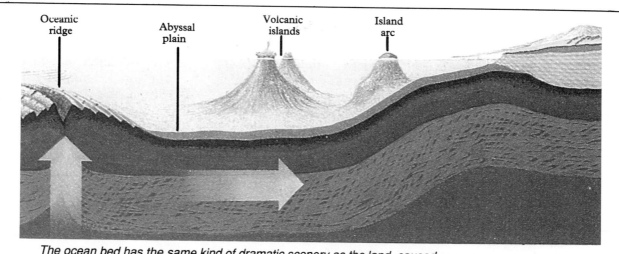

The ocean bed has the same kind of dramatic scenery as the land, caused by movements of the tectonic plates.

Ocean currents Great circular movements of ocean water. Because of the Earth's rotation, the currents move clockwise in the Northern Hemisphere and counterclockwise in the Southern Hemisphere. Currents are set in motion by the winds.

Ocelot A wild, spotted cat of South America. It is 3.5 to 4 feet (1.1 to 1.2 meters) long.

Octopus A sea animal with eight arms, called tentacles, which it uses to seize prey.

Ohio Located in the east central United States, Ohio became the 17th state in 1803. Farmland covers much of the state. Soybeans and corn are leading crops. Coal and some oil are mined. The main source of income is manufacturing. Leading products are transport equipment, farm machinery, and metals. Area: 41,330 square miles (107,044 square kilometers). Capital: Columbus.

Oil Any of a large group of sticky, greasy liquids that do not dissolve in water. Oil can come from animals (whale oil), vegetables (corn oil), or minerals (heating oil). It is used for cooking, heating, and many other purposes.

Oklahoma Located in the south central region of the United States, Oklahoma became the 46th state in 1907. It is a major producer of oil and natural gas. Farming and manufacturing of machinery and metal products also make a large contribution to the economy. Area: 69,919 square miles (181,089 square kilometers). Capital: Oklahoma City.

Oklahoma City State capital of Oklahoma. Livestock, grain markets, and food processing are major activities.

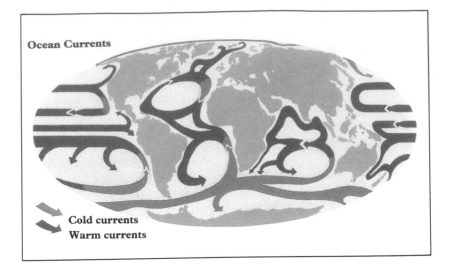

Ocean Currents

Cold currents
Warm currents

Olive A small fruit produced by the olive tree, which grows mainly in the eastern Mediterranean region. Some olive trees are more than 2,000 years old. Olives are eaten and used for making olive oil.

Olympic Games An international sports competition held every four years, based on the games of ancient Greece. The first modern Olympics were held in 1896. Since 1924, Winter Games as well as Summer Games have been held.

Oman Country on the southeastern coast of the Arabian peninsula. Most of Oman is desert, but the country has rich deposits of oil and natural gas. Area: 82,030 square miles (212,441 square kilometers). Capital: Muscat.

Ontario One of the four provinces that made up the original Dominion of Canada in 1867. Manufactured goods include transport equipment and metal products. Gold, nickel, copper, iron ore, silver, and uranium are mined. Beef cattle, fruit, pigs, and vegetables are leading farm products. Forestry is also important. Area: 412,582 square miles (1,068,580 square kilometers). Capital: Toronto.

Opera A musical drama in which the words are sung rather than spoken. Opera was first performed in Italy around 1600. Wolfgang Amadeus Mozart, Richard Wagner, Giuseppe Verdi, and Giacomo Puccini are among the great composers of opera.

Opossum An American marsupial. It is the only pouched mammal that does not live in Australia. Female opossums carry their young in pouches on their abdomens.

Orange A citrus fruit, rich in vitamin C, which grows on the orange tree. The orange can be eaten or squeezed for juice. Originally from China, the common sweet orange is grown in many parts of the world. Florida produces almost three fourths of the oranges grown in the United States.

Orangutan A rare ape that lives on the islands of Sumatra and Borneo in southeastern Asia. Its name means "man of the woods." It has reddish hair and stands upright at up to

5 feet (1.5 meters) tall.

Orbit The curved path that a planet, moon, or other object makes as it travels around another object in space.

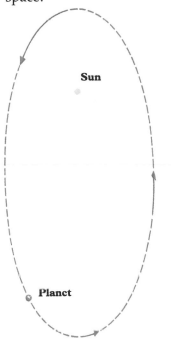

The orbit of a planet around the sun.

Orchestra A group of musicians who play together on various instruments. Symphony orchestras have stringed, woodwind, brass, and percussion instruments. Some symphony orchestras have about 100 musicians. They sit in a semicircle and follow the directions of a conductor.

Orchid A large family of over 20,000 kinds of beautiful flowering plants. Most orchids grow in the tropics.

Oregon Located on the coast of the Pacific Ocean, it became the 33rd US state in 1859. Behind the rugged coastline is the Coast Range, with the Klamath Mountains in the southwest. Inland, the Cascade Mountains contain volcanoes. Forests cover much of Oregon. Wood products are the leading manufactured goods, followed by food products. Livestock products and wheat are important. Area: 96,981 square miles (251,180 square kilometers). Capital: Salem.

Organization of Petroleum Exporting Countries (OPEC) An association of 13 countries that produce and export oil. Eight of the countries are Middle Eastern or Arab states. Two are in South America, two are in Africa, and one is in Asia.

Oscilloscope An electronic instrument that shows changing electrical signals as a moving graph on a screen. Oscilloscopes are used to test electronic equipment and to study electrical activity in the brain and heart.

Osmosis The passing of a liquid through a membrane, which is a thin layer of animal or plant tissue. In animals, digested food passes from blood vessels into body cells by osmosis. Plant roots soak up water from the soil by osmosis.

Osprey A large bird of prey that hunts fish. It is also known as the fish hawk and fishing eagle. It is mostly brown, with white mottled (spotted) underparts. It is found in North America, Europe, and Asia.

Ostrich The largest living bird. Some males are 8 feet (2.5 meters) tall and weigh more than 300 pounds (140 kilograms). The ostrich cannot fly but can run 40 miles (65 kilometers) an hour. It has a long neck and long legs. Ostriches live in Africa.

Ottawa Capital city of Canada, in Ontario. Founded in 1826 as a small lumber settlement, it became the seat of government in 1857 and capital in 1867.

Otter A member of the weasel family. Otters live on every continent except Australia and Antarctica. They live near water, hunting at night for fish and other water animals. They are excellent swimmers.

Ottoman Empire Turkish state from the 14th to the early 20th century. At its height in the 1600s, the empire included parts of the Middle East, North Africa, and eastern Europe.

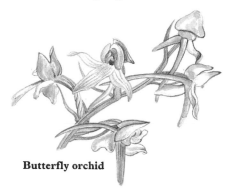

Butterfly orchid

Otter

The empire ended in 1922, when the republic of Turkey was created.

Owl A bird of prey that hunts for small mammals mostly at night. It is found in most parts of the world. The owl's soft, fluffy feathers make its flight noiseless.

Ox A family of hoofed animals that includes domestic cattle, bison, buffalo, and musk oxen.

Oxen pulling the plow in Ancient Rome.

Oxidation A chemical process in which a substance is combined with oxygen. Rust is a product of oxidation.

Oxygen A gas vital to plant and animal life. It makes up about 20 percent of the atmosphere and is essential to the human body. Chemical symbol: O.

Oyster A shellfish found in oceans and shallow, muddy coastal waters. A mollusk, it has a soft body protected by two hard shells. Oysters are a popular food. Some species produce pearls that are used as jewels.

Ozone A form of oxygen. Each molecule of ozone has three atoms instead of oxygen's two. A layer of ozone in the upper atmosphere absorbs harmful ultraviolet radiation from the sun. Some pollutants are destroying the ozone layer.

P

Pacific Ocean The largest and deepest ocean in the world, extending from the Americas to Asia and Australia, and from the Arctic Circle to Antarctica. Area: 63,800,000 square miles (165,200,000 square kilometers). Greatest depth: 36,198 feet (11,033 meters).

Painting A work of art created on a surface, such as canvas. Paintings are done in paint, chalk, ink, or similar material. The oldest paintings known are those left on cave walls from prehistoric times, mostly of hunting scenes.

Pakistan An Islamic republic in South Asia. Its chief industries are textiles, cement, sugar cane, paper, fertilizers, and engineering products. Area: 307,374 square miles (796,095 square kilometers). Capital: Islamabad.

Paleontology The study of fossils of prehistoric life forms. Fossils are the remains of plants and animals.

Palm A family of tropical trees and shrubs. Palms usually have tall, branchless trunks topped with large fans of evergreen leaves, called fronds. Some, such as the date palm and coconut palm, are grown for their fruit and oil.

Panama A country in Central America. The Panama Canal runs across it, linking the Atlantic and Pacific oceans. The country gains most of its wealth from trade passing through the canal. Area: 30,134 square miles (78,046 square kilometers). Capital: Panama City.

Panama Canal A ship canal across the Isthmus of Panama. It connects the Atlantic and Pacific oceans. Before the canal was built, ships traveling between the two oceans had to go around the tip of South America. The canal was built by the United States government. It opened in 1914.

Pancreas A gland inside the body that produces digestive enzymes to break down foods. It also secretes (gives off) two hormones, insulin and glucagon, that control the amount of sugar in the blood.

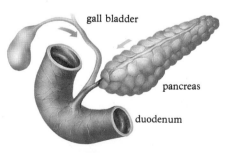

Digestive juice from the pancreas and bile from the gall bladder flow into a tube called the duodenum below the stomach.

Panda, giant A black and white mammal that lives in the bamboo forests of China. It looks like a bear, but some believe it is related to the raccoon. Now carefully protected, its numbers are decreasing because of the destruction of its habitat (the area in which it lives). The main food of the panda is bamboo shoots.

Pansy A flowering plant similar to its close relative, the violet. Pansies have larger, flatter flowers.

Paper A flat sheet made from fibers. Its name comes from papyrus, a plant used in ancient Egypt to make a material for writing upon. The first paper was made by the Chinese around 105 AD. Cheaper paper is made from wood pulp. Fine paper comes from rags. Paper with different kinds of surfaces can be produced by varying the kinds of rollers through which the paper passes as it is made.

Papua New Guinea A country in the Pacific Ocean, north of Australia. It includes the eastern part of New Guinea, islands of the Bismarck Archipelago, two of the Solomon Islands, and several other small islands. Area: 178,704 square miles (462,840 square kilometers). Capital: Port Moresby.

Papyrus A grasslike water plant of the Nile River valley in Africa. The ancient Egyptians used its tough stems to make boats, cloth, and paper.

Paraguay A landlocked republic in central South America. The chief occupation is farming. Nearly 6 million cattle graze the rich pasturelands, and meat products are among the chief exports. Area: 157,048 square miles (406,752 square kilometers). Capital: Asunción.

Parakeet Any of several small, brightly colored members of the parrot family, mostly living in Australia. Parakeets also live in Africa and Asia. The Carolina parakeet is an extinct American bird.

Parasite A plant or animal that lives on or in another species. A parasite takes food from its host without giving anything in return.

Paris The capital city of France, located on the Seine River. It is a major commercial, cultural, and fashion center. Famous buildings include Notre Dame Cathedral, the Arc de Triomphe, and the Eiffel Tower.

Parliament Literally a "talking place" where elected representatives meet to discuss and pass laws. Canada and Great Britain use the parliamentary system.

Parrot Any of a large number of brilliantly colored birds found throughout the tropics. Some can mimic (imitate) human speech. Because of their popularity as pets, many species are now facing extinction.

Partridge A game bird that lives in Europe, Asia, and Africa. It looks like a pigeon. In North America, the ruffed grouse and the bobwhite are sometimes called partridges.

Passover (also **Pesach**) The most important Jewish festival, occurring in March or April. It is a time when Jews remember how God delivered (rescued) them from slavery in Egypt.

Pasteur, Louis (1822-1895) French scientist who invented the process (now called pasteurization) of heating milk to kill any bacteria in it. He also discovered how to vaccinate animals and humans to make them immune to (protect them from) various diseases.

Patton, George S., Jr. (1885-1945) US soldier. During World War II, he commanded the Third Army when the Allies invaded German-occupied Europe. His columns of tanks swept across Europe. They led the drive that liberated France from Germany. Because Patton was a tough general, he earned the nickname "Old Blood and Guts."

Parrot

Pauling, Linus C. (1901-) US chemist. He won the Nobel prize for chemistry in 1954. He also won the Nobel Peace Prize in 1962 for his support of nuclear disarmament.

Pea A group of flowering plants. Peas include the edible garden pea and the black-eyed pea or cowpea. The sweet pea is cultivated (grown) only for its flowers.

Peace Corps An organization sponsored by the United States government. People of all ages and occupations may volunteer to join. They are sent to countries that need help with farming, education, health, and economic programs.

Peacock A spectacular bird about the size of a turkey. The male has a magnificent train of turquoise feathers marked with a bold pattern, which he raises into a fan during courtship. Females, called peahens, have brown feathers.

Pearl A valuable gem formed inside oysters and other mollusks. The oyster's shell is lined with a substance called nacre, or mother-of-pearl. When a piece of grit gets inside the shell, the animal coats it with smooth nacre, eventually forming a pearl.

Peccary A small piglike mammal of North and South America. It has small tusks and bristly hair. Peccaries travel in packs. There are three different kinds of peccaries. They live in forests or dry regions. The collared peccary, or javelina, lives in the southwestern United States.

Pelican The world's largest web-footed bird. It has a large pouch under its beak into which it scoops fish. It lives in North America, Australia, Europe, and Africa. The American white pelican is the largest, with a wingspan up to 10 feet (3 meters) wide.

Pendulum A weight on the end of a piece of string or rod that will swing backward and forward in a fixed, even time called its period. A pendulum is often used to control the movement of a clock. It was

Independence Hall, in Philadelphia, Pennsylvania.

discovered by the Italian scientist Galileo.

Penguin A flightless, black and white bird that lives on ocean coasts from the equator south to Antarctica. Penguins eat krill (tiny shrimplike animals) and fish. They raise their young on land, gathering on the ice in large groups, called rookeries.

Penicillium A green, mat-forming mold that grows on bread, overripe fruit, and many other foods. The mold produces penicillin, the antibiotic that is used in medicine to fight infection.

Penn, William (1644-1718) English Quaker who founded Pennsylvania. In England he was persecuted for his religious beliefs. King Charles II had borrowed a great deal of money from Penn's father. He paid the debt in 1681 by giving Penn a grant of territory in America. Thousands of Quakers moved there from England, Germany, and other parts of Europe. Penn visited the colony in 1682. He founded the city of Philadelphia.

Pennsylvania A Middle-Atlantic state in the United States. Pennsylvania was first settled by people from Sweden and the Netherlands. In 1681 the Quaker William Penn founded a colony where Quakers and others could enjoy religious freedom. Pennsylvania became the second state in 1787. Coal is mined, and manufactured goods include metals, machinery, and food products. The largest city is Philadelphia. Area: 45,333 square miles (117,412 square kilometers). Capital: Harrisburg.

Pentagon The headquarters for the United States Department of Defense. It was built between 1941 and 1943 and is one of the largest office buildings in the world. It is called the Pentagon because it has five sides.

Perch Any of a group of small, spiny-finned, edible freshwater fishes, especially the yellow perch of North America.

Perching bird A member of the largest order of birds, whose toes are adapted for gripping branches. They include most familiar garden birds.

Percussion instrument A musical instrument that produces a sound when struck or shaken. A drum and a tambourine are examples.

Perfume A substance that gives off a fragrant (sweet-smelling) odor. Perfumes have been used since ancient times to make the body smell pleasant. They are made largely from plant and animal oils blended in alcohol.

Periodic table An arrangement of the chemical elements in order of increasing atomic number. The atomic number is the number of protons in the nucleus of each atom.

Periscope A device for seeing objects out of the line of vision through an arrangement of mirrors and lenses. Complex periscopes are used in submarines; simple ones are used to see over the heads of people in a crowd.

Perry, Matthew Calbraith (1794-1858) US naval officer. He sailed to Japan with a naval squadron in 1853. At that time, Japan's ports were closed to all countries. Perry persuaded the Japanese to sign a treaty that gave the United States trading rights at two ports in Japan. Soon Japan began trading with other Western nations.

Pershing, John Joseph (1860-1948) US soldier. He was commander-in-chief of the American Expeditionary Forces (AEF) in Europe in World War I. The two million men of the AEF turned the tide against the Germans. After the war, Pershing was chief of staff of the United States Army.

Peru A republic in South America. Most of its wealth comes from minerals such as copper, iron, silver, lead, zinc, and oil. Area: 496,225 square miles (1,285,216 square kilometers). Capital: Lima.

Petroleum (Also called **crude oil**) A fossil fuel. It is pumped from the earth, refined, and turned into gasoline, kerosene, diesel oil, fuel oil, lubricating oil, and many plastic products.

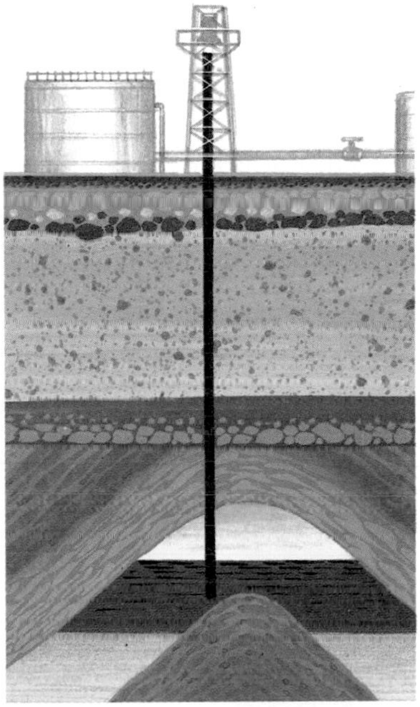

Petroleum and natural gas are found together in underground pools trapped between layers of rock.

Pharaoh A ruler of ancient Egypt. The pharaohs were believed to be gods as well as kings. When they died, they were buried with great ceremony in a pyramid, or rock tomb.

Pheasant A large bird with colorful feathers and an unusually long tail. It came originally from Asia, but is now found worldwide. The male is much more colorful than the female.

Philadelphia A port city in Pennsylvania, on the Delaware River. It was once the most important city in the United States and briefly the capital (1790-1800). The Declaration of Independence was signed here in 1776.

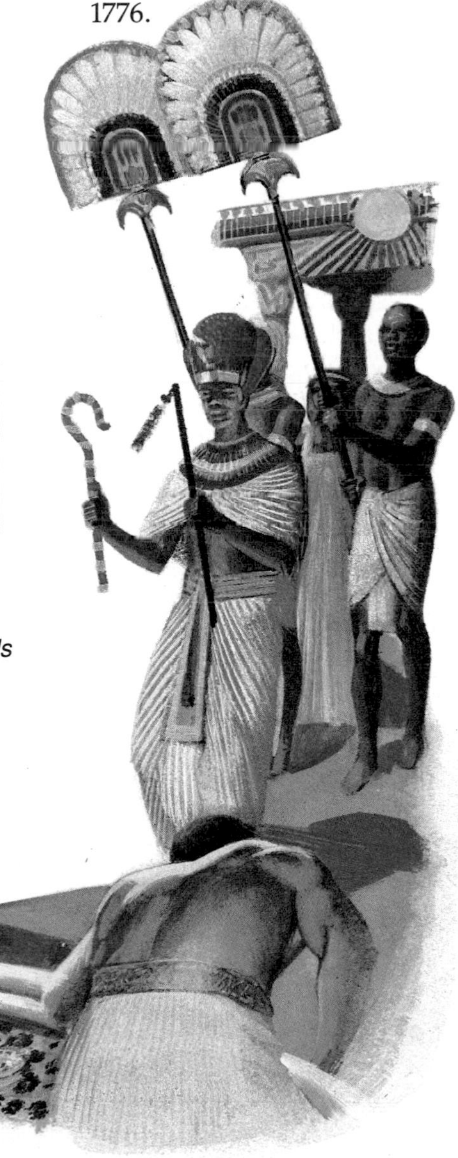

The warrior pharaoh Tuthmose III receives tribute of gold, leopard skins, and ivory from his subjects.

Philippines A republic in Asia, separated from the continent by the South China Sea. It is made up of more than 7,000 islands. It has a rich variety of minerals including copper, oil, iron, and gold. Area: 116,000 square miles (300,000 square kilometers). Capital: Manila.

Philosophy The study of learning itself. The word *philosophy* comes from two Greek words meaning "love of wisdom."

Phoenicians Ancient people who lived on what is now the coast of Syria, Lebanon, and Israel beginning about 2,000 BC. Great sailors and merchants, they controlled trade in the Mediterranean Sea from the 12th to the 6th century BC.

Phoenix A mythical (imaginary) Egyptian bird said to have lived in the Arabian Desert. According to Greek mythology, every 500 years it burned itself to ashes, and rose anew from those ashes.

Phosphorus A nonmetallic element that glows in the dark. It bursts into flame on contact with air at room temperature. Chemical symbol: P.

Photography The art of producing images of objects on a light-sensitive surface, such as film, using a camera. The image shows up once the film is developed.

Photon A tiny packet of energy (measured in units called quanta) of electromagnetic radiation, such as light.

Photosynthesis The food-making process of green plants. Chlorophyll (the green material) in the leaves absorbs sunlight, using the energy to make glucose (sugar) from water and carbon dioxide. Oxygen is given off during the process.

Phylum The second largest category used in the classification of plants and animals. All members of a phylum have basically the same structure, although they may differ greatly in size and appearance.

Physiology The study of the ways in which plants and animals function (operate) and of the various processes involved.

Piano A musical instrument in which wires are struck by hammers when keys are pressed on a keyboard. The word *piano* is short for pianoforte.

Picasso, Pablo (1881-1973) Spanish painter and sculptor who had a great influence on 20th century art. He was the pioneer of cubism. Perhaps his most famous work is *Guernica*, which depicts the horror and bloodshed of the Spanish Civil War.

Pierce, Franklin (1804-1869) Fourteenth president of the United States. A New Hampshire Democrat, he was a member of the House of Representatives and of the Senate. In the Mexican War (1846-48) he was a brigadier general. Pierce was president of the United States from 1853 to 1857. Trade with Japan was opened during his presidency.

Pig Also known as the hog. A stout domestic animal that developed from the wild boar. Pigs are raised for their meat (pork and bacon), fat (lard), and leather (pigskin). The United States is a leading producer.

Pigeon Any of a family of plump, seed-eating birds. Pigeons have been used to

The ancient Greeks began the science of philosophy. Here, a teacher discusses the nature of things with his pupils.

Common pigeons are related to the less wild rock dove.

carry, messages and are raced in several parts of the world.

Pigment A substance used to color other substances, such as paper or cloth. Most pigments occur in plant or animal tissue (especially skin), but some are made artificially.

Pike A freshwater predatory fish known to reach 4 feet (1.2 meters) in length, with large jaws bristling with teeth. Pike are found in the Northern Hemisphere.

Pike

Pilgrims The first colonists in New England. They moved to America where they would not be persecuted (mistreated) for their religion. Sailing in the Mayflower, they founded Plymouth Colony, Massachusetts, in 1620.

Pine A group of evergreen, cone-bearing trees with needle-shaped leaves. They are found mainly in the cooler, northern parts of the world.

Pineapple A tropical plant with sharp, sword-shaped leaves and a cone-shaped flower spike, which develops into a large, juicy fruit. Pineapples are produced commercially in Hawaii.

Piranha A carnivorous (meat-eating) fish of South American rivers, ranging in length from 4-16 inches (10-40 centimeters). Piranhas have razor-sharp teeth. A school of 1,000 can eat the flesh of a large animal in a few minutes.

Pirates Seafaring robbers, mainly of the 16th and 17th centuries. One famous pirate was Edward Teach, known as Blackbeard, who terrorized the southeastern coast of the United States.

Pittsburgh Steel-producing city in Pennsylvania. It is the second largest city in the state.

Plague An infectious disease, uncommon today, that caused terrible epidemics (illness in many people at one time) in Asia and Europe in the 14th to 17th centuries. It was nearly always fatal. See also Black Death.

Planet A heavenly body that orbits the sun and shines by reflected sunlight. There are nine planets in our solar system.

Plankton The tiny, free-floating plants and animals that live in the surface waters of seas, lakes, and ponds. Plankton are the food source of many sea creatures.

Plant Any organism of the plant kingdom able to make its own food, using sunlight, through a process called photosynthesis.

Plasma The fluid part of blood. In physics, plasma is an extremely hot gas whose atoms have been stripped of their electrons. The atmospheres around the stars are plasmas.

Plastic A synthetic (man-made) material made up of long chains of molecules, called polymers, produced mainly from oil or coal. It is very malleable (soft) when hot. Plastic products are usually molded.

Platinum A scarce, precious metallic element that has a high resistance to corrosion (being worn away by chemicals). Platinum is used mostly in jewelry and as a catalyst (activator) in the chemical industry. Chemical symbol: Pt.

Plato (427?-347? BC) A Greek philosopher. He was a pupil of Socrates and the teacher of Aristotle. He believed in a world of ideas superior to the material world. His theories had a great effect on Western philosophy.

Platypus An egg-laying mammal with a bill like a duck, a furry body, and webbed feet. It lives in Australia, in riverbank burrows where the females nurse their newly hatched young.

Pluto The smallest and most distant of the planets in the solar system. Pluto and its moon Charon are believed to be giant snowballs of frozen gas and dust. Diameter: 1,460 miles (2,350 kilometers). Mean distance from the sun: 3.7 billion miles (5.9 billion kilometers).

Pocahontas (1595-1617) An Indian princess. She became a Christian, married English colonist John Rolfe, and went to England with him in 1616.

Poe, Edgar Allan (1809-1849) US short-story writer, poet, and critic. He wrote tales of mystery and horror. Poe's "The Murders in the Rue Morgue" is the world's first modern detective story. His most famous poem is "The Raven."

Poetry A work of literature, mostly using rhythmical forms and sometimes rhyme. Ancient stories and events were often told in poems, since rhyme and rhythm are good memory aids. Modern poetry, though rhythmical, does not necessarily rhyme.

Poisons Substances that kill or sicken living things. Poisons can come from plants (belladonna, strychnine), animals (the venom of snakes, spiders, or fish), or metals (arsenic, mercury, lead).

Poland Republic in Europe, bordered by the Baltic Sea. Poland became independent in 1918. After World War II, a Communist government was introduced despite considerable opposition. Democratic elections took place in 1989.

Area: 120,728 square miles (312,683 square kilometers). Capital: Warsaw.

Polar bear A large white mammal that lives in arctic coastal regions, feeding on fish and seals. During winter, the female hibernates (sleeps) in a snow den, giving birth to two or three cubs that remain with her for up to three years.

Polar bear

Poles The geographic North and South poles are imaginary points on the Earth's surface at the axis of the spinning Earth. The magnetic poles do not exactly match the geographic poles. Their position changes over the years.

Police Organization for law enforcement. Police forces in the United States are run by town, county, or state governments. Police usually wear uniforms and carry guns.

Polk, James Knox (1795-1849) Eleventh president of the United States. A Democrat, he was a member of the House of Representatives and governor of Tennessee. During his presidency (1845-1849), the Mexican War was fought. The peace treaty added California and most of the Southwest to the territory of the United States.

Pollination The transfer of pollen by wind or insects in a flower. This results in fertilization and the formation of seeds.

Pollock, Jackson (1912-1956) US painter. Pollock made many of his paintings by dripping or pouring paint onto huge canvases placed on the floor. He created colorful patterns. This type of painting is called "abstract expressionism."

Polo, Marco (1254-1324?) Merchant from Venice, Italy, who traveled all over Asia. He is famous for his journey to China which lasted from 1271 to 1295.

Pompeii A small Roman city in southwestern Italy. In 79 AD, a nearby volcano named Mount Vesuvius erupted. Many people were killed, and much of the city was buried in volcanic ash. Since the 1700s, scientists have been digging out the city. The ash preserved many buildings and objects. These help show what daily life was like in ancient Rome.

Pony A horse less than 14 hands (56 inches or 142 centimeters) high. The Shetland pony is one of the smallest of all. It stands only 40 inches (100 centimeters) high.

Pope The leader of the Roman

Catholic Church. *Pope* means "father."

Poppy A family of plants, usually with bright red, yellow, or white flowers. The common poppy has red petals and is often grown in gardens.

Porcupine A hairy rodent with sharp quills on its back. Once a quill is stuck in an enemy's flesh, it is very painful and difficult to remove.

Porpoise Any of several small whales less than 6 feet (2 meters) long. They are distinguished from the dolphins by their blunt snouts.

Portugal A republic in western Europe, bounded by Spain and the Atlantic Ocean. It includes the islands of Madeira and the Azores. Portugal is the world's chief producer of cork. Area: 34,340 square miles (88,941 square kilometers). Capital: Lisbon.

Postage stamp A small piece of paper issued by a government. Stamps are printed on one side and sticky on the other. They are sold to be attached to pieces of mail to show that a fee has been paid for sending a letter or package from one place to another. Stamps are also collected as a hobby.

Potassium A soft, silvery metallic element that reacts violently with oxygen and water. It is essential for plant growth and is widely used in fertilizers. Chemical symbol: K.

Potato A widely grown vegetable, rich in starch. It originated in the Andes Mountains of South America. The USSR is the world's largest producer of potatoes.

Pottery A handicraft in which wet clay is shaped into objects. A wheel is used to make round pots. Pottery is baked slowly in an oven, called a kiln, to harden it. A coating of shiny, colored glaze may be applied.

Poultry The name given to chickens, turkeys, ducks, geese, and other birds raised for their meat or eggs.

Pound, Ezra (1885-1972) US poet, critic, and editor. He lived most of his life in England and Italy. Pound had a strong influence on many important writers in England and the United States. During World War II, he made broadcasts for the Italian Fascist government. After the war, he was brought to the United States and charged with treason. He was declared insane and held in a mental hospital. After his release, he returned to Italy.

Power plant A building where electric power is generated. Many power plants use oil or coal power for steam turbines that drive the generators. Nuclear plants use heat from controlled nuclear reactions.

Prague The capital city of Czechoslovakia, on the Vltava River.

Prairie Wide, open grasslands. Prairies in North America are the Canadian plains and the Mississippi River valley. The word prairie is French in origin and was first used by French explorers to describe the area.

Prairie chicken A brown and white bird that looks like a chicken. It belongs to the grouse family. Prairie chickens once lived in great numbers on the North American prairies. Most prairie land is now being farmed, so there are fewer prairie chickens.

Precious stones Those minerals that, when cut and polished, are used as gemstones in jewelry. Examples are diamonds, emeralds, rubies, and blue sapphires.

Prehistoric life The first plant and animal forms on Earth. Fossils show that the earliest life forms existed about 3.5 billion years ago. Humans emerged only about 2 million years ago, and writing did not develop until around 3,500 BC. Therefore prehistoric life dates roughly from 3.5 billion to 3,500 BC.

President of the United States The person who is head of state, leader of the government, and commander-in-chief of the armed forces. The first US president was George Washington, who was unanimously elected in 1789.

Washington crossing the Delaware River–a painting by Emmanuel Leutze.

Presley, Elvis (1935-1977) US rock and roll singer and movie actor. In the 1950s he became one of the first big stars of rock and roll. His songs included "Hound Dog," "Blue Suede Shoes," and "Love Me Tender." He also made many movies.

Pressure The pressing or pushing of one body on another.

Primates The order (related group) of mammals that includes lemurs, monkeys, apes, and humans.

Prime Minister (Also called **Premier**) The chief executive in a parliamentary system of government. The prime minister also appoints and heads the cabinet ministers.

Primrose A common woodland flowering plant. It has a single five-petaled flower and long, oval leaves.

Prince Edward Island Smallest province of Canada, which joined the Dominion of Canada in 1873. Area: 2,184 square miles (5,660 square kilometers). Capital: Charlottetown.

Printing A mechanical process for reproducing text (words) or pictures. Printing as we know it began in about 1440 when Johannes Gutenberg, a German, invented the printing press. He used a piece of metal, called type, for each letter of the alphabet.

Prism A block of glass or other transparent material used to split up (refract) light or other rays. Different wavelengths of light are refracted at different angles, producing a rainbow of colors.

Prison A place of confinement for people who have been found guilty of a crime. Penitentiaries and jails are prisons.

Probability A measure of the likelihood that something will happen. If an event cannot happen, its probability is zero. If an event is certain to happen, its probability is one.

Prohibition A ban on alcoholic drinks. In 1919, the 18th Amendment to the Constitution made the manufacture and sale of alcoholic drinks a crime. The law could not be enforced. Liquor was smuggled into the country and manufactured in secret. This was called "bootlegging." Illegal saloons called speakeasies opened in towns and cities. Bootlegging was controlled by gangsters, and there were fierce gang wars. In 1933, the 18th Amendment was repealed, ending Prohibition.

Propaganda The one-sided information given out by governments or other organizations to assist their cause. Often propaganda stretches the truth to make a government or organization look good.

Protein A group of amino acids that are linked together. Proteins are a vital part of every animal and plant cell. Proteins are found in foods such as milk, eggs, meat, fish, nuts, and beans.

Protestantism The religion of Christian churches other than the Roman Catholic and Orthodox churches. Protestantism resulted from the Reformation, when reformers protested against the authority of the Roman Catholic Church.

Protozoan Any of the many very tiny organisms whose bodies consist of just a single cell. Few can be seen with the naked eye.

Psychology The study of the mind and behavior, and the ways in which people react with their environment.

Pterosaur An extinct flying reptile of the Mesozoic Era, with batlike wings. Pterodactylus was the size of a sparrow but its relative Quetzalcoatlus had a 32-foot (10 meter) wingspan.

This pterosaur must have been a clumsy creature with its heavy body and a wing span of only 5 feet (1.5 meters)

Ptolemy (100?-165?AD) A Greek astronomer of the 2nd century. His claim that the Earth was stationary and that the universe revolved around it remained unchallenged until the 16th century.

Pueblo A community dwelling built by Hopi and Zuñi Indians in the southwestern United States. It is made of stone or adobe (sun-dried brick) and a flat roof. Pueblos can be as high as five stories.

Pulley A small wheel on an axle. It has a grooved rim into which a rope or cable can fit. A pulley is used to lift heavy things. It is a kind of simple machine.

Pulsar A rapidly rotating star that emits an immensely strong radio wave or visible light as it spins.

Puma Also known as the cougar or mountain lion. A large cat that stalks the mountains of South America and western North America.

Pump A machine for moving liquids or gases by using suction or pressure. Some pumps have pistons that move back and forth in a cylinder to produce the required pressure. Valves allow the fluid to pass in one direction only.

Punctuation The use of marks in writing that make the meaning of a sentence clearer. A period (.), quotation marks (" "), and a dash (–) are examples of these marks.

Puppet A small doll of a person or animal that can be made to move. Some puppets move when a person puts his or her hand inside the body to control the arms and head. Others have strings attached to them to make them move. Puppets can be used to act out a story.

Purple Heart A United States military medal awarded for wounds received in action. It was established in 1782 by George Washington and was revived in 1932.

Pygmy Small people who live in parts of central Africa, near the equator. They have dark skin and rarely grow more than 5 feet (1.5 meters) tall. Some also live in Asia and on islands in the Indian and Pacific oceans.

Pyramids A group of gigantic stone tombs like flat-sided cones, built by the ancient Egyptians for their kings. The largest is the Great Pyramid at Giza. It was

Ancient Egyptian peasants labor in the fields while behind them dead pharaohs lie entombed in treasure-filled pyramids.

originally 481 feet (147 meters) high and 754 feet (230 meters) long on each side.

Pyrenees A mountain range that forms the natural boundary between France and Spain. It runs from the Bay of Biscay to the Mediterranean Sea. Highest peak: Pico de Aneto, 11,168 feet (3,404 meters).

Python A group of constricting (squeezing) snakes. Some are over 30 feet (9 meters) long. They are found in the tropics of Asia, Africa, and Australia. They eat small mammals and birds. Pythons are expert climbers and swimmers. The boa constrictor is a python.

Q

Qatar A small country on a peninsula that juts into the Persian Gulf. Rich from oil, its people have a very high standard of living. Area: 4,416 square miles (11,437 square kilometers). Capital: Doha.

Quahog A large edible clam found on the east coast of North America. It has a thick, hard shell.

Quail A small game bird related to the pheasant and partridge. There are about 45 species living all over the world. Quail fly very little and normally keep within 3 feet (1 meter) or so of the ground.

Quarry A large, open pit where rocks are cut or blasted out of the ground. Slate, granite, and marble are mined in quarries.

Quasar (Stands for **quasi stellar radio source**) A brilliant

Quasars are believed to be galaxies at an early stage in their evolution.

starlike object far off in space. Quasars produce the energy output of 100 bright galaxies in a space not much larger than our own solar system.

Quayle, J. Danforth (1947-) Vice-president of the United States (1989-) under President George Bush.

Quebec Port and capital city of the province of Quebec, Canada, on the Saint Lawrence River. Quebec was founded in 1608 as Quebec City.

Quebec One of the original four provinces of Canada. Most people in Quebec speak French and many of their customs are French. Quebec is rich in gold, iron, and other minerals. Its main industries include paper products, machinery, chemicals, and clothing. Area: 594,860 square miles (1,540,680 square kilometers). Capital: Quebec.

Quetzal Spectacular bird of Central and South America. The male has a long train of green feathers.

Quito Capital city of Ecuador. It is situated on a plateau in the Andes Mountains, 9,350 feet (2,850 meters) above sea level and about 15 miles (25 kilometers) south of the equator.

R

Rabbit A small, furry animal with long ears and a short tail. It is a close relative of the hare. Rabbits live in burrows or warrens that they dig in the ground. They eat grass and other green vegetation, including crops.

Rabies An infectious disease of the central nervous system in mammals. Humans can catch rabies if they are bitten by an animal that has the disease. Victims have convulsions, choke, and are unable to swallow.

Raccoon An American carnivore related to the panda. Raccoons are about 2-3 feet (.6-1 meter) long, with dark bands on the tail and head. They live in forests but often venture near where people live to look for food at night.

Radar (Stands for **Radio Detection And Ranging**) A device used to locate airplanes and other objects. Radar uses radio waves, which are sent out in short pulses and reflected back from a distant object. The reflected waves show up on a cathode-ray tube. Radar is used in the military and navigational fields.

Radio A device for communicating without using wires. In radio, sounds and signals are changed into electromagnetic waves. The invisible radio waves are transmitted through space and can be picked up by aerials (antennas) on radio receivers.

Radioactivity The giving off of energy by some atoms in the form of particles and waves. Radium and uranium are radioactive elements.

Radio astronomy The study of radio waves emitted naturally by objects in space. Radio astronomy has led to the discovery of objects such as quasars and pulsars.

Radio telescope A device for collecting radio waves from space. Most are dish-shaped and work in a similar way to the mirrors inside a telescope. They collect radio waves and focus them onto a detector.

Radium A rare, naturally occurring, radioactive metallic element. It was discovered in 1898 by Marie and Pierre Curie and a co-worker, Gustave Bémont. Radiotherapy, the use of X rays from radium, is used in the treatment of cancer. Chemical symbol: Ra.

Railroad An important means of transportation. British engineer George Stephenson built the first public railroad in 1825. Soon railroads were opened up all over the world. They spread across the United States beginning in the 1850s.

Rain Drops of water that fall to earth from clouds. As the moist air forming a cloud cools, its water droplets grow too heavy to remain suspended in the air. They then fall to the ground as rain.

Water droplets in a cloud increase in size until they fall as rain.

Rainbow An arc of colored light seen in the sky. It occurs when sunlight is reflected and refracted (bent) by falling raindrops or the spray of a waterfall. Refraction splits the light into red, orange, yellow, green, blue, indigo, and violet.

Raleigh, Sir Walter (1552?-1618) English explorer and writer. He sent expeditions to explore and settle new English land in North America. He introduced potatoes and tobacco to Ireland.

Ramadan A holy month in the

religion of Islam. Muslims fast between sunrise and sunset each day.

Ranching The raising of cattle and sheep. The animals roam free and graze on the land.

Rat A rodent with large ears and a long, almost hairless tail, found worldwide. Rats do enormous damage to food and spread disease.

Rattlesnake A poisonous snake of the pit viper family, found in the Western Hemisphere. The "rattle" is the sound made by horny rings of cast-off skin at the end of its tail.

Ray A fish related to the shark. The skeletons of rays are made of cartilage, not bone. Rays have flattened bodies that are shaped like a disk.

Stingray

Reagan, Ronald W. (1911-) Fortieth president of the United States. He had a successful career as a motion-picture actor. Long interested in politics, he campaigned for the Democrats in the 1940s. He later became more conservative. In 1962 he became a Republican. From 1967 to 1975 he was governor of California. He was president of the United States from 1981 to 1989. In 1987 he and Mikhail Gorbachev of the Soviet Union signed a treaty to do away with intermediate range nuclear missiles in Europe.

Recording The sounds of voices or music that are turned into electronic signals by a microphone. These signals are put on a record, tape, or laser disc so that they can be played back later.

Record player A machine which plays back pre-recorded sound from a flat vinyl disc or record. Thomas Edison and Emile Berliner were pioneers of sound recording. Berliner manufactured his first "gramophone" in 1887 in the United States.

Red Cross An international organization that helps relieve suffering in war or during a disaster. It was founded through the efforts of Swiss citizen Jean Henri Dunant in 1863. During wars, Red Cross workers are guaranteed safe conduct by the Geneva Conventions.

Redwood A large cone-bearing tree of the western United States. Redwoods are among the tallest trees in the world, growing to over 300 feet (100 meters) high. Many live for thousands of years.

Reflection The return of a light wave, or other kind of energy wave, from the surface that it strikes. Light, for example, is reflected by mirrors. In radar, radio waves are reflected from airplanes and other objects.

Reformation A religious revolution in the Roman Catholic Church in Europe in the 16th century. It resulted in a division in the Church that led to the establishment of the Protestant churches.

Refraction The bending of light waves when they pass from one clear substance into another. When light passes from air into water, for example, or from air into glass, it changes speed slightly. When the speed changes, the light rays bend.

Refrigeration The process of reducing the temperature of substances by taking heat away. Refrigerators work because heat flows from a warm object to a colder object.

Reindeer A large domesticated deer of northern Europe, Asia, and North America. Reindeer provide meat, milk, and clothing. North American reindeer are also called caribou.

Relativity A theory about time, space, and the motion of objects. It was first proposed by Albert Einstein in 1905 who added a second part to the theory in 1915. He said that length, mass, and time are all affected by motion. Relativity explains why objects fall to the ground, how heavenly bodies move, why satellites stay in the sky, and many other things about the universe.

Religion An organized set of beliefs, usually in God or gods, with rules for earthly conduct. The main world religions include Christianity (1.5 billion followers), Islam (840 million), Hinduism (650 million), Buddhism (308 million), and Judaism (18 million).

Rembrandt (1606-1669) Dutch painter whose vast output includes numerous self-portraits, group scenes, and landscapes. His mastery of light and color has placed him among the world's greatest artists.

Renaissance (14th-17th centuries) A period in European history when people became very interested in literature, art, music, science, and architecture. Explorers and traders also traveled to new parts of the world.

Reptile A member of a group

Respiration

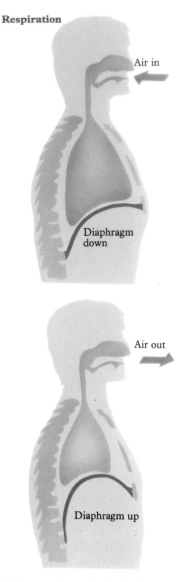

When you breathe in (top), your chest muscles raise your ribs and a flat muscle called the diaphragm moves downward. This pulls air into the lungs. When you breathe out (bottom), the diaphragm relaxes and rises, pushing air out.

of animals with backbones that includes snakes, lizards, tortoises, and crocodiles. All are covered with scales, are cold-blooded, and are active only in warm weather.

Republican Party One of the two main political parties of the United States. The other is the Democratic Party. The Republican Party was founded in the 1850s by members of other parties to unify the growing anti-slavery forces.

Respiration The act of breathing, or the taking in of oxygen and the release of carbon dioxide. Respiration is also the chemical process that takes place inside the cells, resulting in the production of energy.

Revere, Paul (1735-1818) US patriot. He took part in the Boston Tea Party and fought in the American Revolution. He is best remembered for his famous ride on April 18, 1775, at the start of the Revolution. Revere rode from Boston to Lexington to warn the people that the British were coming. Revere was also a skilled silversmith.

Rhinoceros A huge, lumbering mammal of Asia and Africa. It has an exceptionally thick hide and one or two horns. There are five kinds of rhinoceroses. The Indian rhinoceros, weighing about two tons, is the largest in Asia.

Rhode Island Smallest state in the United States. In 1790, Rhode Island became the 13th state to ratify the Constitution. Located in southern New England, it has much beautiful scenery and many historic buildings to attract tourists. Manufacturing dominates the economy. Jewelry, silverware, and metal products are the most valuable manufactured goods. The state has nurseries and dairy, poultry, and potato farms. Fishing is important on the coast. Area: 1,214 square miles (3,144 square kilometers). Capital: Providence.

Rhododendron A large evergreen shrub with large clusters of flowers that come in a range of colors. It grows in northern temperate climates and mountainous areas.

Rice A cereal grass with nutritious, starchy grain. It is the staple diet of more than half the world's people. Rice is mostly grown in the hot, wet regions of Asia.

Richter Magnitude A special scale for measuring the strength of earthquakes. It was devised in 1935 by the US seismologist (earthquake scientist) Charles Richter.

Rio de Janeiro A seaport and former capital city of Brazil. It is situated on beautiful Guanabara Bay, a natural harbor dominated by Sugar Loaf Mountain.

A view of Providence, Rhode Island, in 1872.

Rio Grande A river in North America flowing from Colorado to the Gulf of Mexico. It forms part of the boundary between Mexico and the United States. Length: 1,885 miles (3,034 kilometers).

River A large stream of water. Rivers are used for transportation, fishing, and recreation. They provide drinking water and water for irrigation. Rivers also drain water from the land and carry rock debris to the sea.

They are important in industrial production. Robots are used, for example, in some automobile assembly lines. The design and production of robots is called robotics.

Rock The hard material of the Earth's surface. There are three different kinds of rock: metamorphic, igneous, and sedimentary. Metamorphic rock is formed by heat, igneous rock by cooling, and sedimentary rock by water.

Rocky Mountains (Also known as the Rockies) The longest chain of mountains in North America. The range is more than 3,000 miles (4,800 kilometers) long and extends from Alaska to New Mexico. It consists of a number of parallel ranges with numerous peaks. Highest peak: Mount Elbert, 14,433 feet (4,399 meters).

Rodent Any of a group of mammals that have large front teeth for gnawing. Rats, mice, squirrels, beavers, hamsters, and porcupines are rodents.

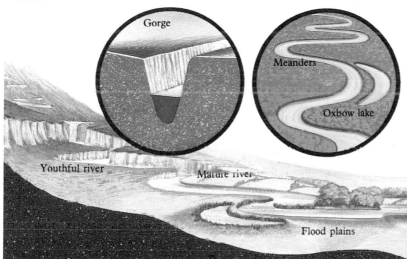

Youthful rivers (left and left inset) cut deep gorges in rock. Mature rivers (right and right inset) form meanders, or bends. Oxbow lakes occur when a bend of the river gets cut off.

Road A strip of land that is used for the passage of people and vehicles. The first great roads were built by the Romans. It was not until the 1700s that Scotsman John McAdam introduced the macadam surface, which consisted of layers of crushed rock. Today's roads have solid foundations such as cement and bitumen. Surfaces may be tar, concrete, or asphalt.

Robin Birds of the thrush family that live in different parts of the world. Males have red breasts.

Robot A machine that can do certain tasks automatically.

Rockefeller, John D. (1839-1937) US oil businessman. He founded the Standard Oil Company and became very rich. He gave a lot of money to charities.

Rocket A powerful engine that can propel vehicles into space. Rocket propellants consist of a fuel and a substance with oxygen in it. This enables the rockets to work in the airless conditions of space. The Saturn rockets that launched Apollo astronauts to the Moon were 363 feet (111 meters) high and had as much thrust as 40 jumbo jets.

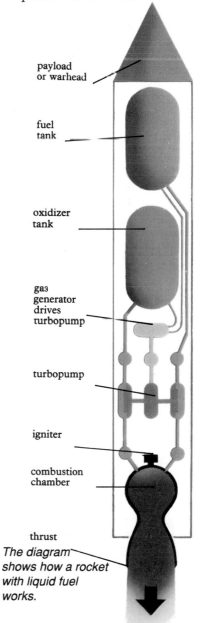

payload or warhead

fuel tank

oxidizer tank

gas generator drives turbopump

turbopump

igniter

combustion chamber

thrust

The diagram shows how a rocket with liquid fuel works.

Rodeo A show or sport in which cowboys and cow-girls compete in horseback riding, roping, and other skills of the Old West. Popular in North America, rodeos developed from the contests staged by cowboys after rounding up cattle.

Roentgen, Wilhelm Konrad (1845-1923) German physicist who discovered X rays in 1895. He was awarded the Nobel prize for physics in 1901.

Roman Catholicism The largest division of Christianity. Roman Catholics acknowledge the Pope as the spiritual leader of the Church. They believe him to be the successor of Saint Peter, the apostle appointed by Jesus to be the head of the church.

Roman Empire The dominant civilization in Europe, North Africa, and the Middle East from about the 1st century BC to the 5th century AD. Roman engineering, architecture, and technology had a great effect on European culture.

Romania A republic in southeast Europe. The Carpathian Mountains cover much of the country. They are forested and rich in minerals, among them oil, natural gas, coal, and iron. Area: 91,700 square miles (237,500 square kilometers). Capital: Bucharest.

Roman mythology A set of stories and beliefs of the people of ancient Rome telling about their many gods and heroes. Jupiter was the king of the gods; Juno was his queen. Vulcan was the god of fire. Venus was the goddess of love. Aeneas was a legendary hero.

Rome Capital city of Italy, situated on the Tiber River. It is a major government, religious, cultural, and tourist center.

Roosevelt, Franklin Delano (1882-1945) Thirty-second president of the United States. He served the longest term as president (1933-1945). His 12 years in office saw the Depression (for which he developed the New Deal) and World War II. He pioneered many social programs, reformed taxes, and developed more open relations with foreign countries. He kept the US out of World War II until the United States military

This 3rd-century coin shows Romulus and Remus, the wolf-reared twins said to have founded Rome in 753 BC.

base at Pearl Harbor (in Hawaii) was attacked. Reelected for a fourth term of office, he died suddenly in 1945.

Roosevelt, Theodore (1858-1919) Twenty-sixth president of the United States (1901-1909). Popularly known as "Teddy," he was one of the youngest presidents (aged 42). Vice-president to William McKinley, he became president when McKinley was assassinated. His conservation program expanded national forests. He won the 1906 Nobel Peace Prize. He retired from politics to lead an expedition into South America.

Root The part of a plant that anchors it in the ground. It absorbs water and minerals from the soil.

Rose A flowering shrub. Roses are grown for their colorful, fragrant blooms. Roses have thorny stems and many-petaled flowers which can be any of several colors.

It was the army which made Rome a great power. Victorious generals were allowed to hold a "triumph." They drove through the streets with their troops, their prisoners, and their booty.

Rowing The use of oars to move a boat forward. In some rowing races, called sculling, each rower uses two oars. In other kinds of races, each rower uses a single, large oar.

Rubber An elastic substance made from the latex sap of rubber trees. It is also produced synthetically from chemicals. Rubber is airtight, resistant to water, shock-absorbent, and does not conduct electricity.

Ruminant Any mammal that chews its cud and has split hoofs. Cud is food that is first taken into the stomach chamber, and then brought back into the mouth to be chewed and digested at leisure. Deer, sheep, goats, camels, giraffes, and cows are ruminants.

Rush-Bagot Agreement An 1817 agreement between the United States and Great Britain to limit fortifications on the Great Lakes.

Russia The largest of the Soviet republics of the USSR, and a name sometimes used to mean the USSR itself. Russia is the northern and eastern part of the USSR, stretching from the Baltic Sea to the Pacific Ocean, and from the Arctic Ocean to the Caspian Sea. Area: 6,592,849 square miles (17,075,400 square kilometers). Capital: Moscow.

Rust A reddish-brown crust that forms on iron and steel. It is caused by moisture or salt in the air, and by air pollution.

Rwanda A small East African republic. It is the most densely populated country in Africa. Most Rwandans are Hutu, a farming people who grow bananas, sweet potatoes, corn, and other crops. Coffee is the most important export crop. Area: 10,169 square miles (26,338 square kilometers). Capital: Kigali.

S

Saber-toothed tiger An extinct prehistoric cat that lived in Africa, Europe, and North and South America. Larger than a modern tiger, it had a pair of 8-inch (20 centimeter) teeth, sharp and curved like a saber (sword).

Sahara The largest desert in the world, situated in North Africa. It stretches from the coast of the Atlantic Ocean to the Red Sea and is rich in oil and mineral deposits. Area: over 3.5 million square miles (9 million square kilometers).

Saint A person who is regarded as being very holy and sacred. Such a person may be declared a saint (canonized) by a church.

Saint Lawrence River A river in Canada and along the Canada-United States border. It flows from Lake Ontario to the Gulf of Saint Lawrence. Length: 800 miles (1,287 kilometers). The Saint Lawrence Seaway, opened in 1959, has made the river passable by oceangoing vessels from the Great Lakes to the Atlantic Ocean.

Salamander An amphibian that looks like a lizard but has a soft skin. Salamanders live in moist spots over much of the northern hemisphere. Most are under 6 inches (15 centimeters) long, but the giant salamander of Japan may reach 5 feet (1.5 meters) long.

Salem (Massachusetts) A city on the Atlantic Ocean. It was the site of the witchcraft trials of 1692, when 20 persons were executed as witches. During the late 1700s and early 1800s, Salem was an important port in the East Indies trade.

The Custom House, Salem, Massachusetts.

Salinger, J.D. (Full name **Jerome David** (1919-) US writer. The first book he published, *The Catcher in the Rye* (1951), was about a teen-aged boy in New York City, Holden Caulfield. Many of his short stories are about a warm-hearted family named Glass, especially the three brothers Seymour, Buddy, and Zooey, and their sister Franny.

Salk, Jonas (1914-) US scientist. In 1953 he developed a vaccine against polio, a disease that can cause paralysis.

Salmon A game fish related to the trout, found in North America, Europe, and Asia. After living in the ocean, adults return to lay their eggs in the upland stream where they were hatched.

Salt A chemical compound formed by the reaction of a base with an acid. Common salt is a compound of sodium and chlorine, and is known chemically as sodium chloride. Chemical symbol: NaCl.

SALT (Stands for **Strategic Arms Limitation Talks**) Meetings held between the United States and the Soviet Union. In the SALT I agreement they agreed to limit the number of antiballistic missiles. A similar agreement, SALT II, was never ratified by the United States Senate. But in 1987, President Ronald Reagan and Soviet leader Mikhail Gorbachev signed an agreement to do away with intermediate range nuclear missiles in Europe.

Salvation Army A religious organization run like a military group. It provides food, shelter, and counseling to the poor. It was founded in England in 1865 by William Booth.

The old Santa Fe trail – a painting by John Young-Hunter.

San Andreas Fault A fracture of the earth's crust that extends from southern California north to San Francisco and into the Pacific Ocean. Movement along a fault causes earthquakes. There are several thousand small movements a year along the San Andreas fault. Most of these are too weak to be felt or to do much damage. In 1906, however, an earthquake destroyed San Francisco. Another earthquake caused great damage in the San Francisco area in 1989. Experts believe that there will be more earthquakes along the San Andreas Fault in the future.

Sandstone One of the most common sedimentary rocks. It consists of grains of sand, mostly quartz, which have been pressed down and cemented together by pressure or by minerals.

San Francisco A city located on a peninsula between the Pacific Ocean and San Francisco Bay in California. The scenic waterfront and the Golden Gate Bridge attract many tourists.

San Marino One of the smallest republics in the world. It grew from a 9th century religious community in Italy. It earns money largely from tourism and the sale of postage stamps. Area: 24 square miles (61 square kilometers). Capital: San Marino.

Santa Fe Trail The trade route that ran from Independence, Missouri, through Kansas and Colorado to Santa Fe, New Mexico. It was about 780 miles (1,260 kilometers) long. In 1821 the trail was first used as a trading route. Later, wagon trains made the trip each year. It took 40 to 60 days each way. In 1850 a monthly stagecoach line was started. In 1880 the Santa Fe Railroad reached Santa Fe, and the trail was soon a thing of the past.

Sardine A small fish of the herring family that lives in vast shoals in the Mediterranean and around the coasts of western Europe. Sardines are an important food fish.

Sardinia Island in the Mediterranean Sea. It is a self-governing region of Italy. Area: 9,301 square miles (24,090 square kilometers). Capital: Cagliari.

Saskatchewan A Canadian

Prairie province since 1905. It is the leading wheat-growing province. Mining and manufacturing are also important. Area: 251,700 square miles (652,330 square kilometers). Capital: Regina.

Satan In religion, the king of evil and the enemy of God. Also called the devil. Satan is represented in Judaism, Christianity, and Islam.

Satellite An object in space that moves in orbit around a larger object. For example, Mars is a satellite of the sun. Weather satellites orbit the Earth.

Saturn The second largest planet in the solar system, sixth in line from the sun. It is known for its system of rings. Diameter: 74,600 miles (120,000 kilometers). Mean distance from the sun: 885 million miles (1.4 billion kilometers). Number of moons: 20.

Saudi Arabia A country occupying most of the Arabian Peninsula. Oil wealth has paid for industrial and social development. Area: 830,000 square miles (2,149,690 square kilometers). Capital: Riyadh.

School A place where children or adults go to learn.

Science A system of facts about nature and the universe that have been learned through observation and experimentation. Biology, geology, and physics are kinds of science.

Scorpion A poisonous arachnid of the spider family, up to 8 inches (20 centimeters) long. It is found in most hot, dry parts of the world. The sting is carried in the tail, which arches over the back.

Scotland The northernmost part of the United Kingdom. Highlands and moors cover most of the country, with towns and industries in the valleys. Area: 30,414 square miles (78,772 square kilometers). Capital: Edinburgh.

Sculpture An art form. It involves carving and modeling in different materials, such as stone and bronze.

Sea horse A small, oddly-shaped fish with a long snout and a tail for gripping. Most are less than 6 inches (15 centimeters) long, but some can reach twice that size. The male has a pouch in which eggs spawned by the female are hatched.

Seal Any of a group of meat-eating mammals that are specialized for life in the sea, with tapering bodies and powerful flippers. Most find movement on land difficult.

Gray seal

Pup

Season One of four periods (spring, summer, autumn, winter) into which a year is divided. The weather in each season is caused by the Earth's axis tilting 23 degrees toward the sun and then 23 degrees away from it during a year. When the northern hemisphere tilts toward the sun, it brings summer; when it tilts away, winter comes.

Seaweed A large group of marine algae, found mostly around the shore. Seaweeds do not have leaves as such, though many are shaped like leaves.

Secession The withdrawal of the Southern states from the others in the United States because of a disagreement about slavery. In December 1860, South Carolina seceded. It was followed by Mississippi, Florida, Alabama, Georgia, Louisiana, and Texas. These states established the Confederate States of America. After the Civil War started in April, 1861, Virginia, Arkansas, North Carolina, and Tennessee also joined the Confederacy.

Secret Service, United States A division of the United States Department of the Treasury. It was formed in 1865 by Congress to fight against the counterfeiting of money. After President William McKinley was assassinated in 1901, the Secret Service also began protecting the president. Later the Secret Service began protecting vice-presidents, former presidents, visiting heads of state, and others. A uniformed division guards the White House. The Secret Service also investigates such things as credit card fraud and computer access fraud.

Sedimentary rock A rock formed from the remains of once-living things, or of minerals. These tiny pieces of matter, called sediments, are moved from their original location by water and wind and accumulate in layers that are compressed and slowly cemented together by minerals.

Seed The reproductive part of flowering plants and conifers. It consists of a miniature plant, known as the embryo, surrounded by a tough coating, and a store of food.

Seismology The study of shock waves traveling through rocks. The largest shock waves result from earthquakes. The force of an earthquake can be measured using a table of measurement called the Richter scale and an instrument called a seismograph.

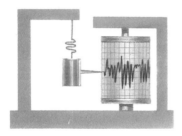

A seismograph: the heavy weight stays still while the support shakes. The tremors are recorded on a drum.

Semiconductor A material that is neither a good conductor of electricity nor an insulator. Its resistance grows less as its temperature increases.

Senate The upper house of the United States Congress. Two members are elected to the Senate from each state by popular vote. Senators serve six-year terms.

Senegal A republic in West Africa. Peanuts are its main export, but unreliable rainfall has led to droughts and famines in recent years. Area: 75,750 square miles (196,192 square kilometers). Capital: Dakar.

Seoul The capital of South Korea, on the Han River.

Sequoia, giant A coniferous tree that grows wild in the mountains of California. The sequoia is among the world's largest and oldest living things. It is estimated to live for more than 3,000 years.

Seven Wonders of the Ancient World Seven of the most remarkable objects of ancient times. The seven wonders included a Greek temple, statue and tombs; the Hanging Gardens of Babylon; a huge statue at Rhodes; a lighthouse at Alexandria, Egypt; and the Egyptian Pyramids.

Sextant An instrument used in navigation that measures the altitude of stars or the sun. Using an altitude table, the navigator can then find out the latitude at which his or her ship is located.

Shakespeare, William (1564-1616) English poet and dramatist whose works are performed all over the world. His plays include *Hamlet, Othello, A Midsummer Night's Dream*, and several histories of English kings.

Shale One of the most common sedimentary rocks, formed from silt or clay. Shale splits easily into thin layers. It has few uses, but some deposits contain petroleum.

Shanghai A major port and the largest city in China, on the Huangpu River near the delta of the river Yangtze. It is China's leading manufacturing center.

Shark A predatory fish with a torpedo-shaped body, a large tail, and a fin that sticks up from the water. Sharks can reach up to 40 feet (12 meters) in length.

Sheep A four-legged mammal with a woolly coat. Some kinds of sheep live wild in the mountains. Other kinds are raised for their wool, meat, and skin. The wool is used to make clothing. Meat from sheep is called lamb or mutton.

Shell A hard outer covering. Shells are found on some animals that do not have an inside skeleton, such as lobsters and snails. The hard outer coverings of eggs and some kinds of fruits, nuts, and seeds are also called shells.

Shellfish An animal with a hard outer covering that lives in the water. They are not really fish. Shellfish include clams, crabs, and scallops.

Sherman, William Tecumseh (1820-1891) US soldier. Sherman graduated from West Point in 1840. When the Civil War started, he was made a colonel in the Union Army. In 1864 he was made commander of all Union forces in the West. With an army of about 100,000 men, he captured Atlanta, Georgia. The city was set ablaze. Then, in his famous "march to the sea," Sherman captured Savannah and then invaded the Carolinas. Wherever he went, Sher-

General Sherman at the battle of Atlanta.

man ordered his soldiers to destroy everything that could be of use to the Confederate Army. Finally, Confederate General Joseph E. Johnston was forced to surrender. In 1869 Sherman became commanding general of the United States Army.

Ship A seagoing vessel for carrying cargo and passengers. Some ships are built for war. Today's ships are made of steel and run on diesel engines, turbines, and even nuclear reactors.

Shipbuilding The construction of ships. Modern ships are often prefabricated, sometimes in sections, away from the shipyard. Once the outer construction is complete, the ship is launched down a greased ramp into the water. Engines and furnishings are then installed.

Shorthand A method of rapid handwriting. It employs a variety of symbols that represent sounds of the language.

Shrew One of the smallest of all mammals. Shrews look like mice but have more pointed snouts. The common shrew is about 3.5 inches (9 centimeters) long.

Shrimp A marine crustacean resembling a tiny lobster. Shrimps are an important food for many fish, and are also eaten by people.

Siberia A vast, desolate area in northern Asia, part of the Soviet Union. It is rich in mineral deposits, but its fierce climate makes it difficult for people to live and work there. Area: 4,235,000 square miles (10,968,600 square kilometers).

Sicily The largest island in the Mediterranean. It is a self-governing region of Italy, separated from the mainland by the Strait of Messina. Area: 9,926 square miles (25,708 square kilometers). Capital: Palermo.

Sierra Leone A country in West Africa, on the Atlantic Ocean. Its products include palm kernels, coffee, and ginger. Area: 27,699 square miles (71,740 square kilometers). Capital: Freetown.

Sikhism A religion founded in the 16th century in India. It combines the beliefs of the Hindu and Muslim religions. Its holiest shrine is the Golden Temple at Amritsar.

Silicon A nonmetallic element abundant in the Earth's crust. With the addition of certain impurities, silicon becomes a semiconductor and the raw material for the manufacture of microchips. Chemical symbol: Si.

About 300 separate and identical chips are obtained from a single "wafer" of silicon.

Silk A natural fiber produced by silkworms. A silkworm spins a cocoon from a strand of silk over 900 feet (275 meters) long. China and Japan are leading silk producers. Because it is expensive to make, the fiber has been largely replaced by synthetic materials.

Silver A white, precious metal that can be easily shaped and has a high resistance to corrosion. It is also the best metallic conductor of heat and electricity. Silver is also used in making jewelry, eating utensils, and many other things. Chemical symbol: Ag.

Silverfish A small wingless insect with a three-pronged tail. It is often seen in homes, where it is a pest because it feeds on the starch in cloth and paper. It belongs to a group of insects known as bristletails.

Singapore An island republic in Southeast Asia, at the tip of the Malay Peninsula. It is a busy, prosperous port and manufacturing center. Banking and communications are also important. Area: 209 square miles (620 square kilometers). Capital: Singapore.

Siphon A bent tube for transferring liquid from one container into another whose surface is at a lower level. The different levels cause a difference in pressure so that the liquid is sucked from the higher to the lower container.

Sitting Bull (1834?-1890) US Indian leader. He was a chief of the Sioux tribe. Sitting Bull was the main medicine man when the Sioux, led by Crazy Horse and Gall, defeated General Custer at the battle of Little Bighorn. After the battle, he fled to Canada. He returned to surrender in 1881 and was put on a reservation. He later toured the country as a star in Buffalo Bill's Wild West Show. In 1890, he was killed by Indian police in an uprising.

Skating, Ice A way of moving over ice wearing skates (boots with a metal blade). Skating is an event in the Winter Olympic Games, with competitions for speed skating, figure skating, and ice dancing.

Skeleton The bones of an animal. In the case of vertebrates (animals with backbones), the skeleton acts as a framework for the body.

Skiing The art and skill of sliding over and down snowy slopes using a pair of long narrow runners called skis attached to the feet. Skiing is a winter sport and an Olympic Games event with races and jumping.

Skunk A black and white, North American mammal, known for its unpleasant odor. When frightened, skunks raise their bushy tails and squirt a bad-smelling mist at enemies from a distance of 10 feet (3 meters) or more.

Sky diving A sport in which people wearing parachutes leap from airplanes. Divers can "fly" for a brief time as they fall towards the ground, before pulling the cord that opens the parachute.

Skyscraper A tall building built around a framework of concrete and steel. The high price of land in big cities makes it worthwhile to build upward instead of outward. Skyscrapers were made possible by the development of safe electric elevators and iron girders that could support many floors.

Slate A fine-grained metamorphic rock derived from shale. It splits into thin layers and is sometimes used for roofing.

freed by the passage of the 13th Amendment to the US Constitution.

Sleep A time of rest for the mind and body of people and animals.

Sloth A slow-moving, coarse-haired mammal of Central and South America. It uses hooklike claws to hang upside down in the trees of the tropical rain forests. The two main species are the two-toed and the three-toed sloth.

Slug A gastropod mollusk, closely related to the snail but usually without a shell. Found in damp places, they usually come out at night and eat mainly plants.

Smallpox An often fatal viral disease that left its victims with disfiguring scars. Today the disease has disappeared, thanks to the use of vaccination programs.

Smuggling Bringing something secretly from one country to another. Smuggling is usually done to avoid paying a tax on the goods or because it is illegal (against the law) to have the goods.

Snail A gastropod mollusk found on land, in fresh water, and in the sea. Thousands of species of snails are known. Most eat plants, but some eat other animals. The snail's shell protects it from enemies.

Snake A legless reptile related to the lizard. It has a long, slim body, a tail, and a scaly skin. Some snakes kill their prey by squeezing it to death. Others have poisonous fangs.

Snipe A wading bird found in marshes. Snipe have mottled brown plumage with dark stripes on the head. They fly in a zigzag manner when alarmed.

Snow Precipitation (con-

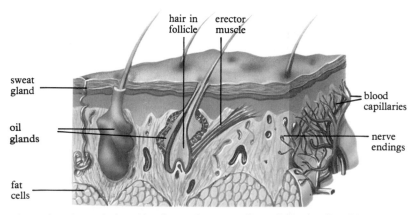

A section through the skin: the surface consists of dead cells which flake off.

Skin The outer covering of the body. It protects the internal organs from physical damage and infection by harmful bacteria and viruses.

Slavery The practice of holding people as property and making them work without pay. Slaves were used in parts of the United States until 1865, when they were

Snow crystals

densed water) in the form of delicate ice crystals with a variety of hexagonal (six-sided) shapes. Snowflakes form in air that is below the freezing point and then fall to the ground.

Soap and detergent Materials that can be added to water to make it "wetter." They are used to remove dirt and grease. Soaps are made from alkalis such as caustic soda, caustic potash, or vegetable oils. Detergents are synthetic products made from oil by-products treated with sulfuric acid and alkalis.

Soccer A game played by two teams of eleven players. Each team tries to move a round ball into the other team's goal by kicking or hitting the ball with any body part except the arms

and hands.

Social insect Any of those insects that live in an organized community. Ants, termites, bees, and wasps are social insects.

Socialism An economic system based on the principle of sharing wealth and resources. Resources such as mines and factories are owned by the government, which distributes goods and provides jobs.

Social Security Act The Act of Congress, passed in 1935, that set up a system of compulsory old-age insurance. It provides monthly cash payments to retired or injured people.

Socrates (469?-399 BC) A Greek philosopher whose ideas were written down by his pupil, Plato, and others. He believed that people could find the meaning of life by learning about themselves.

Sodium A very soft, white metal. Combined with other chemicals, it is very plentiful. Sodium chloride

is ordinary table salt. Sodium bicarbonate is used in medicine and to make baking powder. Chemical symbol: Na.

Sofia The capital of Bulgaria, located close to the Yugoslavian border. It is Bulgaria's chief commercial center.

Soil The topmost layer of the Earth's surface. It consists of broken-down rock which is either sandy or clay; air; water; and organic material (humus) which provides nutrition for plants.

Solar energy The energy of the sun. Only a tiny fraction reaches the Earth, but this is still an immense amount of energy. Some can be collected and converted to supply power for homes.

Solar system The sun and the natural objects that orbit around it. The solar system includes the nine planets, their moons, and countless smaller heavenly bodies such as asteroids, comets, and meteors. It has a circular shape.

The planets of the solar system showing their relative distance from the sun (from left to right): Pluto, Neptune, Uranus, Saturn, Jupiter, Mars, Earth, Venus, and Mercury. On the far right is the Earth as seen from space.

Sole A flatfish found mostly on sandy or muddy seabeds. The fish is about 16 inches (40 centimeters) long. By day it lies buried in the sand. It hunts at night.

Solid One of the three states of matter, the others being liquid and gas. The atoms or molecules of most solids are arranged in fixed patterns called crystals.

Solomon, King (? - 922? BC) The son of King David, he became King of the Jews in about 965 BC. He was very wealthy and was revered for his wisdom. He built the Temple at Jerusalem.

Solution A mixture of two or more substances. They cannot be separated by being filtered or left to settle.

Somalia An arid country in East Africa. Sheep, camels, and goats graze in large herds. Drought and famine are serious problems. Area: 246,201 square miles (637,657 square kilometers). Capital: Mogadishu.

Sonar A device that uses sound waves to measure the depth of water under ships and to locate underwater objects.

Sound Vibrations which travel through air or some other medium and can be detected by the ears. Sound travels through air at about 740 miles (1,190 kilometers) an hour.

Sound recording The reproduction and storing of sound on discs or tapes. In 1877, Thomas Edison invented the first machine to record sound. The first electric recording appeared in 1925. Today, using laser technology, compact discs offer almost perfect reproduction in a durable form.

Sousa, John Philip (1854-1932) US bandmaster and composer. In 1880 he became conductor of the United States Marine Band. His own band, formed in 1892, was world famous. Sousa wrote 100 marches, including "The Washington Post March" and "The Stars and Stripes Forever."

South Africa A country at the southern tip of the African continent. It is a world leader in gold production and is also rich in minerals, including diamonds. Area: 471,445 square miles (1,221,037 square kilometers). Capitals: Pretoria (administrative); Cape Town (legislative); Bloemfontein (judicial).

South America The fourth largest continent, occupying about 12 percent of the world's land area. It is located entirely in the Western Hemisphere. Much of it is below the equator. It is divided into 12 independent countries, the Falkland Islands, and French Guiana. Area: 6,887,000 square miles (17,837,000 square kilometers).

South Carolina In the southeastern United States, South Carolina was one of the original 13 states. The Atlantic coastal plain contains swamps and forests. Inland, the hilly Piedmont plateau rises to the Blue Ridge, part of the Appalachian Mountains. Textiles, chemicals, and machinery are manufactured. Area: 31,055 square miles (80,432 square kilometers). Capital: Columbia.

South China Sea Part of the Pacific Ocean. It is bordered by Vietnam, the Philippines, Malaysia, and southern China.

South Dakota Located in the north central United States, it became the 40th state in 1889. It is mainly a flat region drained by the Missouri River. The Black Hills in the west are the site of the Mount Rushmore National Memorial. Farmland covers most of the state. Barley, beef cattle, pigs, oats, sheep, and wheat are major products. Area: 77,047 square miles (199,551 square kilometers). Capital: Pierre.

Soy A native plant of China. It is now cultivated in many

Mount Rushmore, in South Dakota.

parts of the world for its nutritious beans, which are rich in protein and oil.

Space Also called outer space. The area beyond the Earth's atmosphere or beyond the solar system.

Space probe A space vehicle used to explore beyond the Earth's atmosphere. Explorer I was the first US space probe, launched in 1958. Following the first successful moon landing in 1969, the United States landed the Viking probe on Mars in 1976. The Voyager probe photographed Jupiter's moons in 1979. Voyager II reached Saturn in 1981, Uranus in 1986, and Neptune in 1989.

Space shuttle A reusable spacecraft developed by the United States. It takes off like a rocket, aided by an external fuel tank and two solid fuel boosters. When landing, it glides to a halt on a runway, like an airplane.

Space station An artificial satellite designed to orbit the Earth. In it people can carry out scientific experiments and other projects. In 1971 the Soviet Union launched its first space station, Salyut I, followed by a whole series of manned Salyuts. In 1973 the United States launched the Skylab space station, which was abandoned the following year.

Spain A country in southwestern Europe. High inland plains and mountains are surrounded by coastal plains. Many people in Spain are farmers, fishermen, or work in the tourist trade. Area: 194,889 square miles (504,759 square kilometers). Capital: Madrid.

Sparrow Any of a large group of small, streaky brown

Bird-eating spider
Black widow spider
Garden spider
Crab spider
Tarantula

birds with pale underparts, which live in large flocks. They have short, stout beaks for cracking seeds.

Species The smallest group classification of animal or plant. All the individuals in a species can interbreed to produce more of the same kind, but normally cannot breed with any other species.

Specific gravity The density of a substance compared with the density of water at 39 degrees Fahrenheit (4 degrees Celsius). If a substance is three times as dense as water, it has a specific gravity of 3.

Spectrum The band of rainbow colors produced when white light is passed through a prism or spectroscope.

Speech The ability to use spoken words to tell thoughts, feelings, and ideas to others.

Sphinx An imaginary creature of Egyptian, Greek, and Near Eastern myth. Most Egyptian sphinxes had the head of a human and the body of a lion.

Spice An aromatic plant substance used to flavor food. The most popular include pepper, mustard, cinnamon, cloves, nutmeg, and ginger.

Spider An arachnid whose body is divided into two parts. Spiders have four pairs of legs. Some spiders spin sticky webs to catch their prey.

Spinning The process of gathering and twisting fiber together to make long yarns for weaving.

Sponge One of a group of simple animals found mainly in warm, shallow seas. Most look like plants but are in fact made up of colonies of tiny animals with chalky, fibrous, or glasslike skeletons.

Spruce A group of coniferous trees of the pine family. There are about 40 kinds in the Northern Hemisphere. The Norway spruce is a traditional Christmas tree. The Sitka or silver spruce comes from western North America.

Squid A marine mollusk related to the octopus, with eight short arms and two tentacles to seize prey. Squids move by squirting out jets of water and hide themselves by giving off a cloud of inky liquid.

Squirrel A bushy-tailed rodent common to most parts of the world. American gray squirrels are tree-dwellers who make their nests in trees.

Sri Lanka An island state off the southeastern tip of India. Crops include tea, rubber, coconuts, and cinnamon. Emeralds and rubies are mined there. Area: 25,332 square miles (65,610 square kilometers). Capital: Colombo.

Stalactite An iciclelike growth from the roof of a limestone cavern. It is created by the continuous evaporation of water containing dissolved calcium carbonate. Columns of calcium carbonate growing from the floor of a cavern in the same manner are known as stalagmites.

Stalin, Joseph (1879-1953) A Soviet political leader. He succeeded Lenin and became dictator in 1929. A ruthless dictator, Stalin got rid of political opponents by executing them or sending them to labor camps. He led the Soviet Union through World War II.

Joseph Stalin

Star A glowing ball of intensely hot gas. The energy of a star is derived from the nuclear fusion of hydrogen atoms to form helium atoms. Unlike a planet, a star does not orbit.

Starch A substance produced by plants, commonly found in cereals and root vegetables. An important energy food, it is also used to stiffen fabrics and in many industrial processes.

Starfish One of a class of spiny sea animals. They usually have five arms radiating from a central body.

Starling A common European songbird that forms huge, noisy flocks in the fall and winter months. It was introduced into the United States, where it is now considered a pest.

Statistics A collection of facts, usually expressed as numbers. The statistics are drawn from data to give information about a subject.

Statue of Liberty A large copper statue of a robed woman that stands on Liberty Island in New York Harbor. It is 151 feet (46 meters) high. The statue was a gift from the French people to the United States. It was designed by the sculptor Frédéric Auguste Bartholdi. Dedicated in 1886, it has become a symbol of freedom.

Steamboat A boat moved by steam power. In 1807, Robert Fulton built the first commercially successful steamboat.

Steam engine An engine worked by steam pressure that pushes pistons up and down in their cylinders. Rods from the piston turn a wheel. The first practical steam engine was patented by James Watt in 1769.

Stegosaurus A plant-eating dinosaur of the Jurassic period. It was about 20 feet (6 meters) long and weighed about two tons. It had huge plates on its back for defense that also may have helped control its body temperature.

Stockholm A port and the capital city of Sweden, located on Lake Mälaren near the Baltic Sea. Industrially, Stockholm developed rapidly during the 19th century and is now a modern, commercial city.

Stocks A certificate issued by a company that represents a share in the company. Companies sell shares in their business when they need money for development. The shares owned by someone are called stocks. The New York Stock Exchange, on Wall Street in New York City, was established in the 18th century to handle the buying and selling of the stocks of many corporations. Other stock exchanges are located in cities throughout the world.

Stomach The part of the body where food is stored and digested after swallowing. It looks like a bag of muscle that is open at both ends.

Stone Age The period of development from about 2 million BC to about 3,000 BC. During this time humans learned to use stone tools and weapons, to live in settlements, and to domesticate (tame) animals.

Stonehenge A prehistoric monument on a plain outside of Salisbury, England. It was originally made of two large circles of huge standing stones. One circle is inside the other. It may have been used as a religious temple or as a way of observing and keeping track of the sun, stars, and planets.

Stork A large, long-legged wading bird. It has a long neck and bill.

Stowe, Harriet Beecher (1811-1896) US writer. She is best known for *Uncle Tom's Cabin*, an antislavery novel. This best-selling book helped increase opposition to slavery in the Northern states.

Stringed instrument A musical instrument that produces sound when strings are plucked or stroked with a bow. Such instruments include the harp, violin, viola, cello, guitar, double bass, and others.

Stuart, Gilbert (1755-1828) US painter. He studied art in London and became a well-known portrait painter. When he returned to the United States, he painted portraits of George Washington, James Madison, John Quincy Adams, and other leading statesmen and citizens.

Sturgeon A large, bony fish, about 20 feet (6 meters) long with armor made up of bony plates. It is the survivor of a prehistoric group of fishes. Eggs from the females are used in making caviar and are a great delicacy.

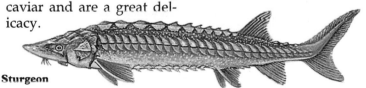

Sturgeon

Stuyvesant, Peter (1610?-1672) Governor of New Netherland, a Dutch colony in North America. It included areas of what are now New York, New Jersey, Connecticut, and Delaware. Stuyvesant was a strict leader who opposed religious freedom, but he helped the colony to prosper, especially New Amsterdam, the small city on Manhattan Island. The English captured New Amsterdam in 1664 and renamed it New York.

A modern attack submarine—The USS Los Angeles.

Submarine An underwater boat. Ballast tanks that can be filled with or emptied of water enable submarines to dive or surface. Nuclear submarines can remain submerged for months.

Subtraction The act of taking away one number from another to find the difference. The mathematical symbol for subtraction is -.

Subway A rapid transit system that runs underground. The world's first subway was opened in London in 1863. Today there are subways in Boston, Paris, New York City, Tokyo, Moscow, Chicago, Toronto, Mexico City, San Francisco, Washington DC, and many other cities. The New York City subway system is by far the largest in North America. It has more than 230 miles (370 kilometers) of lines.

Sudan The largest country in Africa, in the northeastern part of the continent. Muslim Arabs live in the northern part of the country. Christians and believers in traditional African religions live in the South. Crops include cotton, peanuts, sugar cane, and millet. Area: 967,500 square miles (2,505,813 square kilometers). Capital: Khartoum.

Suez Canal A major canal, connecting the Mediterranean Sea with the Red Sea and the Indian Ocean. It was built by French engineer Ferdinand de Lesseps and opened in 1869. Length: 118 miles (190 kilometers).

Sugar A naturally occurring, sweet-tasting carbohydrate, produced by plants during photosynthesis. The main types are fructose (from fruit), sucrose (from sugar cane and sugar beets), and glucose (from starch).

Sulfur A yellow, nonmetallic element sometimes found around volcanoes. It burns with a pungent smell. It is used for matches, gunpowder, and sulfuric acid. Chemical symbol: S.

Sun The star at the center of our solar system. It is a giant powerhouse in which the conversion of hydrogen atoms to helium atoms by nuclear fusion generates enormous energy. Diameter: 865,000 miles (1,392,000 kilometers). Mean distance from the Earth: 92,600,000 miles (149,000,000 kilometers). Surface temperature: about 10,000 degrees Fahrenheit (5,500 degrees Celsius). Core temperature: 27 million degrees Fahrenheit (15 million degrees Celsius).

Supersonic flight An aircraft traveling faster than the speed of sound. When the aircraft reaches Mach I, the speed of sound, a pressure disturbance builds up just ahead of the plane. This is called a shock wave. People on the ground can hear a sonic boom as the aircraft crosses the sound barrier.

Surface tension A force that causes liquids to behave as though an elastic film covered their surfaces. It is because of surface tension that drops of liquid take a nearly spherical shape.

Surgery An operation to mend faulty or injured parts of the body. The introduction of anesthetics and antiseptics in the 19th century led to a great improvement in technique.

Suriname A small country in northeastern South America, on the Atlantic Ocean. It is part of the Guiana region. Chief products are bauxite, sugar, fruit, and rice. Area: 63,037 square miles (163,265 square kilometers). Capital: Paramaribo.

Surveying The science of determining the relative position of points on the Earth's surface. Surveyors measure horizontal and

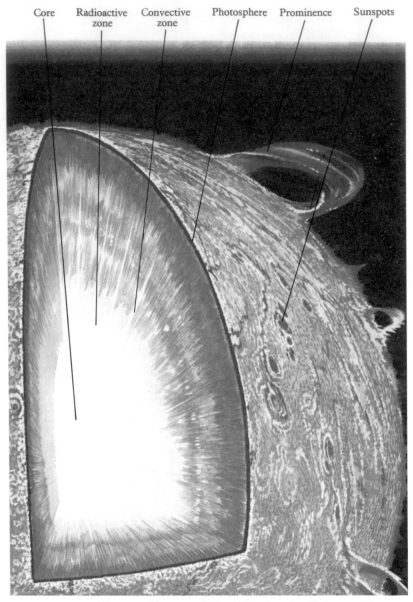

Core   Radioactive zone   Convective zone   Photosphere   Prominence   Sunspots

A cutaway view of the sun. The core is the hottest part, with temperatures of several million degrees Fahrenheit. The visible surface is called the photosphere. The photosphere is marked by cooler and darker areas called sunspots and huge loops of glowing gas called prominences.

vertical distances, and the angle of one fixed point from another.

Swallow A graceful, streamlined bird. It spends most of its time flying to catch insects. Nests are built on, or preferably in, buildings.

Swan A large water bird. It has an elegant, long neck and belongs to the duck family. Swans are powerful birds and strong fliers.

Swaziland A country in southeastern Africa. It is bordered by South Africa and Mozambique. Its main crops are sugar, fruit, and cotton. Asbestos, coal, and iron are mined. Area: 6,704 square miles (17,363 square kilometers). Capital: Mbabane (administrative), Lobamba (traditional).

Sweden A country in northern Europe, part of Scandinavia. It is rich in forests and minerals. Manufactured goods, electrical machinery, and vehicles are the major exports. Area: 173,732 square miles (449,964 square kilometers). Capital: Stockholm.

Swift A fast-flying, streamlined bird that catches its food in the air. The common swift has dark brown feathers, a white throat, and a forked tail. Swifts are among the fastest fliers of all birds.

Swimming The act of moving the body through water by using the arms and legs. It is a popular leisure activity and a sport in the Summer Olympic Games. Various strokes are used in swimming. The fastest is the freestyle crawl, followed by the butterfly, backstroke, and breaststroke.

Switzerland A small, land-locked country in central Europe. Its most famous feature is a large mountain range, called the Alps. Despite having few resources, Switzerland has become prosperous and is a major financial center. Area: 15,943 square miles (41,293 square kilometers). Capital: Bern.

Swordfish A silver and blue game fish, about 7 feet (2 meters) in length. It has a high dorsal fin and a long, swordlike beak.

Sydney The largest city in Australia, situated on the shore of Sydney Harbor near Port Jackson Bay. It was founded in 1788 by the British as a convict settlement, the first in Australia.

Synthetic fiber A fiber made entirely from chemicals. Chips of plastic are melted and forced through spinnerets to produce fibers of varying thickness. A US inventor, Wallace Carothers, developed the first synthetic fiber, called nylon, in 1937.

Syria A country in the Middle East. It is at the eastern end of the Mediterranean Sea. Textiles and oil refining are major industries. Area: 71,498 square miles (185,180 square kilometers). Capital: Damascus.

T

Table tennis A game, originally called Ping-Pong. It is played indoors on a table that has a net across it. The players use round paddles covered with rubber to hit a small, hollow ball back and forth.

Tadpole The larva of frogs and toads. Tadpoles live underwater and breathe through gills like fish. They grow legs as they become adults and develop lungs for breathing when they leave the water.

Taft, William Howard (1857-1930) Twenty-seventh president of the United States. He was the first civilian governor of the Philippines after the United States won them from Spain. He then was appointed US secretary of war. A Republican, he was president of the United States from 1909 to 1913. From 1921 to 1930 he was a member of the Supreme Court, serving as chief justice of the United States of America.

Tahiti One of the Society Islands in the South Pacific. It is a possession of France. Area: 402 square miles (1,041 square kilometers). Capital: Papeete.

Taiwan An island off the coast of China. Taiwan exports many manufactured goods. Area: 13,900 square miles (36,000 square kilometers). Capital: Taipei.

Taj Mahal A building in Agra, India. Some people say that it is the most beautiful building in the world. It was built in the 17th century by the Emperor Shah Jahan as a memorial to his wife, Mumtaz Mahal.

Tank A heavily armored fighting vehicle that runs on continuous tracks. First introduced in World War I, tanks played a major part in World War II.

American M1

German Leopard 2

The Leopard and the M1 tanks have been in active military service for many years.

Tanzania A country in East Africa. It contains Africa's highest mountain, Kilimanjaro, which is 19,340 feet (5,899 meters) high. Diamonds are mined and industry is developing. Area: 364,900 square miles (945,087 square kilometers). Capital: Dar es Salaam.

Tape recorder A machine for recording sound on plastic tape. The tape is coated with magnetic iron oxide. This tape passes over electromagnetic heads which "fix" sounds by magnetizing iron oxide particles into patterns.

Tapestry A piece of fabric woven on a loom using colored threads. Tapestries often form large pictures used for wall hangings, particularly in European castles during the Middle Ages.

Tapeworm A parasitic worm that lives in the stomach of many animals, including humans. Tapeworms look like long white ribbons. They can be up to 30 feet (9 meters) in length.

Tapir A stocky pig-like mammal of the horse family with a long snout. It lives deep in forests of tropical America and Southeast Asia, feeding on plants at night.

Tarantula Any of several large, hairy spiders, particularly the bird spider of the southwestern United States or South America, over 7 inches (18 centimeters) wide. Its bite, which is fatal to small animals, is only painful to humans.

Tasmania An island off southeastern Australia. It is Australia's smallest state. Area: 26,200 square miles (67,800 square kilometers). Capital: Hobart.

Taxation The money raised by a government in the form of charges on people's income or property, the goods they buy, or the services they use.

Taylor, Zachary (1784-1850) Twelfth president of the United States. As a young man, he fought in Indian campaigns and in the War of 1812. In the Mexican War he was commander of the Army of the Rio Grande and won several major battles. A popular hero, he was elected president in 1848. He served from 1849 to 1850, when he became ill and died.

Tea A shrub native to China and cultivated in India, Sri Lanka, China, and elsewhere in Asia. The young leaves are gathered and dried to be steeped (soaked in boiling water) as a beverage.

Teak A large, hardwood tree of Southern Asia. It can grow up to 150 feet (46 meters) tall. Its strong, oily timber is used to make furniture.

Tectonic plate One of the large, rigid sections of the Earth's crust. Shifting of the plates can cause mountains to rise or continents to move. It can also cause earthquakes and the formation of volcanoes.

Tehran The capital of Iran, situated on the southern slopes of the Elburz Mountains. It has grown rapidly since World War II into a modern city.

Tel Aviv-Yafo A city and leading financial center of Israel. It is on the Mediterranean Sea. The state of Israel was proclaimed here in 1948.

Telegram A message transmitted by the electric telegraph and printed on paper. Telegrams that are transmitted over cables under the sea are called cablegrams.

Telegraph A means of sending messages by electrical impulses on radio or wire. In 1844, the US inventor Samuel Morse made the first successful demonstration of a telegraph.

Telephone A device for sending sound messages by wire. It was invented by Alexander Graham Bell in 1876. In modern telephones, the handset is both the transmitter and the receiver.

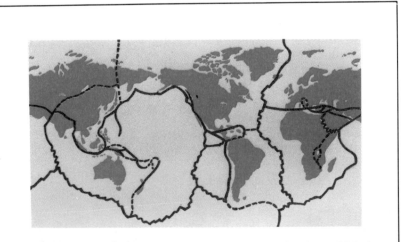

The map shows the continually moving tectonic plates into which the Earth's crust is cracked.

Telescope An instrument that makes distant objects seem nearer. It is mainly used in astronomy.

Television A device that receives images sent from a transmitter in the form of electromagnetic waves. Signals, usually with sound, are received onto a cathode-ray tube in the television set. Dots of light are lined up with those in the studio cameras to reproduce the images.

Temperature The "coldness" or "hotness" of the air or of an object. It is usually measured by either the Fahrenheit or Celsius scale. On the Fahrenheit scale, water boils at 212 degrees and freezes at 32 degrees. On the Celsius scale, the boiling point is 100 degrees and freezing point is 0. The Kelvin scale, used in science, begins at absolute zero.

Tennessee A state in the southern United States. It became the 16th state in 1796. Chemicals, food products, and machinery are its chief manufactured goods. Coal and zinc are among its mining products. Dairy products, meat, soybeans, tobacco, and corn are all important. The largest cities are Memphis and Nashville. Area: 42,114 square miles (109,152 square kilometers). Capital: Nashville.

Tennis A game played on outdoor or indoor courts. It is played by two or four players, who use rackets to hit a ball over a net. The US Open and British Wimbledon championships are internationally famous.

Teresa, Mother (1910-) Roman Catholic nun from Albania. She is known for her work among the poor of Calcutta,

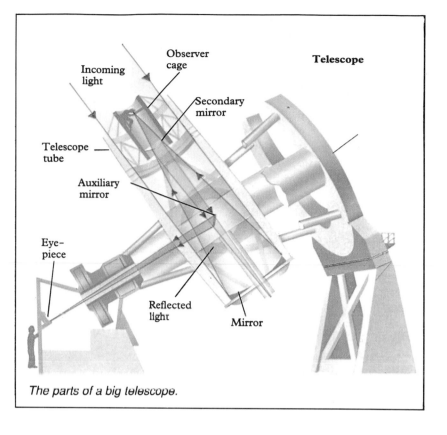

The parts of a big telescope.

India, and for the order of nuns she founded. She was awarded a Nobel Peace Prize in 1979 for her work.

Termite An insect related to the cockroach. It is often called a white ant. Some termites live in mud nests. Termites feed on wood and can rapidly destroy timber.

Terrapin The common name of certain turtles. "Terrapin" was an American Indian name for "turtle." The terrapin is distinguished by its flatter shell and webbed toes.

Texas The second largest US state (after Alaska) and third in population. It is the leading mining state and has huge reserves of oil and natural gas. It is also a major state for agriculture, including cotton and beef cattle. Area: 266,807 square miles (691,030 square kilometers). Capital: Austin.

Textile A woven or knitted fabric. Spinning turns fiber into yarn, which is then knitted or woven into cloth on a loom.

Thailand A country in Southeast Asia, formerly called Siam. Among its crops are rice, corn, cotton, sugar cane, and rubber. It has tin and tungsten mines. Timber and tourism are important industries. Area: 198,500 square miles (514,000 square kilometers). Capital: Bangkok.

Thames River in England, flowing east through London to the North Sea. Length: 210 miles (340 kilometers).

Thanksgiving Day A legal holiday in the United States. It is celebrated on the fourth Thursday of November. Families meet and give thanks for the good things in their lives. The first Thanksgiving celebration was held by the Pilgrims in thanks for a good harvest after a hard winter.

Theater A place where dramatic or musical performances are given. Many modern theaters have space for the audience on three sides of the stage.

Thermometer An instrument for measuring the temperature. A slim glass tube contains a liquid, such as colored alcohol or mercury, which expands or contracts with the rise or fall of temperature. The liquid inside moves up or down a numbered scale of degrees marked on the thermometer.

Thermostat An automatic device that controls temperature. It operates by sensing changes in heat. Thermostats are often used to control central heating switches on fire alarm units and to regulate the heat in buildings.

Third World A group of countries which have little or no industrial development. People in these countries often suffer from poverty, drought, famine, and disease.

Thistle A large group of flowering plants belonging to the daisy family. Thistles have prickly leaves and purplish flower heads.

Thoreau, Henry David (1817-1862) US writer. For two years, he lived in a hut next to Walden Pond near Concord, Massachusetts. He wrote down his thoughts and observations about nature there in a book called *Walden* (1854).

Thrush A common garden songbird that has plain feathers. The most common species in the US are the robin, wood thrush, and hermit thrush.

Thunderstorm A storm associated with towering clouds, thunder, lightning, and often heavy rain.

Tibet A region in central Asia. It is sometimes called the "roof of the world." Since 1951, Tibet has been part of China. Tibet's ruler, the Dalai Lama, has lived in exile since 1959.

Tick Any of a group of tiny parasites related to mites and spiders. Ticks cling to passing animals, feeding on their blood. Ticks often carry diseases, such as Rocky Mountain spotted fever and Lyme disease.

Tide The regular rise and fall in the level of the sea. It is caused by the gravitational pull of the moon and, to a lesser extent, that of the sun.

Tiger A large, striped Asian cat. The largest variety, the Siberian tiger, may reach 13 feet (4 meters) in length.

Time The period during which things happen or continue.

Time zone A geographical area, all parts of which have the same standard time.

These zones were established to give places in one zone the same time. The Earth is divided into 24 time zones, each with a one-hour time difference from the next zone. Some places are in the middle of a time zone or want to keep the same time as another part of their country, so they set their clocks a half hour ahead or behind the time zone's time.

Spring tide

Neap tide

Spring tides occur when the sun, moon, and Earth are in a straight line; neap tides occur when they form a right angle.

During a thunderstorm, lightning can travel from a cloud to Earth. It occurs when a negative (-) and a positive (+) electric charge meet.

Tin A soft, white metallic element that is widely used for plating thin sheet steel (the tin plate of food cans). Tin is also used in many alloys including solder, bronze, and pewter. Chemical symbol: Sn.

Titanium A scarce metal that combines lightness and strength with resistance to corrosion. It is used in the construction of aircraft and rockets. Chemical symbol: Ti.

Toad A tailless amphibian related to the frog. Toads live in fairly dry places, hiding by day and feeding at night on slugs and other small animals. Toads lay their eggs in water.

Tobogganing A winter sport in which people race down icy hill tracks on long, flat-bottomed sleds called toboggans.

Togo A small country in West Africa, between Ghana and Benin. Phosphates are the principal export. Area: 21,925 square miles (56,785 square kilometers). Capital: Lomé.

Tokyo A port city and the capital of Japan. It is in the central part of the island of Honshu. It is a major financial and industrial center. Because it is located on marshy ground, expansion of the city requires expensive land reclamation.

Tomahawk A small ax. It was used by some Indians in North America as a tool and as a weapon.

Tomato A plant of the nightshade family that originated in South America. Tomatoes are rich in vitamins A and C, and in iron.

Tonga A country in the South Pacific Ocean, also known as the Friendly Islands. Copra (dried coconut meat) is the main product. There is some tourism. Area: 289 square miles (748 square kilometers). Capital: Nuku-alofa.

Tongue A movable flap of muscle on the bottom of the mouth. It is used for eating, tasting, and swallowing. People also use the tongue when speaking.

Tooth One of the bony growths in the jaws of vertebrates, used for chewing food. The bony substance of a tooth is called *dentin*. Inside this is the *pulp cavity*, containing nerves and blood vessels. A layer of *enamel* covers and protects the *crown*, which is the visible part of the tooth. The *root* is embedded in the gum.

Parts of a tooth

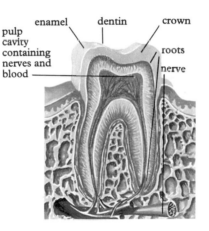

Tornado A small but intense storm in which winds of more than 200 miles (320 kilometers) an hour whirl around a funnel of low pressure. They occur chiefly in central and southern United States. Tornadoes can cause enormous damage, flattening buildings in their path.

Tortoise A shelled reptile renowned for slowness and long life. The Galapagos tortoise of the Galapagos Islands near Ecuador may reach 4 feet (1.2 meters) in length and live for over 150 years.

Toucan A family of large, boldly colored Central and South American birds. The toucan has an enormous bill, which probably plays a role in its courtship. They gather in small flocks in tropical forests and feed mainly on fruit.

Transformer A device for increasing or decreasing electrical voltage. Transformers play an important part in radio and television sets and other electronic apparatus.

Transistor An electronic device for controlling tiny electric currents. Thousands of transistors can be incorporated in a very small wafer of silicon, a few chips of which can contain the entire circuitry of a computer or television set.

Tree A large, woody plant, usually with just one main trunk. Trees are the largest living things in the world. Broad-leaved trees such as oaks shed their leaves. Needle-leaved trees such as pines do not. They are known as evergreens.

Trigonometry A branch of mathematics. It is concerned with the sides and angles of triangles and their relationships. It is used to measure distances to the stars, heights of tall buildings or mountains, and in navigation.

Trillium A North American and Asian plant of the lily family. It has a straight stalk with a collar of leaves, and a single flower with three petals.

Trinidad and Tobago A country in the Caribbean Sea, formed by the two southernmost islands in the West Indies. Tourism is important. Area: 1,980 square miles (5,128 square kilometers). Capital: Port-of-Spain.

Trojan War A war fought in about 1250 BC between the Greeks and the people of the city of Troy. No one is sure if this war really took place. Greek myths and the *Iliad*, a long poem by the Greek poet Homer, tell of its heroes and battles. Events after the war are told in Homer's *Odyssey* and in Virgil's *Aeneid*.

Tropical cyclone A huge revolving storm, sometimes called a hurricane or a typhoon. Winds up to 180 miles (300 kilometers) an hour spiral around a central vortex or "eye" of low pressure.

Tropical fish Small, brightly colored fish that live in warm areas of the world. People sometimes keep them in aquariums as a hobby.

Trotsky, Leon (1879-1940) A Russian revolutionary who served under Lenin. Opposed to Stalin's policies, Trotsky was dismissed from the Communist party in 1927. He went to live in exile in Mexico, where he was assassinated.

Truman, Harry S. (1884-1972) Thirty-third president of the United States. He was an artillery officer in World War I. Truman studied law after the war. A Democrat, he was a senator from Missouri from 1935 to 1945. In 1944 Truman was elected vice-president of the United States under Franklin D. Roosevelt. He became president in April 1945 upon Roosevelt's death. Truman won the presidential election in 1948 and remained in office until 1953. He ordered the use of the atomic bomb to defeat Japan in World War II. After the war he established the CIA. He also initiated the Marshall Plan and worked for the formation of NATO. In 1950 he sent US troops to Korea.

Truth, Sojourner (1797?-1883) US abolitionist and reformer. She was freed from slavery in 1828. Thereafter she spoke throughout the United States against slavery.

Tsetse fly An African blood-sucking fly. As it sucks the blood, it infects its victim with a parasite that causes a disease called *nagana* in cattle and *sleeping sickness* in humans.

Tubman, Harriet (1820?-1913) US abolitionist. She escaped from slavery in 1849. She helped more than 300 slaves to escape to freedom on the Underground Railroad. Because of this she was called "the Moses of her people."

Tuna A large marine food fish. It can grow to about 10 feet (3 meters) long. Tuna feed mainly on herring, mackerel, and garfish.

Tungsten A hard, brittle metal with a high melting point. It is used for making high-speed cutting tools and in electric light bulb filaments. Chemical symbol: W.

Tunisia The smallest country in North Africa, bordered by Algeria and Libya. Fruit, crops, and cattle are raised on the fertile coast. Area: 63,170 square miles (163,610 square kilometers). Capital: Tunis.

Tunnel A passageway through a mountain, under a city, or under water. Tunnels are made by drilling or cutting and blasting through rocks. The inner wall of the tunnel is strengthened with such materials as steel and concrete.

Turbine An engine in which steam, water, gas, or air turns wheels or screws to produce power. Turbines are used in power stations to drive generators, which produce electricity.

Turkey A large American game bird first domesticated by the Aztecs. Farm-raised turkeys can weigh up to 50 pounds (23 kilograms) and are traditionally served at Thanksgiving and Christmas. Turkeys also live in the wild.

Turkey A country composed of a small area in Europe and a much larger area in Asia. Separated by water, the two areas are linked by a bridge. Industries include mining, textiles, paper, and ancient crafts such as carpet weaving. Area: 301,382 square miles (780,576 square kilometers). Capital: Ankara.

Turtle

Turtle A reptile that usually lives in or near water. The turtle's body is encased in a bony shell covered by horny plates called scutes. Most turtles can draw their head and legs into their shell for protection. Baby turtles hatch from eggs.

Tutankhamen (1300s BC) An Egyptian king. Historians believe he died at about the age of 18. His tomb and its great treasures were discovered by the British archeologist Howard Carter in 1922.

Tuvalu An island country in the Pacific Ocean. Area: 10 square miles (26 square kilometers). Capital: Funafuti.

Mark Twain

Twain, Mark Pen name of the US writer and humorist **Samuel Langhorne Clemens** (1835-1910) He worked as a printer, a riverboat pilot on the Mississippi, and a newspaper reporter in Nevada and California. He wrote many books, including *The Adventures of Tom Sawyer* (1876), *Life on the Mississippi* (1883), and *The Adventures of Huckleberry Finn* (1884).

Tyler, John (1790-1862) Tenth president of the United States. He was a member of the House of Representatives from Virginia and later served as governor and senator of the state. Tyler was elected vice-president in 1840. He became president in 1841 when President Harrison died after one month in office. Tyler was president until 1845. During his presidency, the United States annexed Texas, which Mexico claimed. This brought on the Mexican War.

Typewriter A keyboard machine that prints letters, numbers, or symbols onto paper when keys are pressed. Today, electric typewriters and word processors are usually used.

Typhoid fever A disease transmitted by salmonella bacteria sometimes found in food and water. It is most common in poorer parts of the world where sanitation is not good. Typhoid causes fever and can be fatal.

Tyrannosaurus A ferocious, carnivorous (meat-eating) dinosaur. It had large, powerful back legs and a huge head. Its massive jaws contained razor-sharp fangs 6 inches (15 centimeters) long.

Triceratops

Tyrannosaurus

Only a heavily armed beast like Triceratops would dare attack a Tyrannosaurus.

U

Uganda A small country in east central Africa. Most people work in agriculture, growing coffee, tea, and cotton. Area: 91,134 square miles (236,036 square kilometers). Capital: Kampala.

Ultrasound The use of sounds higher than those the human ear can hear in medicine, industry, and scientific research. Scientists can locate solid objects underwater, such as submarines or schools of fish, with ultrasound. Engineers use ultrasound to detect flaws in metals.

Ultraviolet radiation Invisible radiation from the sun. Exposure to these rays produces Vitamin D in the body, but too much exposure can be dangerous. However, many kinds of harmful bacteria can be killed by ultraviolet rays.

Ulysses Also called Odysseus. A hero of ancient Greek myths. After fighting the Trojan War, he had many adventures on his journey back home to Greece. These are described in the *Odyssey*, a long poem by the Greek poet Homer.

Uncle Sam A popular symbol for the United States. Uncle Sam is a cartoon drawing of a tall, thin man with a short beard, who is dressed in red, white, and blue. The name was first used during the War of 1812. It may have been suggested by the initials "US" on army uniforms and government property, or it may have come from the nickname of an army inspector of beef named Samuel "Uncle Sam" Wilson, of Troy, New York.

Underground Railroad A network of escape routes that helped slaves escape from the South before the Civil War. Harriet Tubman, its most famous "conductor," led hundreds of slaves to freedom.

Unicorn A mythical white horse with a horn in the middle of its forehead. Unicorns were described in stories during the Middle Ages.

An artist's impression of a U.F.O."invasion."

Unidentified Flying Objects (UFOs) Flying objects, believed by some people to be alien spacecraft. Many have been reported, but most sightings have been explained as tricks of light or weather balloons. Some sightings have not been explained.

Union of Soviet Socialist Republics (USSR) Largest country in the world. About one-quarter is in Europe and three-quarters in Asia. After the Russian Revolution in 1917, it came under communist rule. It is more than twice the size of the United States. Area: 8,649,500 square miles (22,402,000 square kilometers). Capital: Moscow.

United Arab Emirates Group of states on the eastern Arabian Peninsula. It is made up of seven small states called emirates. Its people, who once lived as desert nomads, now prosper on the money earned from oil sales. Area: 32,278 square miles (83,600 square kilometers). Capital: Abu Dhabi.

United Kingdom Short name for the United Kingdom of Great Britain and Northern Ireland, off the western coast of Europe. It is made up of England, Scotland, Wales, and Northern Ireland (see individual entries). Area: 94,250 square miles (245,050 square kilometers). Capital: London.

United Nations International organization formed to settle disagreements between nations peacefully. Set up in 1945, its headquarters are in New York City. The Food and Agricultural Organization (FAO) and the World Health Organization (WHO) are part of the United Nations.

United States of America The world's fourth largest nation. It is a federal republic of 50 states. The United States has very good land for agriculture and produces many kinds of food. It also has great mineral wealth. The United States has one of the highest standards of living in the world. Area: 3,618,770 square miles (9,372,571 square kilometers). Capital: Washington D.C.

The Great Seal of the United States.

Universe Space and everything in it, including the solar system, stars, and galaxies. It is also called the cosmos. Many astronomers believe that the universe was created by an enormous explosion about 20 billion years ago. This is known as the Big Bang Theory.

University A place for the highest levels of education. Students, called undergraduates, receive degrees when they graduate. They may go on to study for higher degrees called masters or doctorates.

Uranium A radioactive element. One form, uranium-235, can be made to undergo nuclear fission. Uranium is used in atomic bombs and to produce nuclear energy. Chemical symbol: U.

Uranus The seventh planet from the sun. Through a telescope, Uranus appears as a featureless green disk. The Voyager II spacecraft photographed it in 1986. Diameter: 31,570 miles (50,800 kilometers). Mean distance from the sun: 1.8 billion miles (2.9 billion kilometers). Number of

A view in Bryce Canyon National Park, Utah.

moons: 15.

Uruguay A small country on the southeastern coast of South America. Its flat, grassy plains are ideal for cattle and sheep ranching. Area: 68,037 square miles (176,215 square kilometers). Capital: Montevideo.

USSR See Union of Soviet Socialist Republics.

Utah A west central state, Utah became the 45th US state in 1896. Utah has spectacular scenery and five national parks. Copper, petroleum, coal, uranium, gold, and other metals are mined. Metal products, machinery, and transport equipment are manufactured. Farming is also important. Area: 84,899 square miles (219,889 square kilometers). Capital: Salt Lake City.

The planet Uranus.

V

Vaccination An injection into a person's body that protects him or her against certain diseases. Vaccines are made from dead or weak disease germs. They cause the body to build up resistance to different diseases, such as measles, smallpox, mumps, influenza, and polio. The process of vaccination was developed by the English physician Edward Jenner in 1796.

Vacuum A space that is completely empty of air or other gases. Actually, there is no such thing as a perfect vacuum. Partial vacuums are used in electric light-bulbs and vacuum cleaners.

Valentine's Day February 14, the day on which people send valentine cards to their loved ones. It probably began as an ancient Roman festival called Lupercalia. In the late 5th century, this festival became a day honoring St. Valentine.

Valley Forge An area along the Schuylkill River in southeastern Pennsylvania. During the American Revolution, George Washington's Continental Army camped there from December 1777 to June 1778. The winter was bitterly cold and the soldiers suffered a great deal. Nearly one fourth of the troops died.

Vampire A legendary dead person who rises from the grave at night to suck the blood of living people and turn them into vampires as well. Also, any of several types of bats, only some of which actually feed on blood.

Vanadium A rare metallic element. It is used in very hard alloy steels from which tools and vehicle parts are made. Chemical symbol: V.

Van Buren, Martin (1782-1862) Eighth president of the United States. A Democrat, Van Buren served as a senator from New York and governor of that state. From 1829 to 1831, he was United States secretary of state. A close ally of Andrew Jackson, he was Jackson's vice-president during his second term. He was president from 1837 to 1841, the first to be born a citizen of the United States.

Vanuatu Independent republic made up of 80 islands in the western Pacific Ocean. It was formerly called the New Hebrides. Area: 5,700 square miles (14,763 square kilometers). Capital: Port-Vila.

Vatican City The world's smallest sovereign (independent) state. It lies within the city of Rome, Italy. Vatican City is the spiritual and administrative (business) center of the Roman Catholic Church and the residence of the Pope. Area: 109 acres (44 hectares).

Vegetable A plant whose parts are eaten as food. Spinach, beans, and carrots are kinds of vegetables.

Velocity The rate at which something moves in a given direction. The velocity of a moving object changes if either its speed or direction changes. When an object is moving at a constant velocity, it is moving in a straight line at a constant speed.

Venezuela Country on the northern coast of South America. Its wealth comes from oil. Since 1958 it has had the most democratic and progressive government in South America. Area: 352,145 square miles (912,050 square kilometers). Capital: Caracas.

Venice Port and city in Italy, built on a group of islands in a lagoon. Instead of streets, it has a network of canals. It is known for its splendid architecture and art treasures.

Venus The second planet from the sun. It is about the same size as the Earth. Venus has sulfuric acid clouds, a primarily carbon dioxide atmosphere, and a surface temperature of

Venus is covered by unbroken clouds. Beneath the cloud layer is a world with a choking atmosphere and fierce temperatures.

about 850 degrees Fahrenheit (500 degrees Celsius). It has no moons. Diameter: 7,520 miles (12,100 kilometers). Mean distance from the sun: 67 million miles (108 million kilometers).

Verb A word that tells action (swim, giggle, grow) or being (am, was).

Vermont A New England state, it became the 14th US state in 1791. Its mountains attract skiers and other tourists. Manufactured goods include machinery, printed materials, and metal products. Burlington is the largest city and industrial center. Milk, meat, poultry, eggs, potatoes, and grains are important farm products. Area: 9,614 square miles (24,900 square kilometers). Capital: Montpelier.

Versailles A city in France, near Paris. It is famous for its magnificent palace, built for King Louis XIV. The Treaty of Versailles, which ended World War I, was signed in the palace.

Vertebrate Any animal with a backbone. Fishes, amphibians, reptiles, birds, and mammals are all vertebrates.

Vespucci, Amerigo (1454-1512) Italian explorer. He made several voyages to newly discovered lands in the New World. North America and South America are named after him.

Vesuvius A volcano in southern Italy, on the Bay of Naples. Its eruption in 79 AD buried the cities of Pompeii, Herculaneum, and Stabiae. Numerous eruptions have since been recorded. Height: 4,190 feet (1,277 meters).

Veterans Day November 11.

Arlington National Cemetery, in Virginia.

This legal holiday in the US was once called Armistice Day. It was established in memory of the signing of the Armistice (end of fighting) that ended World War I on November 11, 1918. In 1954 the name was changed to Veterans Day to honor all veterans of the United States armed forces.

Victoria, Queen (1819-1901) Queen of the United Kingdom. She reigned for 63 years, from 1837 until her death, longer than any other British ruler.

Video recording A recording method that uses magnetic tape (called videotape). Electrical signals are stored on the videotape, which can be played back immediately. Video recording is used to record sound and pictures, unlike audio tape recording, which only records sounds.

Vienna Port and capital city of Austria, on the Danube River.

Vietnam A country in southeast Asia. After the 1957-1975 war between North (communist) and South Vietnam, the country was united under a communist government. The United States was involved in the war from 1965-1973. Area: 127,242 square miles (329,556 square kilometers). Capital: Hanoi.

Vikings Scandinavian warriors who began raiding the coasts of Europe in about 800 AD before settling there. They established colonies in Iceland and Greenland.

Virginia Located on the east coast of the United States, Virginia was founded in 1607 and was one of the original 13 states. Tobacco is a major crop. Corn, soybeans, wheat, and livestock products are important. Manufacturing dominates the economy. Manufactured goods include chemicals, food products, transport and electrical equipment, and machinery. Area: 40,767 square miles (105,586 square kilometers). Capital: Richmond.

Virus A tiny living thing that can cause disease in people, plants, and animals. Viruses live and grow only inside of other cells. Colds, chicken pox, and influenza are some of the illnesses caused by viruses.

VISTA (Stands for **Volunteers in Service to America**) A program organized in 1965. Volunteers are trained for special projects to help poor people improve their lives.

Vitamins Organic substances found in most foods. They are known by letters of the alphabet (Vitamin A, B, C, etc.) Vitamins are needed by the body in proper quantities for health. A lack of vitamins may cause illness.

Volcano An opening in the Earth's surface through which molten lava, gases, and ash may erupt. Many volcanoes look like cone-shaped mountains.

The inside of a volcano. The cone-shaped mountain has alternate layers of rock formed from lava and ashes from previous eruptions.

Voting Rights Act of 1965 A law enacted by the United States Congress that extended the voting rights of minority groups. It was signed by President Johnson in 1965 and extended by President Reagan in 1982. It struck down local laws and practices that prevented minorities from voting.

Vulture A large bird of America, Europe, Africa, and Asia. Vultures eat carrion, or dead animals. They are often seen circling in the sky, looking for a meal. The largest vultures are the California and Andean (South American) condors.

W

Wales A part of the United Kingdom. Wales is a land of mountains and river valleys. Sheep are raised on the hillsides. Steel and coal mining industries, once important, are now declining. Area: 8,018 square miles (20,768 square kilometers). Capital: Cardiff.

Wallaby A small marsupial of Australia and New Guinea related to the kangaroo. Some are only the size of rabbits.

Walrus A bulky seal-like mammal of Arctic, North Atlantic, and North Pacific coasts. Walruses have leathery skin, whiskers, and long tusks. A bull (adult male) may weigh over a ton.

Warbler A family of small insect-eating birds. Many are good singers. The yellow warbler and American redstart are two well-known examples.

Warning coloration A bold color or pattern exhibited by an animal. This warns predators that the animal is poisonous or distasteful. A skunk's black and white coloring is one example.

War of 1812 (1812-1815) A war between the United States and Great Britain. It began when the United States became involved in trade problems between Britain and France. Battles were fought along and on the Great Lakes, on Lake Champlain, at Washington, D.C., and at New Orleans, Louisiana.

Warsaw The capital city of Poland, on the Vistula River. It is an important industrial and communications center.

Wart hog An unusual-looking wild African pig. The wart hog has warts on its cheeks, upturned tusks, a mane of bristly hair, and a tufted tail.

Washington A Pacific Coast state in the United States. Washington contains magnificent coastal and mountain scenery. It became the 42nd state in 1889. Resources include forests and coal. Manufacturing is the chief activity, producing transportation equipment, timber, and food products. Crops are also important. Beef cattle and chickens are raised. The largest cities are Seattle, Spokane, and Tacoma. Area: 68,192 square miles (176,616 square kilometers). Capital: Olympia.

Washington, D.C. The capital city of the United States, on the Potomac River. It is named after the first President, George Washington, who chose its location in 1791. Washington is the site of the White House, the president's residence. It is a

The south face of the White House, in Washington, D.C.

federal district called the District of Columbia (D.C.).

Washington, George (1732-1799) First president of the United States. He was a delegate to the Continental Congress, commander-in-chief of the Continental Army in the Revolutionary War, and the presiding delegate at the Constitutional Convention. He was president from 1789 until 1797.

Wasp A group of stinging insects related to ants and bees. Wasps often have striking black-and-yellow markings that warn other animals that they are not good to eat.

Watch A small portable machine that shows and tells the time. Time is measured in hours, minutes, and sometimes seconds. Watches have faces that show the time by numbers or a marked dial over which two hands pass. A watch may be worn on the wrist or carried in a pocket.

Water The most important compound on Earth. It can be a solid (ice), liquid, or vapor (fog and steam). It covers more than 70 percent of the Earth's surface. Water makes up about 65

percent of the human body. Chemical symbol: H_2O.

Water buffalo Any of several kinds of wild oxen, most of which have been domesticated as draft animals. They like to wallow in mud and water, so they are ideal for plowing flooded rice fields.

Water cycle A process of nature. Water from the oceans, rivers, lakes, and other sources passes into the atmosphere through evaporation, falls to the ground as rain or snow through condensation, and flows back to the sea again in streams and rivers.

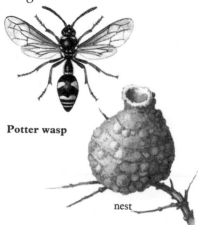

Potter wasp

nest

A simplified diagram of the water cycle.

121

Waterfall A step in a river bed that water tumbles over. Often a series of ledges are formed over which the river flows swiftly in rapids.

Water lily A family of aquatic flowering plants that are not related to true lilies. Water lilies float on the surface of slow-moving or stagnant water such as lakes and ponds.

Wave A moving ridge or line of liquid, sound, or light. Waves travel across the surface of the oceans without taking water along with them. Sound and electromagnetic waves travel by the wave motion of air molecules.

Weasel A small, slender mammal, the smallest of the carnivores. It is only about 9 to 18 inches (23 to 46 centimeters) long, with short legs and a bushy tail. Weasels eat mice, rats, birds, and eggs.

Weather The condition of the air around us. This includes the temperature, humidity (moistness), and pressure of the air, together with winds, clouds, snow, and rainfall.

Weather forecasting The science of predicting the weather. Weather information from ground stations and satellites is sent to forecast centers. Meteorologists (weather scientists) analyze the information and prepare forecasts for the following days.

Weaving The interlacing of yarn on a loom to make fabric. One set of threads (the weft) is passed under and over a set of lengthwise threads (the warp).

Webster, Daniel (1782-1852) US lawyer, statesman, and orator. Webster was a member of the House of Representatives from New Hampshire. After he moved to Massachusetts, he represented that state in the House of Representatives and the Senate. He also served as secretary of state under three presidents. As a lawyer, Webster argued and won many cases before the Supreme Court. An outstanding orator, he made many speeches in support of a strong national government.

Weevil Any of a group of small beetles with pointed snouts. Weevils infest flour and other food. Some, such as the cotton boll weevil, are serious pests.

Weights and measures A system used to find and describe the weights and sizes of things. The two most commonly used systems are the English system, based on feet, pounds, and pints; and the metric system, based on the meter, the gram, and the liter.

Welding The permanent joining together of two pieces of metal by melting them. When cooled, the pieces are fused together with a joint that should be as strong as any other part.

Werewolf A creature of superstition in many cultures, made popular by the movie industry. A werewolf is supposed to be a man who is transformed into a wolf. When there is a full moon, the werewolf is supposed to hunt humans.

Western Samoa A country in the Pacific Ocean, part of the Polynesian island group. It is rich in forests. Cacao and bananas are grown. Area: 1,097 square miles (2,842 square kilometers). Capital: Apia.

West Indies (Also called the Indies.) A group of islands located in the Atlantic Ocean between North and

Weaving–a traditional occupation of Navaho Native Americans.

Sperm whale

devices from windmills to steam turbines, and in machines from simple pulleys to automobiles.

White House Formerly called the Executive Mansion. The official home of the President of the United States. It is located in Washington, D.C. It has 132 rooms and is painted white.

Whitman, Walt (1819-1892) US poet. One of his books of poetry is called *Leaves of Grass* (1855).

Wildcat A carnivore that resembles a domestic house cat. It is found in mountain forests from western Asia to southern and central Europe.

Wildcat

South America. The countries of Cuba, Haiti, the Dominican Republic, Jamaica, Puerto Rico, the Bahamas, and a number of small nations make up the West Indies.

West Virginia A southern state in the United States, it was admitted as the 35th state in 1863. It lies in the Appalachian Mountains and is mostly rugged, scenic country. It is a major mining state, producing coal, oil, and natural gas. Farming is less important, but a variety of crops are grown. Area: 24,181 square miles (62,629 square kilometers). Capital: Charleston.

Whale One of a group of marine mammals that look like large fish but that must come to the surface to breathe. The largest animal that has ever lived is the blue whale, which may grow to 100 feet (30 meters) long. Sadly, whaling has led to a serious decline in several kinds of whales.

Wheat A cultivated grass grown in temperate regions as a cereal crop. The main producers include the United States, Canada, the USSR, and China. Grains of wheat are ground into flour or meal and used to make foods, especially bread.

Wheel A disk of hard material that can turn on an axle. A wheel can be solid or have spokes radiating from its center. The invention of the wheel, about 10,000 years ago in Asia, was one of the most important discoveries in human history. It is used to harness energy in

Willow A group of deciduous (leaf-shedding) trees and shrubs. Most have long, narrow leaves and like damp soil. Willows bend easily in the wind.

Wilson, Woodrow (1856-1924) Twenty-eighth president of the United States. In his early career he was a lawyer, a professor, and then president of Princeton University. From 1911 to 1913 he was the Democratic governor of New Jersey. From 1913 to 1921, he was president of the United States. During his administration, the United States fought in World War I. After the war, Wilson's Fourteen Points were used as the basis for the peace settlement with Germany.

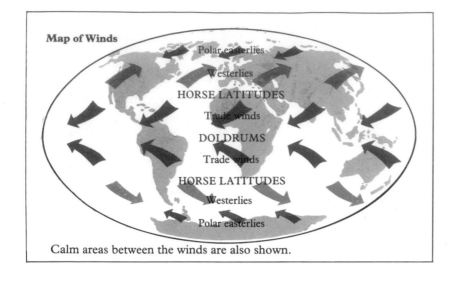

Map of Winds

Polar easterlies

Westerlies

HORSE LATITUDES

Trade winds

DOLDRUMS

Trade winds

HORSE LATITUDES

Westerlies

Polar easterlies

Calm areas between the winds are also shown.

Wind A current of air blowing from an area of high atmospheric pressure to an area of low pressure. The strength of the wind depends upon the difference and distance between the pressure areas.

Wind instrument A musical instrument that produces a sound when air is blown through or across it. This group includes the flute and the reed instruments (bassoon, clarinet, oboe, and saxophone). Brass wind instruments include the French horn, trombone, and trumpet.

Winnipeg The capital city of the Canadian province of Manitoba, at the junction of the Red River and the Assiniboine River, south of Lake Winnipeg. It is one of the world's major wheat markets.

Wisconsin A north central state, it became the 30th US state in 1848. Wisconsin is known especially for its dairy products. However, manufacturing is the most valuable activity. Machinery, food products, paper products, metals, and transport equipment are all produced. Milwaukee is the largest city and one of the country's top industrial centers. Area: 56,154 square miles (145,438 square kilometers). Capital: Madison.

Witchcraft The practice of magic and casting of spells by people who believe they are witches.

Wolf A carnivorous (meat-eating), doglike animal that ranges over remote areas of North America, Europe, and Asia. Wolves live in family groups and work together in packs when hunting large animals.

Wolverine A carnivorous (meat-eating) animal that belongs to the weasel family. It grows up to about 30 inches (75 centimeters) long, and has dark brown fur. It lives in northern forests in most parts of the world.

Wombat A stocky, burrowing marsupial of southern Australia and Tasmania. It is a nocturnal plant-eater (feeding at night) with teeth similar to those of a rodent. It looks like a small brown bear.

Wood The material that makes up the trunk and branches of a tree or shrub. Many softwoods come from evergreens such as the pine, fir, and spruce. They are used for building, furniture, and paper. Most hardwoods come from broad-leaved trees with distinctive colors and grain. They are also used for furniture and for decoration.

Woodpecker A bird renowned for the rat-a-tat noise it makes while hammering into a tree trunk with its sharp bill. Woodpeckers climb up tree trunks, drilling large holes into the wood to build their nests and search for insects to eat.

Wool The coat (fleece) of sheep and some other animals. People have used wool to keep warm since ancient times. Wool is spun into yarn, which can then be knitted or woven into cloth.

Word processor A typewriter with a keyboard linked to a computer, a VDT (video display terminal), and a printer.

Wolverine

A stretcher party bringing in wounded from the World War I battlefield of Passchendaele.

World War I (1914-1918) A war in which nearly all the countries of Europe and many other nations were involved. On one side were the Allies, which included Great Britain, France, the USSR (then called Russia), and Italy. On the other side were Germany and Austria-Hungary. Millions of people were killed. The entry of the United States into the war in 1917 helped the Allies win the war.

World War II (1939-1945) The largest war in history, which involved most of the countries in the world. It was fought in Europe and Asia as well as on the Atlantic and Pacific Oceans. Germany, Japan, and Italy fought against Great Britain, France, the Soviet Union, and the United States. Most other countries helped one side or the other. Some countries were neutral (did not choose either side). The war finally ended when the United States dropped two atomic bombs on Hiroshima and Nagasaki, Japan, in August, 1945.

Worm Any of a wide range of long, slender animals without a backbone or legs. They belong to many different classifications of animals.

Wounded Knee A creek in the Pine Ridge Sioux Reservation, South Dakota. In 1890 United States troops attacked a peaceful gathering of Sioux Indians there. They massacred more than 200 men, women, and children. In 1973 members of the American Indian Movement occupied the village of Wounded Knee for more than two months. They wanted to dramatize Indian grievances. Two Indians were killed. The Indians surrendered when officials agreed to investigate their complaints.

Wren A tiny, brown bird. It nearly always holds its tail straight up as it runs through the undergrowth. Wrens hunt for insects on the ground, but otherwise hide in bushes.

Wren, Sir Christopher (1632-1723) An English architect. After the Great Fire of London in 1666, he was responsible for the rebuilding of Saint Paul's Cathedral and more than 50 other London churches.

Wrestling One of the most ancient sports, dating back thousands of years. The aim in wrestling is to throw, unbalance, or pin your opponent to the mat. Hitting and punching are not allowed.

Wright, Frank Lloyd (1867-1959) US architect. He created unusual and new designs for private homes and public buildings. His ideas influenced many other architects.

The world's first powered flight by the Wright brothers, on December 17th, 1903. It took place at Kitty Hawk, North Carolina.

Wright, Orville (1871-1948) and **Wilbur** (1867-1912) American brothers who invented the airplane. In 1903 they made the first powered flight at Kitty Hawk, North Carolina, covering a distance of 852 feet (260 meters).

Writing The act of using the hand to form symbols or letters with a pen, pencil, or other instrument.

Wyoming A Rocky Mountain state, it became the 44th US state in 1890. Minerals are important to the economy, notably petroleum, natural gas, and uranium. Beef cattle are raised, and manufacturing is also important. The Grand Teton and Yellowstone national parks are among tourist attractions. Area: 97,914 square miles (253,596 square kilometers). Capital: Cheyenne.

X

Xenon A chemical element and one of the rare gases that occurs in tiny quantities in the atmosphere. Chemical symbol: Xe.

X rays A kind of radiation that can pass through substances that regular light rays cannot pass through. X rays can pass through human tissue but are partially blocked by the bones. Doctors use X rays to take pictures of bones and other parts inside of the body.

Y

Yak Wild ox of the Himalayas and Tibet, in Asia. It has a very shaggy coat and horns which extend sideways. The domesticated yak is a beast of burden. Its milk is used for drinking and for cheese. Its hair is woven into cloth.

Yalta Conference A meeting in 1945 between United States President Franklin D. Roosevelt, British Prime Minister Winston Churchill, and Soviet Premier Joseph Stalin. The three leaders met near the end of World War II. They made plans to occupy Germany at the end of the war. They also made plans to form the United Nations. Stalin agreed that free elections would be held in the liberated countries of eastern Europe, but he never allowed this to happen. He also agreed to join the fight against Japan.

Yangtze River (Also known as **Chang Jiang**). The longest river in China and the third longest river in the world. It flows from Tibet across China into the East China Sea. It is a major commercial waterway. Length: 3,915 miles (6,300 kilometers.)

Year, Solar A solar year is the time it takes for the earth to complete one orbit of the sun (365 days, 5 hours, 48 minutes and 46 seconds). This is about one-quarter of a day more than the calendar year.

Yeast A group of single-celled fungi. Yeast is used in baking to make bread rise. In the fermentation process, yeast acts on sugar to make alcohol.

A view of the Grand Geyser frightening early visitors to Yellowstone National Park.

to spread out widely.

Yoga A system of Hindu religious philosophy. People who practice yoga aim to liberate their souls from their minds and bodies. This is done by meditating and by doing certain physical exercises. Many non-Hindus do the exercises to relax and to obtain peace of mind.

Yogurt A nutritious dairy food. It is made by adding certain types of bacteria to milk. The bacteria thicken the milk and give it an acidic taste.

Yom Kippur The day of atonement, when Jews fast and ask God's forgiveness. The 10th day of the Jewish New Year, it falls in either September or October because the Jewish calendar is based on cycles of the moon.

Young, Brigham (1801-1877) US religious leader of the Mormon Church. He was baptized into the Mormon faith in 1832. He then did missionary work in England and the United States. In 1844 he became head of the Church after Joseph Smith, its founder, was killed. Young led the mass migration of Mormons from the Midwest to Utah in 1847. He chose the site for Salt Lake City. Young was the first governor of the Territory of Utah.

Yellowstone National Park A park in northwestern Wyoming and nearby parts of Montana and Idaho. It is known for its hot springs, geysers, beautiful scenery, and Yellowstone Canyon. Area: 3,458 square miles (8,955 square kilometers).

Yemen, Republic of Country in the Middle East, occupying the southern corner of the Arabian Peninsula. For many years, Yemen was divided into two separate nations: the Arab Republic of Yemen (North Yemen) and the People's Democratic Republic of Yemen (South Yemen). On May 22, 1990, the two nations unified, becoming the Republic of Yemen. In fertile areas of the country, crops of dates, wheat, millet, barley, coffee, cotton, fruits, and vegetables are grown. There is also some fishing and oil. Area: 203,887 square miles (530,106 square kilometers). Capital: Sana.

Yew An evergreen tree or shrub. It is commonly used as a decorative planting. The yew can grow to a height of 83 feet (25 meters). Its branches tend

Yew tree

Prospectors pose with their gear before setting out for the Yukon in the Gold Rush of 1897.

Yugoslavia Country in south-eastern Europe. Industries include iron, steel, timber, and manufacturing. It is made up of six republics, the largest of which is Serbia. Area: 98,766 square miles (255,804 square kilometers). Capital: Belgrade.

Yukon Territory A vast mountainous region in northwestern Canada. It attracted world attention during the Klondike Gold Rush in 1897. Minerals, mainly lead, zinc, silver, and gold, are the main source of income. Tourism is also important. Area: 186,661 square miles (483,450 square kilometers). Capital: Whitehorse.

Z

Zaire Third largest country in Africa. Located in the center of the continent, it has valuable minerals. Copper, diamonds, cobalt, uranium, and crude oil are the country's most important exports. Area: 905,365 square miles (2,344,885 square kilometers). Capital: Kinshasa.

Zambezi River in southern Africa. It originates in Zambia and empties into the Indian Ocean at Mozambique. Length: 1,700 miles (2,736 kilometers).

Zambia Landlocked country in south-central Africa. The economy is based on mining, and the most valuable mineral is copper. Area: 290,586 square miles (752,614 square kilometers). Capital: Lusaka.

Zebra African mammal with distinctive dark and white stripes. Related to horses, they are grazing animals and live in herds.

Zero Population Growth An estimate of how many people are needed to keep the world population at the same level. Calculations are made based on how many people have died and how many will need to be born to replace them.

Zimbabwe Country in southern Africa. Most people work in agriculture, but industry is developing. Area: 150,804 square miles (390,580 square kilometers). Capital: Harare.

Zinc A bluish-white metallic element. It is coated on iron to prevent rusting, a process known as galvanizing. Chemical symbol: Zn.

Zodiac An imaginary band in the heavens, that seems to circle the Earth. The zodiac is divided into 12 parts, which are named after 12 constellations. These are Aries (Ram), Taurus (Bull), Gemini (Twins), Cancer (Crab), Leo (Lion), Virgo (Virgin), Libra (Scales), Scorpio (Scorpion), Sagittarius (Archer), Capricorn (Goat), Aquarius (Water bearer) and Pisces (Fishes).

Zoology The science and study of animal life. Together with botany it forms the science of biology.